HARVARD HISTORICAL MONOGRAPHS

LVII

*Published under the direction of the
Department of History from the Income of
The Robert Louis Stroock Fund*

IVAN AKSAKOV

1823-1886

A STUDY IN
RUSSIAN THOUGHT AND POLITICS

Stephen Lukashevich

HARVARD UNIVERSITY PRESS

CAMBRIDGE · MASSACHUSETTS

1965

TO MY FATHER
AND
TO MY WIFE

ACKNOWLEDGMENTS

The original version of this biography of Ivan Aksakov was my doctoral dissertation. I would like, therefore, to acknowledge my deep and sincere gratitude to my teachers Professor Nicholas V. Riasanovsky and Professor Martin Malia of the University of California, Berkeley, who guided and helped me through my graduate years. In particular I must thank Professor Nicholas V. Riasanovsky for encouraging me to prepare this work for publication and for his many invaluable criticisms and suggestions. I am also grateful to Professor Oleg Maslenikov of the Department of Slavic Languages and Literatures of the University of California, Berkeley, for serving as a member of my thesis committee. I would like to express also my gratitude to Professor Valentin Riasanovsky who, although retired and in poor health, has read this work and enriched it with many comments and remarks.

For the material side of this research I must thank the Ford Foundation for a generous fellowship that enabled me to complete my thesis and the University of Delaware for helping me to prepare the manuscript.

I dedicate this book to my father to whom I owe everything and to my wife, Olga, for her help, loyalty, and understanding.

S. L.

Newark, Delaware
September 1, 1964

Contents

Ivan Aksakov
1823–1886

A STUDY IN
RUSSIAN THOUGHT AND POLITICS

The following abbreviations are used throughout the footnotes:

I. A., *Pisma*   I. Aksakov, *Ivan Sergeevich Aksakov v ego pismakh,* 4 vols., Moscow, 1888–1892.

I. A., *Sochineniia*   I. Aksakov, *Sochineniia,* 7 vols., Moscow, 1886–1887.

Barsukov, *Pogodin*   N. Barsukov, *Zhizn i trudy M. P. Pogodina,* 22 vols., St. Petersburg, 1888–1910.

Introduction

This work is an attempt to portray the life and ideas of a militant Slavophile who participated actively in the many great changes that occurred in Russia and Europe in the second half of the nineteenth century. It is an attempt also to describe the interplay between the ideas, personalities, and challenges of that rapidly evolving society. Moreover, Ivan Aksakov (1823–1886) was so prominent as a Slavophile tribune and civic leader that his biography cannot help but enrich our knowledge of Russia's social history during the reigns of Alexander II and Alexander III.

Ivan Aksakov's name is indissolubly linked with Slavophilism, but he should not be put in the same group with his elders— Khomiakov, the brothers Kireevski, Konstantin Aksakov, and even Iuri Samarin.[1] Unlike them he was not a Slavophile ideologist; indeed, his contribution to Slavophilism in the domain of ideas was almost nil. His only innovation was perhaps his reinterpretation of the role of conscious society, or *obshchestvo,* which the elder Slavophiles had neglected or even condemned in the reign of Nicholas I.

The real significance of Ivan Aksakov can be measured only in terms of his lifelong efforts to transform Slavophilism into a popular movement. His earliest biographer and contemporary, S. Vengerov, noted pointedly: "Ivan Aksakov did not give Slavophilism a single new idea, he did not enrich its arsenal with a single new argument, and he did not advance a single significant detail in the field of theory." However, the same Vengerov hastened to add: "Ivan Aksakov has done more for the triumph of Slavophile ideas than all the theoreticians of Slavophilism put together, although they

---

[1] A. S. Khomiakov (1804–1860); I. V. Kireevski (1806–1856); P. V. Kireevski (1808–1856); K. S. Aksakov (1817–1860); Iu. F. Samarin (1819–1876). To this group we could add A. I. Koshelev (1806–1883) and the Slavophile historian I. D. Beliaev (1810–1873).

excelled him by the breadth of their thinking and the depth of their education." [2] In a similar vein one of the political enemies of Ivan Aksakov wrote: "By his nature, by the qualities of his talent, Ivan Aksakov was not an innovator but a propagandist; he was not a thinker but a preacher." [3]

These two evaluations are meaningful inasmuch as Slavophilism continued to influence Russian thought long after Aksakov's death. In this respect, for all that he lacked original creativity, he appears to have been an important link between the older Slavophiles and the neo-Slavophiles of the end of the nineteenth and the beginning of the twentieth century. [4]

In the case of Ivan Aksakov, to be unoriginal meant perforce to be eclectic. His position, perhaps, can be explained in the following way. As the recognized head of the Slavophile movement, Aksakov attempted to translate Slavophilism into a language that could be readily understood by laymen. It was his self-appointed duty to discuss the issues of his day from the Slavophile point of view. To succeed in this task he chose from Slavophilism only those ideas he thought would be convenient, expedient, or necessary for his purpose. This meant, since Slavophilism was a teaching based on dialectically reconciled contradictions, that Aksakov could use antithetically opposed arguments without betraying the content of Slavophile ideology. But, if this sort of flexibility was convenient for Aksakov or had its place in the realm of philosophical thinking, it was sometimes galling and confusing for the average, unsophisticated reader who searched in the Slavophile publications for a firm foundation on which to build a stable world view. Slavophilism is dialectical in nature and, consequently, its puzzling effect on readers in search of a revelation may help to explain why it did not lead to a popular

[2] S. Vengerov, *Kritiko-biograficheski slovar russkikh pisatelei i uchenykh*, 6 vols. (St. Petersburg, 1889–1904), I, 319–320.

[3] Anonymous, "Ivan Aksakov," *Vestnik Evropy* (1886), no. 3, p. 443. The same article can be found in K. Arseniev, *Za chetvert veka* (1871–1894) (St. Petersburg, 1915), pp. 251–264.

[4] See "Estimates and Influence of Slavophilism," in Nicholas V. Riasanovsky, *Russia and the West in the Teaching of the Slavophiles* (Cambridge, Mass., 1952), ch. vi, pp. 187–213.

political movement, and why it was frequently misunderstood by all those who tried to place it either to the left or the right of the political scene. Indeed, in his lifetime, Aksakov was accused frequently of being a liberal and a reactionary at the same time. In fact, he was a strange mixture of both, and, because the divide between apparent inconsistency and opportunism is often impossible to determine and the temptation to mistake the one for the other so great, it is necessary to attempt a preliminary clarification of this problem.

Slavophilism was a complex phenomenon that possessed several levels of significance. The first and the most striking of these was its intellectual and religious aspect. Slavophilism was the child of romanticism or, as Professor N. Riasanovsky says, "To speak of the influence of the romantic spirit on the Slavophiles is not quite adequate: it would be more correct to say that spiritually the Slavophiles were a part of the romantic movement."[5] However, if romanticism in the West can be seen as a reaction against the principles of the Enlightenment, Slavophilism itself was a protest against the Europeanization of Russia that had begun at the end of the seventeenth century. The eighteenth century in Europe was rationalist, freethinking, cosmopolitan, and materialist; the romantic reaction to it, including Slavophilism in Russia, was permeated with religiosity, faith, spirituality, and national self-consciousness. Indeed, Slavophilism cannot be separated from Orthodoxy and from *narodnost*. For the Slavophiles the word "narodnost" meant both the spirit of Russia and belief in this spirit; it was both the cult and the essence of Russian national identity, a problem the Slavophiles pursued with the same fervor as that with which the German romantics sought to determine the significance of the German *Geist* and the virtues of *Volkstümmlichkeit*.[6]

As a corollary to their quest for the meaning of the existence of

[5] *Ibid.*, p. 166.

[6] D. Chizhevski, *Gegel v Rossi* (Paris, 1939); B. Iakovenko, *Geschichte des Hegelianismus in Russland* (Prague, 1938); A. Koyré, *La philosophie et le problème national en Russie au debut du XIXe siècle* (Paris, 1929).

Russia, the Slavophiles, like their western counterparts, believed that those nations which had an "interesting" history, a history appealing to one's imagination, were historical nations; all other nations were unhistorical—capable of being part of a culture but not of building one. From this concept sprang their mystical belief that every historical nation has a mission to fulfill among the other nations of the world. The Slavophiles believed that now it was Russia's turn to bring to the world a new culture, which would blossom as soon as Russia rediscovered her narodnost and the principles that were "organically" correct for her growth. Russia had not yet contributed to European culture because her normal historical growth and development had been stunted by the unnatural introduction of foreign "western" bodies into the Russian organism during the reign of Peter the Great. Thus the Slavophiles looked back with yearning at the Muscovite period of Russian history, in order to find in it the seeds of Russia's cultural fertility. In the West the romantics had chosen the Middle Ages as their favorite time in history.

Slavophilism is often connected with the history of religious thought in Russia. Indeed, the Slavophiles, A. Khomiakov, I. Kireevski, and, to a lesser extent, Iu. Samarin, contributed not only to the religious aspect of Slavophilism, but they initiated also a tradition of high-level lay theological thought in Russia.[7] These three men influenced such thinkers as Berdyaev as well as other representatives of the twentieth-century religious revival. Berdyaev himself declared: "Among us only the Slavophile philosophy is original and full of creative spirit," and A. Volzhski traced the religious ideas of Leontev, Solovev, and Dostoevski to a common Slavophile origin.[8] In fact the contribution of the Slavophiles to Orthodox spirituality is perhaps their most lasting heritage.

Another important aspect of Slavophilism was its preoccupation

[7] A. Gratieux, *Khomiakov et le Mouvement Slavophile,* 2 vols. (Paris, 1939), vol. I: *Les hommes;* vol. II: *Les doctrines;* B. Nolde, *Iuri Samarin i ego vremia* (Paris, 1926).

[8] N. Berdyaev, *A. S. Khomiakov* (Moscow, 1912), p. 123, and A. Volzhski, "Sviataia Rus i russkoe prizvanie," *Voina i kultura* (Moscow, 1915) are both quoted in Riasanovsky, *Russia and the West,* p. 209.

with the problem of national identity. The Slavophiles sought to discover "correct" social principles that would serve as antidotes to the errors committed by the Europeanization of Russia and that would put Russia back on a genuine historical path. Upon these principles depended the future cultural mission of Russia. However, these national and religious aspects of Slavophilism have been well explored; it is the social implications of the movement that have either been neglected or misinterpreted. The only socioeconomic studies of Slavophilism have been made by Soviet scholars; these are often crude and inadequate because they do not take into account any motivation other than group interest and lucre.

The purpose of this chapter is to advance a tentative explanation of the social aspects of Slavophilism, since it is possible to view Slavophilism as a movement in part motivated by the discontent that its exponents experienced with the society in which they lived. However, one difficulty of an attempt of this sort is the fact that we are dealing with a fluid situation. The social conditions of the forties were not the same as those of the fifties or the sixties, and to trace in detail the evolution of the social and economic views of the Slavophiles through three decades is beyond our scope. Instead, an attempt will be made to give a synthetic picture of the underlying social assumptions of Slavophilism in general, with all the limitations that such a loose method entails. However, before even attempting to synthesize the social and economic views of the Slavophiles, the following must be noted.

First of all, it is not possible to understand the social and economic aspects of Slavophile ideology by searching for a meaning in the relevant writings of the Slavophiles. Indeed, one notices that Ivan Aksakov, Koshelev, and Iu. Samarin were much more interested in social and economic questions than the other Slavophiles. Secondly, they wrote on these questions only in the late fifties and in the sixties, after the death of the older Slavophiles. It would not be fair, therefore, to generalize, by assuming that the writings of these people expressed the essence of the socioeconomic thoughts of all the Slavophiles. What can be done, however, is to point out the possibility of interpreting Slavophilism, not through direct quotations from the writings of the Slavophiles, but through a study of the significance of the relations existing among the Slavophile arguments.

The Slavophiles, who were only a small group—A. S. Khomiakov, the brothers P. and I. Kireevski, the Aksakovs, and Iu. Samarin— belonged to the landowning gentry. The estates they owned were either small or of medium size and the number of their serfs was correspondingly modest. The gentry as such had reached its economic and political apogee during the reign of Catherine the Great. The reign of Paul I, although short, marked the beginning of apprehension on the part of the gentry. This was aggravated by growth of bureaucratic government under the reign of Alexander I. The Decembrist plot jeopardized even further the status of the gentry; the government became very cautious, and the last vestige of their autonomy was taken away when Nicholas I placed the gentry assemblies under the direct supervision of the local governor-general and restricted the right to vote to the richer landowners.

The average gentry lost much of its social importance as well when the Edict of Liberties of Peter III and the Charter of Nobility of Catherine the Great released them from compulsory service to the state. In other words, the gentry became a class with privileges and no responsibilities. They could still be useful either in the army or the bureaucracy, but a career as a petty official or a low-ranking officer did not offer much incentive and could not keep them in service for long. And the alternative to such service was an obscure and often idle life in the provinces or a ruinous life in the cities where many lived beyond their meager resources. The lesser gentry can be described as the "superfluous men." They enjoyed privileges without earning or deserving them; this abnormal situation added to their insecurity. And at this point it is possible to suggest that a psychopathological study of the "superfluous men" in a rigidly hierarchic society might be a valuable approach for understanding some of the problems of the social history of Russia in the nineteenth century. Indeed, the westernizers, the Slavophiles, the *narodniki,* as well as the representatives of all the other currents of social thought, whether reactionary or radical, might be examined as groups attempting to create a society in which they would be accepted and recognized. In the third chapter of this work this problem will be illustrated by the struggle of Ivan Aksakov for the rights of the poor gentry within the *zemstvo*.

The Slavophiles wanted to see a new Russia in which they would be reintegrated. They wanted to be needed again; they wanted to be useful. For this they had to destroy the barriers that separated them from the majority of the Russians, in particular, they had to forfeit their privilege to own serfs. They had to repudiate their European veneer and to return to a genuinely Russian way of life. The Slavophiles believed that Russia would be able to create a culture of her own as soon as she was restored to social and historical integrity. Thus their desire to abolish serfdom as the first step toward national regeneration may be viewed as having at least three causes. The first was their romantic drive toward national identity; the second was their wish to be reintegrated into a new society that would not begrudge the injustices of the past, and the third was the fact that the abolition of serfdom corresponded also to their economic interests. It is not easy to decide which of these three causes was the prime-mover of the social doctrine of Slavophilism, but it is safe to assume that each of the three might have exerted an influence on the other two. The extent of this influence is of course impossible to determine. Nonetheless, the exclusion of the gentry from a participation in civic affairs was perhaps only second to their economic plight.

The economic impoverishment of a large section of the gentry had many causes. First of all, the absence of a law of inheritance similar to the law of primogeniture allowed the estates to be parcelled out among many. Ironically enough the gentry was opposed to such a law, though it would have preserved the economic strength of their class. They were alarmed at the desire of Paul I to pass a law allowing only one member of a family to inherit an estate.

Another reason for their plight was the collapse of the prices of agricultural products in the markets of Europe—a collapse caused by the competition of agricultural products imported from America or the Danubian areas, after the end of the Napoleonic era. And,

because the Russian gentry had seldom possessed sufficient capital
for the modernization of their estates and for their transformation
into profitable enterprises, this competition was particularly disastrous for the landowning class. In addition to this, it must be said
that the Russian gentry, as a class, were never spurred by an adven-
turesome capitalist spirit; they were bogged down by antiquated
notions and a fear of all innovations. Besides, the Russian government, which under different circumstances, might have helped the
gentry, was itself poor and inefficient; it could not assist or advise
the landowners in the modernization of their estates or in the creation of an adequate transportation system that might have eased the
marketing of their agricultural products. In reality, however, the
lack of capital and of modern technology made competition unbearably difficult in European markets. Furthermore, the absence of an
internal market, which could have absorbed all the products that
could not be sold abroad, made the gentry economy dependent on
foreign trade.

To this frightening problem of survival, there was but one immediate answer: the gentry had to increase their landholding and
decrease their production costs. Only an abundance of goods, obtained at low cost, could provide the gentry with a better position
for competing in the foreign markets. Such an answer could have
been found easily in the emancipation of the serfs. The serfs could
become hired laborers, paid only for their seasonal services; moreover, then they would have had to return a part or all of their land
to their former masters, because their plots of land belonged officially to the landowner. Apparently such a solution was needed very
urgently by the poorer landowners. The Slavophiles were among
the landowners who opposed serfdom. In spite of their claims that
an end to serfdom was needed for the realization of their dreams
of national unity, it is tempting to see just a selfish economic reason
behind their wish to free the serfs. But who can say with authority
that in the fancy of the romantic Slavophiles the price for cereals
on the markets of Europe was any more "real" than their wishful
visions? [9]

[9] For the Soviet point of view see the articles by S. Dmitriev, "Slavianofily i
Slavianofilstvo," in *Istorik marksist* (1941), no. 1, and "Slavianofily," in *Bolshaia*

The founding fathers of Slavophilism had been educated in the European tradition. They had been brought up on European culture, they spoke European languages, and most of them had traveled in the West. Indeed, the Slavophiles were culturally very much a part of Europe. On the other hand, as romantic idealists they brooded about the inferiority of Russia and her lack of creativity in almost every sector of life. The Slavophiles wanted Russia to become the seat of a new culture and they resented the cultural backwardness of their country. Thus their feelings toward Europe were ambivalent. They both admired and envied Europe. On the political level they feared the menace of a materialistic and atheistic Europe; on the cultural level they felt inferior to the West. They perceived Europe as a threat and they wanted to see the West "decay." This can be explained, perhaps, as a simple form of self-assertion—the negation of a menacing external force.

Nonetheless, despite their complex, the Slavophiles believed that Russia, though backward, had a certain advantage over Europe. Russia enjoyed relative stability; she was neither threatened by a revolution from below nor by one from above—engineered either by the bourgeoisie or the aristocracy. A revolution from below was unlikely as long as the peasant commune prevented the peasants from losing their land and becoming a dangerous proletariat. And the tsar as the absolute autocrat of Russia made sure that no constitutional or oligarchical movement could threaten his throne. According to the Slavophiles the tsar, the peasant commune, and Orthodoxy were the institutions that guaranteed social peace in Russia. The Slavophiles felt that such peace was necessary in order to change Russia for the better.

In the Slavophile ideology, Orthodoxy had several meanings; above all, Orthodoxy designated the soul or the spiritual mystery of Russia, just as narodnost represented Russia's self-consciousness and personality. Such an interpretation fitted well in the romantic conception of the state, which was viewed as a living historical organism; and, though the Slavophiles rejected the reactionary con-

sovetskaia entsiklopedia, vol. 51 (Moscow, 1945). See also N. Tsagolov, "Slavianofily," in Istoriia russkoi ekonomicheskoi mysli, 2 vols., A. I. Pashkov, ed. (ANSSSR, Institut ekonomii: Moscow, 1958), vol. I: Chast II—Epokha feodalisma 1800–1861.

clusions of this approach, namely, that the division of Russia's population into estates and the existing inequality between these estates
were just as necessary to the historical organism of Russia as the
specialization and the inequality of the various limbs and organs
were to a body, they preserved the ideas of the higher manifestations
of a living organism, such as personality-narodnost and soul-Ortho-
doxy. At the same time, Orthodoxy also meant to them the Russian
Orthodox faith and the Russian Orthodox Church.

It is clear, therefore, that the meaning of Orthodoxy in the writings of the Slavophiles can be understood only with the help of the
accompanying text. Thus, with respect to what has been said earlier
about social peace, Orthodoxy was assigned several roles in Slavophile sociology. First of all, Orthodoxy fulfilled the role of a spiritual
democracy. The Slavophiles did not believe in *egalité;* as for *fra-
ternité,* it could only be achieved in the bosom of the Orthodox
Church. The Slavophiles wanted to see all Russians equal before
the law, but they also realized that an emphasis on equality was at
the source of all the revolutions that were disturbing the West.
They noticed further that these revolutions did not bring equality
but rather introduced by force new patterns of inequality. The
autocracy that they knew was typically Russian; it had developed
organically throughout one thousand years of Russian history. The
Slavophiles felt that this autocracy was the correct form of government for Russia. The tsar and the autocracy could be seen as sym-
bols of paternal benevolence, whereas, they argued, a constitutional
government would be tyrannical because it had no historical authority. As for the peasant commune, the Slavophiles considered it a
truly national institution preserved by history since the dawn of time.

The Slavophiles hoped to revive the *Zemski sobor* or "Assembly
of all the Land." The *Zemski sobor* of the Slavophiles, like that of
Muscovite Russia, was to be a consultative institution; it would
serve as an expression of the mutual trust that existed between the
tsar and his people. The Slavophiles were certain that the tsar and
his *Zemski sobor* were far superior to any type of constitutional
monarchy or democracy. The Slavophiles imagined their Russia of
the future as a multitude of peasant communes ruled by democratic

principles under the aegis of an autocratic tsar. Democracy at the local level and autocracy at the state level were to coexist harmoniously. The *Zemski sobor* was to serve as a link between these two forms of government. It would discourage the desire for a western-style constitution and would, at the same time, reduce the power of the bureaucracy. But in their writings the Slavophile thinkers did not outline with any clarity the future of the city dwellers and all those who did not belong to the peasant communes. As for workers, they were to organize themselves in producers' cooperatives, or *arteli* modeled after the communes.

The Slavophiles supported their arguments by examples taken from history. Peter the Great was blamed for diverting Russia from her true historical path. He was accused of putting an end to the Golden Age when Russian society was well integrated. And, indeed, this point may have been well taken since the more primitive a society is the less stratified it tends to be.

History was used further to prove that the Russians were apolitical and not state-minded at all (*narod negosudarstvennyi*). The Slavophiles supported the Normanist thesis that claimed that the Novgorodians had summoned the Varangians to rule over them because they themselves were incapable of creating a state.[10] The peasant commune was also historically justified. The Slavophiles saw in the commune a mode of association peculiar to the Slavs alone and preserved by the Russians throughout the centuries. The commune was an "organically correct" expression of the Russian spirit and as such it deserved to become the base of a regenerated Russia. However, this claim met with a violent rebuttal from various historians, in particular, Boris Chicherin. He tried to prove that the commune as a primitive form of association had died in Russia as elsewhere and that the peasant commune, as it existed in the nineteenth century, was a police institution born of economic and historical needs —devised to ensure the payment of taxes and the recruitment of

[10] On Slavophile historicism see N. Rubinshtein, *Russkaia istoriografia* (Moscow, 1941). See also A. Predtechenski, "Slavianofily," in *Ocherki istorii istoricheskoi nauki v SSSR*, 2 vols., M. Tikhomirov, M. Alpatova, and A. Sidorova, eds. (Moscow, 1955–1960), I, 325–331.

soldiers. The collective was responsible for checking the flight of its members. Its nature was coercive, neither Christian nor moral as the Slavophiles would have had it.[11]

Russia had an advantage over Europe also because Russia was young and vigorous, whereas Europe was old and ill. The future could belong to Russia and to Slavdom. The Slavic nations would absorb the new Russian culture; they would be the *tabula rasa* on which Russia would write her contribution to mankind. The Slavophiles had faith that a new era would dawn in Russia as soon as the Russians rediscovered their narodnost.

To this minimum political program, namely, Orthodoxy, autocracy, and the peasant commune, the Slavophiles added: emancipation of the serfs, freedom of expression, and narodnost. As already mentioned these six points were closely related. The peasant commune was to minimize the potential dangers of emancipation. It was to preserve the land of the peasant, protect the peasants from becoming landless paupers, and prepare the ground for the integrated Russia of the future. Freedom of expression was included although it was fraught with danger from their point of view. It could invite the creation of a constitutionalist movement, which was in their eyes perhaps the most baneful type of western "lie." But by assigning the chief role in their ideology to an autocratic tsar, the Slavophiles no doubt believed that they could parry this threat. Finally, narodnost, in order not to be the brutal expression of the popular spirit, was at all times to be tempered and guided by Orthodoxy. Otherwise, it might become a source of obstreperous passion, unpredictable and uncontrollable. In other words, narodnost and Orthodoxy were to coexist in an organic symbiosis, and it is only in such a symbiosis that narodnost would be the genuine expression of the true, "historical" spirit of Russia. In this context, Orthodoxy meant above all Christian morality.

From what has been said, it becomes understandable why the

---

[11] B. Chicherin, *Vospominaniia,* 5 vols. (Moscow, 1929–1934), II, 262–266. See also Prof. V. M. Shtein, *Ocherki razvitiia russkoi obshchestvenno-ekonomicheskoi mysli XIX–XX vekov* (Leningrad, 1948)—in particular, "Proiskhozhdenie i soderzhanie ucheniia Slavianofilov o selskoi obshchine," pp. 110–146.

Slavophiles were to a certain extent conservative and progressive at the same time. They wanted to improve on what they thought were Russia's greatest assets—orthodoxy in its manifold manifestations, autocracy, and the peasant commune. They had also to protect these national virtues from further corruption. Therefore, they militated against any further imitation of the West.

In reality, however, the Slavophiles were caught between a monarchy and a regime created by their archvillain Peter the Great, a westernizer *avant le mot,* and the continuing westernization of Russia. By professing Slavophilism they were forced to criticize the established order of things; this attitude made them unreliable in the eyes of the government. Their adherence to the idea of autocracy, their hatred of any constitutional movement, as well as their clinging to archaic visions, made them appear reactionary in the eyes of the more radical elements of Russian society. In fact, both the government and the radicals were right. For instance, Ivan Aksakov would act as a staunch liberal when he thought that the conservatives were a danger to an adequate settlement of serfdom; yet, on the other hand, when he sensed that the established order was threatened by liberal and revolutionary ideas, he lent a generous hand to reaction. In both cases he was consistent within the Slavophile world view.

The life of Ivan Aksakov is an interesting one, because it is complex and rich. Indeed, Ivan Aksakov was not only a man of great talents and boundless energy, but he was also a prominent figure in one of the most crucial periods of Russian history. Moreover, Aksakov had a message to convey to his generation: as a Russian and as a Slavophile, Aksakov suffered at the sight of the Europeanization of Russia. In this respect, Aksakov was not against the modernization of Russia, but he was against the servility of the mind and of the body that often accompanies the admiration and the imitation of one culture by another. By preaching his Slavophile gospel, Aksakov hoped to convince the Russians not to lose their self-respect and their confidence that one day Russia would contribute to the culture of the world. This struggle on behalf of Russia's honor and self-respect became for Ivan Aksakov the justification of his life. And, if toward the end of his life, Aksakov became an embittered hater and a rabid chauvinist, it was because he realized that his life had been wasted in a futile turmoil. This work tries to present the major events and issues that took place during the lifetime of Ivan Aksakov through the prism of Aksakov's mind. And, because of the intensity of Aksakov's beliefs, Russian history acquires in the process a certain poignancy, which often borders on despair.

CHAPTER II

A Reluctant Slavophile

Ivan Sergeevich Aksakov was born on September 26, 1823, on one of the estates belonging to his father—the village of Nadezhino, near Belebei in the province of Ufa. He was the son of Sergei Timofeevich Aksakov, the well-known author of "A Family Chronicle," the "Years of Childhood," and several other works that have earned him fame and a place in Russian literature. The senior Aksakov was blessed with fourteen children—six boys and eight girls—many of whom died in infancy. Of this numerous brood only Konstantin (1817–1860) and Ivan were to become noteworthy in the social and intellectual history of Russia; a third brother, Gregory, became the governor of one of Russia's eastern provinces.[1]

The young Ivan was barely three when his family moved to Moscow where his father had received the office of censor through the good will and protection of A. S. Shishkov, the Minister of Public Education. The task of a censor consisted in perusing, accepting, rejecting, or correcting the poetry and the prose which were destined for publication. No article, poem, or book of any sort could be published without the sanction and the seal of the censor. As a consequence of the father's position the Aksakov home became a

[1] Konstantin, the famous Slavophile, was also a philologist and a playwright. And there was also a sister Vera Aksakova who left a diary: *Dnevnik Very Aksakovoi* (St. Petersburg, 1913). On Konstantin consult: S. Vengerov, *Ocherki po istorii russkoi literatury* (St. Petersburg, 1907), which includes a valuable study: "Peredovoi boets slavianofilstva (Konstantin Aksakov)," pp. 379–492, also published separately (St. Petersburg, 1912). In English, see Edward Chmielewski, *Tribune of the Slavophiles: Konstantin Aksakov*, University of Florida Monographs, Social Sciences, no. 12 (Fall 1961), and N. Riasanovsky, *Russia and the West in the Teaching of the Slavophiles* (Cambridge, Mass., 1952), pp. 49–52 et passim. On the Aksakov family the best work is V. Schenrok, "S. T. Aksakov i ego semia," *Zhurnal Ministerstva Narodnago Prosveshchenia* (1904), nos. 10–12, pp. 355–418, 1–66, 229–290 (in sequence).

focus for the news and gossip of the Moscow literary world, which much interested their many guests, who were for the most part the best that the intellectual society of Moscow had to offer. The Aksakov children, who were never separated from the adults about them, circulated freely in this atmosphere and were frequently exposed to heated debates and spirited talk. This may well account for their mental precocity, for Ivan's in particular.

The Aksakov family was apparently very close knit, sharing many interests and leading a common spiritual life, but it seems that it was Konstantin, the oldest child, who was the center of affection for his entire family. Such familial solidarity and the emotional authority of Konstantin may well explain the attraction that later led Ivan toward Slavophilism. The young Aksakovs were brought up in a patriotic and religious spirit. In this respect, their mother, Olga Semenovna, had an enormous influence on the minds of her children. She taught them patriotic tales as well as songs and poems that extolled the glories of the Russian past. This is somewhat surprising since Olga Semenovna was only half-Russian; she was the daughter of one of Catherine the Great's generals and of a captive Turkish noblewoman. Their father, on the contrary, was "never a patriot . . . he was uninterested or indifferent to public affairs," to quote his own son Ivan.[2]

The games played by the children reflected their upbringing. They were always of a historical and patriotic nature, organized and invented by brother Konstantin. The most striking game he introduced was, perhaps, the "Day of Viachko." Every November 30 the entire family celebrated the glorious death of Viachko, an obscure Polabian Slav prince who had committed suicide instead of surrendering to the conquering Germans. On this day all the boys wore armor that had been made specially for the occasion out of sheet iron. The girls dressed in *sarafans* and all sang a mournful ballad written by Konstantin, relating the heroic deeds of Viachko and his manly death. After singing, Russian refreshments were served. The children played other games as well—one consisted of "sinking" paper boats bearing English and French flags, a children's

[2] Ivan Aksakov, "Ocherk semeinogo byta Aksakovykh" in I. A., *Pisma,* I, 13, 18.

premonition of the Crimean campaign! As Ivan Aksakov recalled later: "No . . . hobbyhorses, nor dolls, nor any other playthings were known in the home of the Aksakovs."[3]

Another example of the spirit in which the children were brought up is that the use of the French language, so widespread in the Russian society of that time, was generally avoided by the Aksakovs and disliked as unpatriotic. This negative attitude so affected the children that when they came across a piece of French correspondence, they confiscated it, took it to the attic, stabbed it with knives borrowed from the family pantry, and burned it triumphantly in an auto-da-fé. The execution was usually accompanied by a chorus singing anathema to the odious foreign language. However, these childhood pranks, to be sure, did not prevent Ivan Aksakov from becoming a consummate linguist later in life.

By comparison with his ebullient brothers and sisters, particularly with Konstantin, Ivan Aksakov was a silent boy of a rather morose disposition. He appeared to be somewhat limited in his mental capacities. The revelation pointing to the contrary came quite unexpectedly. At the age of seven Ivan took ill with scarlet fever and to prevent contagion his parents confined him in a room of the entresol of their house. Lonely and bored, the young boy wrote a long missive to his brothers and sisters. The letter amazed everybody by its length, quality, and liveliness. From that time on, opinion about the young Ivan changed altogether. In one of his letters the old Aksakov prophesied: "What can I say about Ivan? I can only say that I am astonished. Ivan will be a great writer."[4]

At the age of ten Ivan was an avid newspaper reader. He was especially fond of politics. When following the revolutionary activities in Spain, Ivan declared himself a Carlist! To be deprived of newspapers was the worst punishment that his parents could inflict on him. In fact, this predilection for foreign affairs remained with him for the rest of his life.

Ivan received his early education at home. His parents hoped that he would be admitted to one of the schools that would lead him to

[3] *Ibid.*, pp. 21, 22–23.
[4] *Ibid.*, p. 3.

a career in either the administration or the army. The choices were
limited in the bureaucratic and professional military order that
prevailed in Russia under Nicholas I. At first, his parents wished to
place him at the Corps of Pages, which prepared future Court and
Guard officers. When they discovered that Ivan was already too
old to qualify, they decided to let him try the newly created Imperial
School of Jurisprudence. And in April 1838 Sergei Aksakov took
his son to St. Petersburg.

On the day following their arrival, Ivan passed his examinations
brilliantly, whereupon he was admitted to the fourth grade of the
School of Jurisprudence. Later, recalling the examination Ivan's
history teacher Kaidanov said among other things: "How excellently
Aksakov answered all the questions! I listened and he lectured to
me." [5]

At first, Ivan did not like the school or his classmates. He took
refuge in reading and read intensively; his favorite authors were
the French historians Guizot, Capefigue, Michaud, Thierry, and
Barante, all very popular at that time. He also wrote very often to
his father, with whom he discussed the articles and books he had
been reading. Unfortunately, these letters have never been published; perhaps they were not even preserved.

Poetry and reading were not Ivan Aksakov's sole interests. While
a student at the School of Jurisprudence, he became interested in
Old Slavonic. He liked to study and compare the ancient manu-
scripts preserved in libraries or in private collections and corresponded on the subject with Professor M. Pogodin, an eminent
professor of history at the University of Moscow and an ardent
Russian nationalist. He also studied Latin, Greek, English, and
German, as well as the literature of these languages, but how deep
or how successful were his varied studies it is difficult to say. In a
letter to Pogodin, one of Aksakov's schoolmates wrote: "Vania
is a different man, he is more of a man of letters and a philosopher,
although his studies in law are very successful." [6]

Many of the features that characterized Ivan Aksakov in his

[5] *Ibid.*, p. 27.
[6] Barsukov, *Pogodin*, V, 484–485.

mature years could be found already in his school years. Ambitious and energetic, he once wrote: "I wonder what sort of destiny fate has in store for me? . . . I am horrified at the thought that I may live like the rest of them without leaving a lasting memory . . . But after all, you must give a push to your own destiny in one direction or another. Fate then will have to be kind." [7]

Ivan Aksakov led a busy life. In addition to his duties as a student, he devoted much time to the theater. His favorite theater was the Mikhailovski where only French plays were performed. To the dismay of his friends and elders, the young Aksakov was wont to skip church on the eves of great Orthodox holidays in favor of some French vaudeville performance.

It was during his stay in St. Petersburg that Ivan Aksakov became acquainted with Belinski, the famous Russian literary critic, whom he visited frequently. He did not fall under the sway of the "violent Vissarion" (*neistovyi Vissarion*) but the relations between the westernizer and the budding Slavophile were very cordial. And this in spite of the fact that Belinski and Ivan's brother Konstantin had become enemies over questions of ideology. We read in the memoirs of A. Ia. Golovacheva-Panaeva:

In the early forties, in the mornings of the days when the school was closed, the young student of Jurisprudence, Ivan Sergeevich Aksakov, used to come and see Panaev in order to read him his poetry. Panaev was very friendly with the young poet. He acquainted him with Belinski, who encouraged the young man to continue to work in literature. Belinski thought that Ivan Sergeevich Aksakov was much more intelligent and talented than his brother Konstantin.[8]

It was only much later in his life that Aksakov, commenting on Belinski's letter to Konstantin marking the final rupture between the two former friends, exclaimed that the letter of Belinski was "full of the most coarse, the most insane, the most cynical insults against Russia and the Russians." [9]

[7] I. A., *Pisma*, I, 31.
[8] *Vospominaniia A. Ia. Golovachevoi-Panaevoi, Russkie pisateli i artisty—1824–1870* (St. Petersburg, 1890–), p. 99.
[9] I. A., *Sochineniia*, VII, 579–583. See also Barsukov, *Pogodin*, V, 456–457.

In March 1841 Ivan Aksakov experienced a cruel loss. His brother
Mikhail, a cadet at the Corps of Pages, was suddenly taken ill and
died in Ivan's arms. Younger than Ivan, Mikhail Aksakov was a
budding composer of great talent. Ivan faced his death with admirable restraint and courage and took it upon himself to console
his grief-stricken parents.[10]

In 1842, at the age of 19, Ivan finished the Imperial School of
Jurisprudence. His only prospect after graduation was a career in
the bureaucracy and it is not hard to imagine the frustrations that
this would bring him. While preparing for his final examinations,
he wrote: "I want to snatch the tribute of respect that is owed to
me in the field of learning. I have no intention to play the pitiful
role of the man who is not understood, who is not appreciated, who
has been hurt by fate." And in one of his last letters from school,
he further described his state of mind and his expectations:

As far as I can judge, I am completely healthy, both physically and
mentally. I am full of unswerving assurance in myself and I thirst for
work; but what I want is hard work, great and beneficial work. A man
must not be deterred by any circumstances and must follow his path
without waivering as long as he breathes, and live not in continuous fear
and anxiety but in a creative drive toward the goal he has set for himself. So while we are alive, we shall work and undertake such tasks as if
we were not supposed to die at all.[11]

It is clear that the Russian bureaucracy was not exactly the place
where the young enthusiast could carry out such a program, and
it is understandable that he experienced more than a few qualms
before entering official service. These are admirably described in
his famous poem called, "The Life of an Official." The poem was
a lyrical farce describing the inner confusion of a young man about
to start a career in the bureaucracy. The young man is tempted by
the "career demon" and counseled against the fatal step by the
"mysterious voice." But, alas, the young man succumbs to the temptation, joins officialdom, and lives to regret it.[12]

[10] Barsukov, *Pogodin*, VI, 57–58.
[11] I. A., *Pisma*, I, 35, 36.
[12] *Ibid.*, Appendix, pp. 1–19.

Shortly after his graduation, Ivan Aksakov received a position in a branch of the Ministry of Justice, in what was then called the Moscow Senate. Eager to shine, he could not endure the stultifying atmosphere of his office and at the first opportunity he requested to be sent on a mission to the provinces, which became possible in 1844. He was appointed to go with an auditing commission to Astrakhan. The commission stayed in this city from January to November 1844, and from there Aksakov wrote long and detailed letters to his family.[13] These letters were like a diary in which Aksakov recorded his observations and his thoughts. He used to say that "he who does not know me through my letters, knows very little of me."[14] And Peter Struve, speaking of Aksakov's correspondence, said:

There is one other form of literature—the epistolary form—in which the name of Ivan Aksakov ought to be put in the first rank of Russian literature. He left letters remarkable in content and in form, in which was reflected all the wealth of his spirit, of the variety of his problems and interests. These letters are instructive historical documents of their time; they also are an admirable product of our national literature, which sometimes rise to incomparable poetic beauty.[15]

In Astrakhan Aksakov came face to face with Russian provincial life, and it may be said that it was from this time on that he began to ponder about Russia and her problems, although he did not yet think of himself as a Slavophile. In one of his letters he wrote: "Although I am not at all a Slavophile, I collected, just for fun, some money for the churches of Dalmatia and Herzegovina."[16] His conversion to Slavophilism was to be a painful and slow process and to come about ten years later, in the late fifties, when Ivan came under the spell of Khomiakov and his brother Konstantin.

Aksakov was appalled at what he saw in Astrakhan. On more than

[13] "Letters from Astrakhan," I. A., *Pisma*, I, 42–225.
[14] *Ibid.*, p. 2.
[15] P. Struve, "Ivan Aksakov," *Slavonic Review* 2:518 (1924). The Russian text is "Aksakovy i Aksakov" in *Russkaia Mysl* (Prague-Berlin, 1923), no. 6–8, pp. 349–358.
[16] I. A., *Pisma*, I, 192.

one occasion he exclaimed: "Oh, Russia! How full of trash and rottenness you are!" [17] But what grieved him most was the sloth of the Russians and their economic backwardness. He believed that the only solution for this was to be found in the material exploitation of all Russian resources and through hard work on the part of everybody. Aksakov fulminated against the typical Slavophile discourses on the sanctity of the Russian *muzhik*. He refused to entrust the future of Russia to some hidden and problematic qualities of the Russian people. In one of his letters he explained his views in the following way: "Instead of crying with the people from whom I am already separated by consciousness, I would work for the good of the people, be it gradually, be it indirectly, but, nevertheless, realistically and not just talk about it." [18]

Leaving Astrakhan at the end of 1844, Ivan spent the winter and the summer of 1845 in Moscow. During this time he wrote the second of his long poems, "The Winter Road," in which he caricatured the Slavophiles and the westernizers. In this poem he imagined a conversation between two travelers, one pro-Russian, the other pro-western. While they spent their time matching their wits, they were jolted by the news that a new levy of serfs had to be produced for service in the army. This parable probably meant that while the Russian landowners were theorizing on the future of their country, calamity was endured by the people alone.[19]

In September of 1845 Aksakov received an assignment in Kaluga where he was to stay until the end of 1847. During this period he spent most of his free time at the home of Anna Osipovna Smirnova-Rosset, the wife of the governor of Kaluga. She was a woman of great beauty and unusual intelligence. Among her many admirers, Pushkin, Lermontov, Gogol, Khomiakov, Samarin, and even the old Aksakov were infatuated at one time or another with Anna. Her house in Kaluga became a salon where political and literary news was discussed. She corresponded with Gogol and Samarin; Ivan was

[17] *Ibid.*, p. 61.

[18] *Ibid.*, p. 168.

[19] *Ibid.*, Appendix, pp. 23–48. Pogodin noted in his diary: "Ivan Aksakov read to me his poem. Excellent. Here is a budding promising man," in Barsukov, *Pogodin*, VIII, 63. A few pages later Barsukov discusses Aksakov's stay in Kaluga.

able to receive all the news from Moscow. It is quite possible that he fell in love with her, but the latter was so much older than he and had so much experience that the young Ivan thought her lacking in feeling and understanding. However, the poems that Aksakov wrote in Kaluga are the most sensual of all his poems. They point to the unsublimated passion of their author and to his longing state of mind.[20]

The years Ivan spent in Kaluga were years of mental turmoil and confusion. In one of his letters Aksakov moaned: "I do not feel anything young in me. What do I feel then?—Nothing. I have no creative ideas, just an echo, a worthless echo of other people's thought."[21] He tried to escape by reading and writing. He read many theological books and wrote about thirty poems. Anna Osipovna wrote about him to Gogol: "I admit that eccentric people bore me . . . The continuous questioning whether art and social order are consonant with the teachings of the Gospel causes in me an intolerable impatience. Here, Ivan Aksakov indulges in such questions."[22] And in a letter home Aksakov admitted that: "All this time I was horribly tormented and alarmed by the question of how to reconcile art with religion and I felt incredibly despondent . . . Of course, I did not solve the problem and I ceased somehow to think so much about it; this problem is a matter of paganism and Christianity, of religion and life; in short, it may take you far."[23]

In another letter to his father Aksakov wrote: "I feel that I could become at any moment either an atheist or an ascetic. This indifferent resignation which does not solve anything, this moral comfort are repugnant to me."[24] Disgusted with life and with himself, he criticized the state of things in Russia, the immorality of St. Petersburg and its bureaucracy, as well as the lack of freedom to act. He wanted to resign but did not for fear of the enforced idleness that might result.

In May 1846 when Belinski visited Kaluga, he and Ivan renewed

[20] "Letters from Kaluga," I. A., *Pisma*, I, 226–440.
[21] *Ibid.*, p. 297.
[22] Barsukov, *Pogodin*, VIII, 537.
[23] I. A., *Pisma*, I, 384–385.
[24] *Ibid.*, p. 416.

their acquaintance, but Ivan, out of solidarity with his brother Konstantin, treated Belinski rather coldly although personally he admired him. In a letter to his father and brother he wrote: "All the life, all the activities of Belinski were not spent in banal quests. He often changed his views but he was at all times carried by his convictions. I do not like Belinski, but one must be impartial."[25] Ten years later, Aksakov repeated:

I have traveled far and wide in Russia, the name of Belinski is known to any thinking young man . . . There is nothing strange in that, for youth likes violent negation. Every protest, every demand for freedom and justice is accepted with enthusiasm, wherever abomination, oppression, slavery, and cowardice threaten to engulf man. "We owe our salvation to Belinski" I was told by the young and honest people of the provinces everywhere.[26]

In a letter to Herzen written shortly after his visit to Kaluga, Belinski reported: "I met Ivan Aksakov in Kaluga. What a fine young man! He is a Slavophile, but he is as nice as if he never was one. I realize that I am guilty of a horrible heresy when I begin to think that among Slavophiles there can really be decent people."[27]

In Kaluga, Aksakov studied Polish and became very fond of Mickiewicz's poetry. He admitted that the latter's book *Le messianisme* made a profound impression on him and he was filled with joy and admiration when Gogol published his obscurantist *Selected Passages from the Correspondence with Friends*. He saw in this work an answer to his own inner perplexity or as he himself described it, "the reconciliation between life and Christianity." As a result, Ivan clashed with his father over the evaluation of the book. Sergei Aksakov censured Gogol and his work: "The best that can be said about the book is that Gogol is insane," he said in his first letter on the subject. On reading it a second time, the old Aksakov

[25] *Ibid.*, p. 338. See also "Perepiska Aksakovykh s N. S. Sokhanskoi (Kokhanovskoi)," *Russkoe Obozrenie* (February 1897), pp. 591–592. In this letter written in 1858, Aksakov gives a rather unflattering description of Belinski who was, according to Aksakov, a man without stable convictions.

[26] I. A., *Pisma,* III, 290.

[27] A. Herzen, *Byloe i Dumy* (Moscow, 1958), III, 493. A. Pypin, *Belinski: Ego zhizn i perepiska,* 2 vols. (St. Petersburg, 1876), II, 262.

maintained that "Gogol's book is extremely noxious, everything in it is false and as a result the impressions left by this book will have to be spurious. You are the nearest live proof to my words." He branded the book as "not only Catholic but pagan." After an exchange of many letters, Ivan conceded that his father was right.[28]

Marriage was a touchy matter for Ivan Aksakov. When Konstantin suggested to Ivan that he should look for a suitable bride, Ivan was angered. In his answer, Ivan wrote: "Konstantin's point of view on marriage is not worth anything. Marriage becomes something common and banal . . . I do not need the peaceful happiness that makes a person banal. Maybe in a few years I shall be ripe for marriage; in other words, it will be when I become more trivial, more cowardly, and more sedate. Such is the law of nature!" [29]

Ivan Aksakov disagreed with his brother on another point. He did not believe in, as Konstantin said, "returning to the people." "I do not share the dreams of Konstantin that we could entirely sympathize with the people because we have left the sphere of pure nationality. I would become insane if I had to live constantly with a *muzhik* . . . Konstantin's ideas are a Utopia à la Georges Sand." [30] This attitude was to remain at the core of Ivan Aksakov's interpretation of Slavophilism. It was to be a Slavophilism without the people and in spite of the people, or *narodnost* without the *narod*.

From Kaluga Ivan anxiously followed the political events in Europe and was impatient at the lack of change: "Louis-Philippe is quarreling with Victoria; this amuses me—they might even come to blows. For too long a time mankind has been bogged down in idle daydreaming for lack of thundering, frightful, and sobering events." [31] And then came the revolutions of 1848–1849. Aksakov was exultant:

At last we are witnessing breath-taking events. What a time to be alive! History is made under our own eyes and you can hear vaguely

[28] I. A., *Pisma,* I, 406–416. The letters of Sergei Aksakov are in the footnotes on pp. 407–409, 411, 413–415.
[29] *Ibid.,* p. 420.
[30] *Ibid.,* p. 418.
[31] *Ibid.,* p. 339.

the great destinies of the world! Who could expect it? Now that the West has turned away from its guiding principles, that it is so enmeshed in the labyrinth of its own intellectual tinkering as not to find a way out, the importance of Russia becomes paramount. Our salvation resides in our independence.[32]

Commenting on Ivan Aksakov's world view in Kaluga, V. Schenrok remarked: "His Slavophilism was quite moderate and reasonable; if later, after the death of his brother, he made many mistakes and fell into extremes, this cannot be said of him in the late forties, when he expressed ideas about cherished Slavophile topics that could have pleased any non-Slavophile."[33] Ivan Aksakov admitted in 1848 that: "If there is anything good in me, I owe it to the Moscow movement but I am completely independent and I would not put on Russian national dress."[34]

When his mission in Kaluga was fulfilled, Ivan Aksakov returned to Moscow, but in the fall of 1848, a few months after his return, Aksakov was forced to resign from his position in the Moscow Senate. His resignation was a direct result of his refusal to countersign a court order that acquitted a young aristocrat of the murder of his mistress during a drunken orgy. Aksakov's protest against such a flagrant injustice reached the ears of Nicholas I; the case was reviewed and the culprit was punished with utmost severity. Vindicated, Aksakov could have returned to his post in the Moscow Senate, but he declined to do so, because he was already working for the Ministry of the Interior.[35]

His first mission for the Ministry of the Interior took him to Bessarabia, where he was sent to investigate the organization of the Old Believers or Dissenters (*Raskolniki*) and their contacts with their bishop who lived across the border in one of the Rumanian principalities. It was on this occasion that Ivan became acquainted

---

[32] *Ibid.*, p. 439.

[33] V. Schenrok, "S. T. Aksakov i ego semia" in *Zhurnal Ministerstva Narodnago Prosveshchenia* (1904), no. 11, p. 56.

[34] I. A., *Pisma*, I, 458.

[35] I. A., *Pisma*, II, 2. More details on this *cause célèbre* can be found in A. K. Borozdin, "I. S. Aksakov v Iaroslavle (Otryvok iz vospominani)," *Istoricheski vestnik* (1886), no. 3, p. 264.

with two new peoples—the Ukrainians and the Jews. He felt at once a great aversion for both groups, but he thought that the Jews could be converted to Christianity as soon as enlightenment reached them. As for the "lazy" Ukrainians with their "distrust of the Muscovites," they were beyond redemption.[36]

In January 1849 Aksakov went to St. Petersburg to give a secret report on his findings in Bessarabia. Remaining there for a few months he became more intimately acquainted with the Slavophile Iuri Samarin. It is from this period that we gather the first evidence of Ivan Aksakov's views on serfdom, though it is hard to say whether these views were prompted or influenced by Aksakov's acquaintance with Iuri Samarin, who later worked in an official capacity on the emancipation of the serfs, both in Russia and in Poland. Upon learning that his elder brother, Gregory, was settling as a landowner, Aksakov wrote:

If I were married and had children, I would naturally strive for their security but in Russia this security is acquired through landownership. As for me, I give my word of honor that I will never own serfs or peasants; no matter what people say, the tempting benefits of the status of landowner are detrimental to a clear view on the peasant question . . .

My opinion is that the landowners should suffer a certain loss at the emancipation of the serfs because for centuries they have enjoyed scandalous rights . . . My conscience tells me that a peasant who toils on the land . . . has more right to this land than I do . . . One brother is becoming a landowner, the other will strive with all his might to deprive him of many of his benefits! [37]

In fact during his stay in the capital, Aksakov even toyed with the idea of writing a book about all the atrocities committed by the landowners known to him and his friends through their personal or professional experience.

Ivan Aksakov was in St. Petersburg when news reached Russia that Louis-Philippe was overthrown, and that the revolution, traveling eastward, was delivering blows on Prussia and Austria. Needless to say that the revolutionary fever of 1848 occasioned grave concern

[36] "Letters from Bessarabia" in I. A., *Pisma*, II, 3–95.
[37] *Ibid.*, p. 108.

for the autocratic regime of Nicholas I. Yet, the revolutionary storm
of 1848–1849 did not directly endanger the Russian Empire although
it had many less direct consequences. Autocracy was ready to defend
itself. The control of the life of the country by the police was
tightened. Any departure from the prescribed way of thinking was
hunted down and persecuted. The Slavophiles were among the chief
suspects on the list of the state police. Samarin was arrested in the
first week of March 1849 for his "Letters from Riga" in which he
assumed the defense of the oppressed peoples of the Baltic coast
against the German nobility.[38] Ivan Aksakov was arrested a little
later on March 18. The police had opened his letters and found a
few rash expressions that rendered Aksakov subversive in their eyes.
Moreover, Slavophilism was falsely believed to be connected with
the Czech Pan-Slav movement. Pan-Slavism was a reprehensible
attempt of the subjects of the Habsburg or Ottoman empires to
rebel against their God-given legitimate rulers, which Nicholas I
could not tolerate.

On the day of his arrest, Aksakov was ordered to submit a detailed
answer to a questionnaire submitted to him by Prince A. Orlov, the
Chief of Gendarmes. Fortunately his answers have been preserved.
They are valuable because they represent the Slavophile views at
that particular time, although it is difficult to say whether the
opinions expressed by Aksakov were really his. This suspicion arises
because there is a significant difference of tone in his letters before
and after his arrest, and in the tone of his answers to the police. In
his letters Ivan appears to be a man whose ideas on the problems
faced by the Slavophiles have not yet crystallized. In the report submitted to the Third Department Aksakov appears to have taken a
firm stand on behalf of all the Slavophile principles and his hatred
of the West is expressed most prominently.

Ivan saw the West as bad because its history was built upon
"false principles"; it lacked faith, and because of this, it had developed such ills as "anarchy, a proletariat, egoistical materialism . . .
Catholicism, Protestantism, rationalism and so forth . . . ," whereas
Holy Russia "was saved by Orthodoxy, which introduced altogether

[38] B. Nolde, *Iuri Samarin i ego vremia* (Paris, 1926), pp. 43–49.

different principles into the life of the people." One of these great principles was that the Russian people "looked upon the Tsar as the autocratic head of the great Orthodox commune." But Russia was not perfect. The gentry was completely divorced from the Russian people. It was the duty of the educated class "to recant, to re-educate themselves morally and become Russians again." Guilt and a longing desire to be accepted seem to be the predominant notes of these words.

Nevertheless, in spite of all this there was a brighter side to Russia. The Russian people nurture an aversion to revolution: ". . . the Russian people hate all upheavals, all violent revolutionary means, because these are contrary to the very foundation of their way of life, which is permeated by faith." Only the Russian government could do something to remedy the evil heritage of the reforms of Peter the Great. And, as for Pan-Slavism, Aksakov did not believe in it because Catholic and Orthodox Slavs were basically opposed to each other and could not be reconciled: "I must admit that Russia concerns me more than all the Slavs put together; as for my brother Konstantin, he is accused of being totally indifferent to all Slavs except Russians, and not even all Russians—just Great Russians." [39]

The answers of Ivan Aksakov were sent to the tsar. They pleased him much, insofar as one can judge by such marginal comments as: "absolutely correct," "the holy truth!," "thank God," and others in the same vein. Thus after a four-day detention, Ivan Aksakov was released on March 22, 1849. Speaking of the arrest of Aksakov, Professor B. Chicherin has concluded: "The half-educated jurist lambasted the free institutions and the civilization of the West about which he did not have the slightest idea. It goes without saying that such answers pleased Nicholas. Aksakov was freed and given an important mission." [40]

The Ministry of the Interior now dispatched Aksakov to Iaroslavl

[39] I. A., *Pisma,* II, 147–163. Also in M. I. Sukhomlinov, "I. S. Aksakov v sorokovykh godakh," *Istoricheski Vestnik* (1888), no. 2, pp. 324–348.
[40] "Perepiska Aksakovykh s N. S. Sokhanskoi (Kokhanovskoi),"*Russkoe Obozrenie* (February 1897), p. 594; B. Chicherin, *Vospominania: Moskva sorokovykh godov* (Moscow, 1929), p. 241.

on a multiple assignment. He was appointed to work with a commission auditing the administration of the town, but he had a secret
assignment as well. He was to help reintroduce a single faith into
a province where religious dissent was rife and, at the same time,
to investigate the mysterious sect of the *Beguny* or Runners.[41]
Aksakov was to remain in the province of Iaroslavl from May 1849
until the end of March 1851, a period of almost two years.

Aksakov's years in Iaroslavl have been described by the editor of
his letters as difficult years for the inner life of Ivan Aksakov, years
in which he was tortured by doubts on religious and social matters.
It appears that the events of 1848 had produced a violent turmoil in
his thinking. His disillusionment was bitter. In a poem entitled,
"After 1848," Aksakov wrote: "We have experienced a trying year/
there was strife and blood was spilt/ The destiny of our last dreams
was at stake/ But the decrepit world did not find rejuvenation." In
another of his poems called, "Let Everything Perish" (*Pust sgibnet
vse*), Aksakov exploded: "Let falsehood be exultant and submit
us/ reckless ones, to a bitter trial/ Brand us with the name of free-
thinkers/ Kill us! Reign! Triumph!" [42] This last outcry was not
the result of frustrated revolutionary dreams but rather the outcome
of a painful ambivalence. Aksakov, like the rest of the Slavophiles,
abhorred the conditions in Russia and yet could not welcome the
victory of the revolution. The joy he expressed on the occasion of
the victorious campaign of the Russian troops in Hungary clearly
confirms the latter point of view. His letters reflect the same confusion. In one of them he wrote:

I am completely off-balance. All this time, during the entire year of
1848, the beliefs that I acquired so painfully were shattered. Now I do
not have any human truth left about which I could not argue both for
and against. I have lost all faith in human intelligence, in our own
conclusions and considerations, as well as in logic and life itself.[43]

---

[41] "Kratkaia zapiska o strannikakh ili begunakh," I. A., *Pisma*, VII, 834–847,
and "O raskole i ob edinovercheskoi tserkvi v Iaroslavskoi gubernii," *ibid.*, pp. 848–
864. On Aksakov's stay in Iaroslavl see A. K. Borozdin, "I. S. Aksakov v Iaroslavle
(Otryvok iz vospominani)," *Istoricheski vestnik* (1886), no. 3, pp. 622–633; and
A. Khomutov, "Otryvok iz vospominani," *ibid.*, no. 7, pp. 47–56.
[42] I. A., *Pisma*, II, Appendix, pp. 51–52, 54–55.
[43] I. A., *Pisma*, II, 197.

Religion could not console him: "I know, there is a medicine—religion, but I cannot take it." "There is a moral truth but I cannot reconcile it with life and I have not the strength to renounce life." [44]

Ivan Aksakov set to work to try to rediscover some values and to reorganize his world view. He admittedly failed and confessed to his father:

> I do not have Konstantin's firmness of conviction. I have decided to study humbly and without any preconceived ideas the actual facts and events. I must admit that much of what I thought before has wavered ... I have lost faith in my own conclusions. When formulating a statement, I say like our friend Carolina, "yes, maybe; maybe, no." [45]

Having no strong religious beliefs himself, he nevertheless advised a young provincial autodidact, "to hold onto faith and church as to an anchor of salvation, for otherwise the torrent will tear you away." [46] He felt urgently the need for a discipline but could not find it for himself. There are indications that his ideas might have hurt the cherished beliefs of his family and the Moscow Slavophiles. His agony may have been the result of his failure to reconcile the opposing points of view.

Ivan's tension was released in epistolary clashes with Konstantin over the elder brother's historical views. Konstantin asserted that the cleavage between the upper class and the people was a result of the reforms of Peter the Great. On this point, Ivan tried to convince him that the cleavage had existed long before Peter's time between the men of service (*sluzhilye liudi*) and the rest of the people (*zemskie liudi*). This rift between the men of service and the others could explain the ease with which Peter the Great and Catherine the Great had separated the former group from the latter under the name of gentry. Ivan added that this cleavage was not only of a social but also of a cultural and psychological nature. The *sluzhilye liudi,* or the ancestors of the gentry, "were subjected to the Tartar and Byzantine influence a million times more than the peasants." [47] His point of view about the men of service is important

[44] *Ibid.,* pp. 189, 197.
[45] *Ibid.,* p. 240.
[46] *Ibid.,* p. 243.
[47] *Ibid.,* p. 249.

to this study because it recurs throughout all of his historical thinking and will be seen to form the base of his theory of *obshchestvo*.

Generally speaking, it was during his stay in Iaroslavl that Ivan
Aksakov began to dislike increasingly his brother's way of thinking.
Ivan complained to his father:

> I cannot, like Konstantin, console myself with sentences such as "the
> most important thing is to maintain the principles; the rest is nothing
> more than an accident," or that "the Russian people seek the Kingdom
> of Heaven," and so on . . . Indifference toward the common good,
> idleness, apathy, and a lust for personal gain are called a search for the
> Kingdom of Heaven! As for Konstantin's concern with principles, I
> must say that it amuses me. It amounts to telling to a hungry man,
> "my friend, you will have enough to eat in the next world; for the time
> being, starve—it is a mere accident. Instead of butter spread some
> principle on your bread, sprinkle it with more principle, and lo and
> behold, it tastes good!" . . . But where is this principle, where did it get
> lost? Go, go, Konstantin, and find it in a dusty chronicle of the twelfth
> or thirteenth century.[48]

The two brothers clashed also over the question of appropriate
education for the people. Konstantin proposed to limit elementary
education to the reading of religious books, which meant that he
did not want any modern education for the peasantry. In fact, in
order to teach the peasants the history of their country, every future
village library was to possess a collection of Russian medieval
chronicles! But Ivan wanted to have schools that would impart
to the children some useful and practical knowledge and he wanted
to exclude all religious literature from the curriculum. Religious
books were to remain a source of spiritual relaxation and nothing
else. As for Slavic art appreciation, Ivan told his brother: "I much
prefer Raphael's Madonna to the Russian paintings of saints." [49]

Yet, despite the differences in viewpoint between Ivan and Konstantin, and between Ivan and his father, who seemed to have an
inordinate affection for Konstantin, Ivan was not able to shake off
the influence of his family and its point of view. Commenting on

[48] *Ibid.*, pp. 300–301.
[49] *Ibid.*, pp. 287–288, 362.

his brother's poetry, Ivan declared: "The conviction displayed in these verses is known to me. I carry it in my soul but, I must admit, without faith, just as a man who does not believe thoroughly carries around his neck a holy image or a cross, out of habit and, also, because he likes to carry on his body the sign of faith."[50]

In Iaroslavl Aksakov helped in the creation of a school for the children of the merchant class. It was at this time that Aksakov began to be interested in the merchant class as a link between the peasantry and the upper classes. And it was also during his stay in Iaroslavl that Aksakov became acquainted with Baron von Haxthausen's book on Russia. The baron, on passing through Moscow, had fallen under the influence of the Slavophiles. He became a fervent admirer of the peasant commune and it is interesting to note that his book was used as an authoritative source on the peasant problem. The haters of the West were delighted by this recognition.[51]

Toward the end of the winter of 1851, Aksakov's days in the administration were clearly numbered. The governor of Iaroslavl complained to the Ministry of the Interior that Ivan Aksakov was known to have read a suspicious manuscript to his friends and acquaintances. Aksakov was asked to produce this manuscript, which happened to be a copy of his long poem *Brodiaga* ("The Vagabond" or "The Tramp"). The poem was found to be innocuous, but Aksakov was enjoined to explain his reasons "for choosing a passportless character as his hero" and was warned that "it was indecent for a man invested with the confidence of the government to write poetry."[52] Ivan Aksakov took offense and resigned from his post in spite of Iuri Samarin's efforts to dissuade him. He returned to Moscow where A. Koshelev, a wealthy Slavophile, asked him to

[50] *Ibid.*, p. 358.
[51] A. von Haxthausen (1792–1866): *Studien über die inneren Zustände, das Volksleben und in-besondere die ländliche Einrichtungen Russlands,* vols. I, II (Hanover and Berlin, 1847); vol. III (Berlin, 1852).
[52] S. A. Vengerov, *Kritiko-biograficheski slovar russkikh pisatelei i uchenykh,* 5 vols. (St. Petersburg, 1889–1904), I, 324. The poem was highly thought of by Gogol (see Barsukov, *Pogodin,* XI, 135), and by Turgenev (see *Vestnik Evropy* [1894], I, 334). The poem is in the Appendix to the second volume of Aksakov's letters, pp. 1–49.

edit a journal that the Slavophiles then intended to publish, the *Moskovski sbornik* (Moscow Anthology).

In 1852, the first volume of the *Sbornik* saw the light. The censorship passed it but made copious comments. The censors were particularly annoyed at an article written by Konstantin Aksakov entitled, "On the Old Way of Life of the Slavs in General and the Russians in Particular." In this article, Konstantin argued that a patriarchal way of life was not known among the Slavs. He insisted that the Slavs had always lived in the commune or *obshchina* and that this organization was based on primitive democracy. The mention of democracy alarmed Prince Shirinski-Shikhmatov, the Minister of Education in charge of censorship.[53] In this same issue Ivan Kireevski also published an article entitled, "On the Character of Education in Europe and its Relation to Education in Russia" in which he recommended a great emphasis on religious teachings for the Russians, a theme very dear to Konstantin Aksakov, as we have already seen. Ivan Aksakov, the editor, and Prince Shirinski-Shikhmatov, the censor, were both very displeased with this article, although for different reasons. Aksakov saw in it a call for obscurantism; the prince sensed in it a criticism of all the monarchs, who following Peter the Great, had introduced western methods into Russia.[54] This issue also included a couple of Ivan Aksakov's poems as well as contributions by Khomiakov, Koshelev, the famous historian Solovev, and the Slavophile historian Beliaev.

The second number of the *Sbornik* was not permitted. It was banned by order of the same Prince Shirinski-Shikhmatov, who could not tolerate the articles of the brothers Aksakov. Commenting on Ivan's essay on life in Iaroslavl, the Prince said: "This article is nothing more than an extremely indecent and continuous mockery of the mores and customs of provincial gentry society, which is not so much real as imagined by the author." [55] Perhaps even more dangerous were the annotated byliny or epic songs that Konstantin

---

[53] K. Aksakov, "O drevnem byte u Slavian voobshche i u Russkikh v osobennosti," *Moskovski sbornik* (1852), pp. 49–140. See also Barsukov, *Pogodin*, XII, 117–118.

[54] Barsukov, *Pogodin*, XII, 109–117.

[55] *Ibid.*, pp. 133–151. See also the anonymous article, "Epizod iz istorii slavianofilstva (1852–1853)," in *Russkaia starina* (October 1875), pp. 367–379.

had wanted to publish. In these byliny a tsar, although a Tartar one, was called a dog. As punishment, the authors of the *Sbornik* were forbidden to write or publish and, as a result, the journalistic activities of the Slavophiles were suspended for several years.

At about this time, in the early fifties, the relations between Ivan Aksakov and the other Slavophiles became strained. With a biting irony Ivan debunked the religious ideas of his elders—Khomiakov, Koshelev, and his brother Konstantin. The older Slavophiles were, at that time, strongly influenced by the sermons of Alexandre Vinet whose thesis was: "C'est par les châtiments du péché que Dieu veut nous retirer, individus et nations, des chaines du péché ... Les souffrances, en un mot, sont les preparatifs de la grâce." But Ivan Aksakov ironized:

"God has willed it" will say the pious man who strikes a wall with his forehead in the dark. There is no doubt, however, that had he taken a lamp he would not have bruised his forehead ... If we were to detect in every misfortune of ours a punishment sent by God, it would be sinful to avoid it. In that case, it would be a sin to try to cure oneself from cholera ... God has created a logical order of things which by the very force of its logic will punish anyone who tries to transgress this order.

His friends were appalled at him but could not change his views.[56] It is not for nothing that Professor Miliukov called Ivan Aksakov "the least religiously minded of all the Slavophiles." [57]

With the failure of the *Moskovski sbornik* Ivan Aksakov withdrew to the family estate of Abramtsevo near Moscow in order to study, although his stay there was suddenly interrupted when he learned that a Russian frigate was scheduled to leave St. Petersburg for a voyage around the world. He rushed to the capital and applied to join the expedition, but his desires were to be frustrated once more. He was refused permission as "politically unreliable," but

---

[56] N. Koliupanov, *Biografia Aleksandra Ivanovicha Kosheleva,* 2 vols. (Moscow, 1889–1892), vol. II, Appendix 8, pp. 43–47, 47–48, 53–54, 57–61, 61–68. The letters of A. Khomiakov to Ivan Aksakov are in volume VIII of Khomiakov's collected works. Alexandre Vinet was a Protestant Swiss theologian (1797–1847) who was an ardent defender of freedom of conscience.

[57] P. Miliukov, "Slavianofilstvo" in *Entsiklopedicheski slovar, Brokhaus i Efron,* XXX (St. Petersburg, 1900), 312.

was offered instead a mission to investigate the Ukrainian fairs for
the Imperial Geographic Society. Aksakov was in the South with
this mission when the Crimean war began.[58] At first he was elated
by the war. It was during the early phase of the Crimean campaign
that he wrote his martial poem "On the Danube!" But his glee
soon turned to gloom when he realized that Russia could not win
the war. In one of his letters he wrote: "What a frightful struggle!
They have on their side the sciences, art, talent, bravery, and all
the material means. We have only the righteousness of our cause
and our personal valor and nothing else." [59] On the other hand,
Aksakov believed that Russia deserved a punishment that would
help her "acquire wisdom" in order to mend her ways. Reforms
were urgently needed, particularly with respect to serfdom, "lest
events should catch unawares the landowners and deprive them of
their daily bread." [60]

The death of Nicholas I in February 1855 and the beginning of
Alexander's reign ushered in a softening of governmental policies.
The Slavophiles took advantage of this new situation to resume
their activities. Their new journal was *Russkaia beseda* (Russian
Colloquium). Ivan was irritated by the program of this publication
because "it was written in such a way as to create bewilderment,
repel from us the support of the young people and gain the sympathy of those for whom I have no use—the sympathy of arch-
bishops, monks, and the Holy Synod." [61] He believed that the
emancipation of the serfs should be the first concern of the "Colloquium." Speaking of emancipation, he wrote: "The more I think
of it, the more I am convinced that if this is not carried out in a
very near future, we will be beaten and dishonored more than

---

[58] I. Aksakov, *Izsledovanie o torgovle na ukrainskikh iarmarkakh* (St. Petersburg,
1858). See also his "Vvedenie k ukrainskim iarmarkam" in I. A., *Sochineniia*, VI,
Appendix, pp. 1–71. For this work Aksakov received both a medal from the Imperial
Geographic Society and the Demidov Prize from the Academy of Science.

[59] I. A., *Pisma,* III, 100. Aksakov was almost arrested for the poem "On the
Danube!" See V. Evgeniev, "Tsenzurnaia praktika v gody Krymskoi voiny," *Golos
Minuvshego* (1917), no. 11–12, p. 256.

[60] Barsukov, *Pogodin,* XIII, 251.

[61] *Ibid.,* XIV, 350.

once." [62] This was at a time when Russia was already suffering the agony of defeat and Ivan, prodded by his family and not of his free will, enlisted in the militia (*opolchenie*). However, the war was over before his unit reached the combat zone. He was demobilized and then returned to the South, to the Crimea, in order to investigate the malpractices of the Quartermaster Corps.

By December 1856 Ivan Aksakov was again back in Moscow, where the ranks of the Slavophiles had begun to thin out—the brothers Kireevski had died in that same year. He became more and more aware of the weakness of the Slavophile teachings and tried to think of some ways in which to make Slavophilism a strong movement, but he himself admitted that to rejuvenate Slavophilism was beyond his means:

> We do not know of any other weapons for the eradication of evil than those designed for us by European civilization: railroads, emancipation of the serfs, periodicals, newspapers, freedom of expression. This means, of course, that the railroads, the steamship companies, the telegraph and the rapprochement created by war will cause a complete amalgamation of Russia and Europe, creating a greater Europeanization of Russia than ever before. [63]

It was in this state of mind that Aksakov undertook his first trip to Europe. He enjoyed Europe as a whole but Italy enchanted him. On his return, Aksakov became the unofficial editor of the *Russkaia beseda,* although officially Koshelev occupied that post. Aksakov had to remain in the shadows as long as he was not allowed to have a publication of his own. Finally, in 1859, he received permission to start a paper of his own.

Ivan Aksakov's weekly newspaper was called *Parus* (The Sail). It did not last very long. The censorship ordered it discontinued after two issues, almost certainly because of its strong pan-Slavist policy, as will be further discussed in Chapter V, which is devoted

[62] I. A., *Pisma,* III, 263. The period following the death of Nicholas I was called "the thaw" (*ottepel*) by the poet F. Tiutchev (see V. Aksakova, *Dnevnik,* St. Petersburg, 1913, p. 102). The same expression was used in our time by the writer I. Ehrenburg to describe the softening of the political conditions in Russia after the death of Stalin.

[63] I. A., *Pisma,* III, 291. See also Barsukov, *Pogodin,* XIV, 348–349.

to the investigation of Ivan Aksakov's pan-Slavism. There is, however, another explanation given by the *frondeur* aristocrat, Prince P. Dolgorukov. According to him, the last lines of the introduction were of a humorous nature—they entrusted the *Parus* to all the rulers of the water "from the Old Neptune to the blue Russian water genie inclusively." The Third Department interpreted this remark as an attempt to ridicule the blue uniforms of His Majesty's gendarmes. Dolgorukov claimed that the paper was closed on account of that and not because of the incriminating articles.[64]

The end of *Parus* produced great dismay among the reading public of Moscow. The government, wishing to allay this bad impression, gave Chizhov, a friend of Aksakov, the right to publish a paper that would replace the *Parus*. The new publication was to be called *Parokhod* (the Steamer) but Chizhov had to promise that "the right of the peoples to autonomy" would never be mentioned in it. This proviso alluded to the propaganda of the Slavic Benevolent Committee, created in 1858, with Pogodin as its president and Ivan Aksakov as its secretary and treasurer. Ivan Aksakov turned down the offer and returned to the editorship of the *Russkaia beseda.*

Ivan Aksakov's failure in his journalistic venture was followed by the death of his father and the illness of Konstantin. The death of Sergei Timofeevich seemed to have left Ivan undisturbed. Indeed, in a letter to Turgenev Aksakov wrote: "I can only say that my way of life has not been altered because I have never lived much with my family, spending my school years and most of my life away from it." [65] But the reasons for this outward calm were different. Ivan Aksakov could not endure the close relation between his father and Konstantin. Every time that Ivan was recalled to Moscow

---

[64] P. V. Dolgorukov, *Peterburgskie Ocherki (1860–1867)* (Moscow, 1934), p. 177. This was corroborated in part by the editor of "Neizdannoe piatistishie A. S. Khomiakova" in *Russki Arkhiv* (1866), pp. 770–771. Ivan Aksakov in *Pisma,* IV, 16–24, reported that the closure of the *Parus* was due to the pan-Slav policy of the publication and the desire of "the government to place the pro-Slav organ of the press in St. Petersburg under its direct control so as to gear it to the vacillations of the governmental policies" (p. 16).

[65] Barsukov, *Pogodin,* XVI, 410.

the situation became unbearable for him. On these occasions he thought of every way of obtaining some new assignment away from Moscow. When he was finally forced to resign his government positions, his appearances in the familial home gave occasion to violent quarrels, in particular with Konstantin. His departures, on the contrary, were hailed as deliverances from an evil disturber. The diary of Vera Aksakova furnishes ample proof of the tension between Ivan and the rest of the family. On the other hand, the letters of Ivan Aksakov to his father are evidence of his desire to be loved and admired on a footing of equality with Konstantin. The death of the father bereaved Konstantin to the point of making him seriously ill. This grief was much too meaningful to Ivan Aksakov; he reacted to it by feigning indifference.

Shortly after the death of his father in 1859, Ivan Aksakov deserted his grief-stricken family and left for Europe. This second trip took him to Germany and the Slavic countries. In Belgrade he delivered to the Serbs the "Address to the Serbs" written by Khomiakov and signed by all the Slavophiles. He was enthusiastically received and feted in all of the Balkan lands.[66]

In the meantime, Konstantin's condition was growing worse and his doctors advised him to go for a cure to Europe. Ivan met him in Germany. They went to Switzerland and Bavaria although the rainy weather had a disastrous effect on the tubercular Konstantin. They decided to seek a warmer climate on the island of Zante in the Ionian Sea. Two weeks after their arrival in Zante, in December 1860, Konstantin died. Since Khomiakov had died of cholera in the fall of the same year the Slavophile ranks were now depleted and without leadership.

In 1861, Ivan Aksakov and Iuri Samarin were the only remaining Slavophiles of the former Moscow nucleus. Samarin was not avail-

---

[66] The "Address to the Serbs" can be found in A. S. Khomiakov's collected works, vol. I (Moscow, 1900), pp. 371–408. The first English translation of the "Address" can be found in Peter K. Christoff, *An Introduction to Nineteenth-Century Russian Slavophilism: A Study in Ideas,* vol. I: *A. S. Khomiakov* (The Hague: Mouton, 1961), pp. 247–268. On Ivan Aksakov's trip to Europe see: "Vospominanii Fridrikha fon Bodenstedta—Ivan i Konstantin Aksakovy," in *Russkaia Starina* (September 1887), pp. 571–591.

able for editorial work; he was busy with a commission preparing the emancipation of the serfs. Ivan, in spite of the laxity of his convictions, found himself the sole heir of Slavophilism. Aksakov understood only too well the awkwardness of his position. It was without false modesty that he explained:

> Forced by circumstances and all our friends to replace Konstantin, I have to experience all the time, besides grief, a vexing feeling of my own incapacity . . . In spite of that, I must willy-nilly serve them as a rallying point at least for the sake of appearances . . . I shall endeavor with all my strength to perpetuate the memory and the influence of Khomiakov and Konstantin.[67]

The simplest and perhaps the most misleading explanation of Ivan Aksakov's conversion from a wavering agnosticism to a staunch Slavophilism is given by Professor B. Chicherin:

> Much more intelligent and much more gifted than Konstantin Sergeevich was his brother Ivan . . . But having no serious background and no time to develop his own convictions he easily fell under the sway of his brother . . . Fanaticism more than intelligence or talent appeals to the hesitating.[68]

Such a statement, although correct in certain ways, is a ruthless condemnation of the behavior of Ivan Aksakov. Furthermore, it is weak because it does not try to speculate on the psychological problems that forced the "more intelligent" Ivan to follow the road of the "less intelligent" Konstantin.

It has been already mentioned in this chapter that tension existed between Ivan Aksakov and his family on account of the favoritism enjoyed by Konstantin. Love and jealousy caused Ivan to feel ambivalence toward his father and brother. Moreover, Ivan loved Khomiakov with an almost filial love. Since Sergei Aksakov, Khomiakov, and then Konstantin died in the space of a year and a half, it is not rash to assume that Ivan might have developed a guilt complex for having tormented his father and brother with daily quarrels in the last years before their deaths. Toward Khomi-

---

[67] V. Schenrok, "S. T. Aksakov i ego semia," *Zhurnal Ministerstva Prosveshcheniia* (1904), no. 12, p. 286.

[68] B. Chicherin, *Vospominania-Moskva sorokovykh godov* (Moscow, 1929), p. 240.

akov, Ivan was to preserve throughout his life a feeling of devotion and gratitude. In order to assuage the bitterness of his remorse, he might have decided to make the dead ones live by perpetuating their work and their ideas.[69] This seems to be a psychological explanation for the Slavophile "fanaticism" of Ivan Aksakov, to use Chicherin's expression.

But there was much more than a mere feeling of guilt behind Aksakov's rapid conversion to militant Slavophilism. It must be remembered that until 1861 Ivan Aksakov had been a failure. During the first thirty-eight years of his life he did not achieve any status in the administration or in the intellectual world. The death of his friends and his brother promoted him to civic leadership, gave him a feeling of importance, and made him in a few months a very controversial figure in Russian society. It is possible that Slavophilism was more an expedient than a truly adequate solution for Ivan Aksakov's social and psychological problems. This situation might explain his insecurity within the framework of the Slavophile ideology. This insecurity manifested itself in a sectarian narrow-mindedness akin to fanaticism and in an almost total lack of doctrinal innovation. As a consequence, the personality of Ivan Aksakov underwent a certain change. Whereas previously his friends had noticed his intelligence and his congenial character, they now began to notice his mental shortcomings. Vladimir Solovev, who knew Aksakov very closely, reminisced: "Ivan Sergeevich in spite of all his serious merits always appeared to be unnatural, as if some traditional armor was covering and hiding his wonderful soul."[70] Pavel Golokhvastov, another of Aksakov's close acquaintances, was even more cavalier in his description: "As for Ivan Aksakov, I do not

---

[69] There are some "circumstantial" evidences that seem to support this explanation of Ivan Aksakov's conversion to Slavophilism. For instance, before his brother's death Ivan wore a fancy hairdo and was cleanly shaven; after his brother's death Ivan grew a beard and combed his hair so as to look like Konstantin. [It is instructive to compare the portrait of Ivan Aksakov taken in 1858, which is one of the illustrations in vol. III of his letters, with his portrait taken in 1862, in S. Durylin, "Gogol i Aksakovy," *Zveniia* 3–4:325–364 (1934). This last item contains also a portrait of Konstantin Aksakov.]

[70] V. Solovev, "Iz vospominani—Aksakovy" in *Pisma Vladimira Sergeevicha Soloveva*, E. L. Radlov, ed., 3 vols. (St. Petersburg, 1911), III, 277.

know what to say . . . It would seem strange to call such a man stupid, but I cannot find a better word . . . In other words, when he reaches a certain point he becomes stupid." [71] It is pertinent to remark here that Ivan Aksakov ceased to write poetry about the time he became an unquestioning Slavophile, and poetry for a poet is basically a form of self-analysis. Professor Riasanovsky has justly remarked that Ivan Aksakov negated, toward the end of his life, some of the most cherished Slavophile principles.[72] This negation may be the result of the circumstances that promoted Aksakov's acceptance of Slavophilism.

[71] "Avtobiografiia Konstantina Leonteva," in *Literaturnoe Nasledstvo* (1935), no. 22–24, pp. 455–456.

[72] "Ivan Aksakov was a true Slavophile, the last one; he also served as an introduction to the extreme nationalism, Pan-Slav and otherwise, which became prominent in Russia at the end of his life and which marked a negation of the principles most cherished by the Slavophiles," N. Riasanovsky, *Russia and the West in the Teaching of the Slavophiles* (Cambridge, Mass., 1952), p. 55.

CHAPTER III

The Reforms of the Sixties

I. THE PEASANT AND THE GENTRY QUESTIONS

When Aksakov returned to Europe following Konstantin's tragic death, he petitioned the proper authorities to restore his right to edit and publish. At the time the *Parus* was banned Aksakov had been unconditionally barred from owning a publication or from writing for publication. But now, after many fruitless attempts to have this ruling withdrawn, Aksakov finally received permission to publish a newspaper, which he named the *Den* (Day). His efforts to obtain this permission were greatly aided by Countess Antonina Bludova, daughter of Count Dimitri Bludov, president of the State Council.[1] However, the debut of the *Den* was marked by indecision and by Aksakov's lack of faith in his own ability. In a letter to Countess Bludova, he confessed:

How could I publish a Slavophile periodical without the vivifying guidance and the severe control of Khomiakov and brother Konstantin? Of course, I know better than anybody all the difficulties and the danger of such a venture. I know well that I lack not only their knowledge but also their power of conviction. I think, however, that I shall be able to preserve at least the moral purity of the banner and prevent the interruption of the Slavophile tradition. Perhaps, I shall see the day when a man of greater merit will appear and deserve to take over the spiritual heritage of the Slavophile teaching.[2]

[1] Countess A. Bludova was known for her literary activity and for her championing of Orthodoxy in Volynia where she helped the erection of Orthodox churches and schools. The letters of Ivan Aksakov to Countess Bludova can be found in I. A., *Pisma*, IV, 181–256, and also in *Russki arkhiv* (1915), no. 6, 129–132.

[2] I. A., *Pisma*, IV, 182 (February 1861). Aksakov repeated the same thing in a letter to another friend, see "Pisma I. S. Aksakova k N. A. Elaginu," *Russki arkhiv* (1915), no. 1, p. 9.

Aksakov began to publish *Den* in the fall of 1861. The emancipation of the serfs, which had been proclaimed in February 1861, raised many questions that demanded comment. It did not take long for Aksakov to forget his initial hesitation and rush headlong into the melee.

Aksakov was opposed to serfdom as much or perhaps more than any other Slavophile. At least he was more outspoken than the others on the subject that he considered the greatest evil of the Russia of his day. He also knew that only a correct solution of this problem would guarantee Russia's future welfare. The manifesto announcing the end of serfdom had filled him with joy. In his first editorial Aksakov suggested the introduction of a new Russian calendar that would start a new count for the days and the years from February 19, 1861.[3] But inwardly, Aksakov was far from being satisfied with the Statute of Emancipation. In his letters he could not conceal his apprehensions:

The emancipation of the serfs is indeed a prodigious and hard-to-grasp event, a great and holy act. The important thing is that the word has been uttered: the emancipation of the serfs and the declaration that the peasants will not part with their land. The manifesto itself is written in an ugly fashion, in a Tartarlike language. The statute [*Polozhenie*] is extremely confused and verbose. Neither peasants nor landowners are satisfied. The peasants say: "there is something suspicious about this, there will be eventually genuine freedom but what sort of freedom is it to go and work the corvée for the landowner!"[4]

Aksakov believed that freedom (*volia*) for the peasants had to be freedom from poverty and wretchedness. He knew that they were not seeking political freedom but economic security. This economic security consisted of land—land which was threatened by the statute: "This stupid statute announces on its first page that the land is an inalienable property of the landowners; in other words, it defies

[3] I. A., *Sochineniia,* II, 1. See also V. Ulanov, "Slavianofily i zapadniki o krepostnom prave," in *Velikaia reforma,* 6 vols. (Moscow, 1911), III, 175–193.

[4] I. A., *Pisma,* IV, 48. Aksakov alluded to the period of time, known as the "temporary obligation," when the peasants were obligated to work for the landowners as before in order to allow the landowners to reorganize their economy. This mandatory period lasted until the spring of 1863.

the view evolved by the people on this question . . ."[5] The land belonged to the peasants; therefore, they should not pay any redemption fee for it. The landowners should be remunerated for the loss of their land by the government. Ivan Aksakov was outraged by the governmental decree that forced the state-peasants to pay redemption fees to the government treasury. Aksakov thought that it was just as absurd as forcing "an oak to pay for the ground from which it grew."[6] Answering the bigots who became maudlin over the "moral" decision to give land to the serfs and who waited for the "deep gratitude" of the peasantry, Aksakov raged:

We should not expect any gratitude from them. What for? Because we order them in a sweet voice to irrigate our fields with their sweat? Thank God, there is no gratitude . . . I believe, by the way, that the landowners are not badly off; the peasants are in a much worse position, not as compared with their former life, but as compared with their expectations and their lawful demands.[7]

The emancipation act was good only insofar as it struck a first blow against serfdom; in other ways "it contradicted all the natural and lawful demands of the people." Commenting on the peasant rebellions that had taken place in the spring of 1861, Aksakov reported to his friend, the Rev. M. Raevski in Vienna: "The peasants do not work, the energetic generals and their aides-de-camp whip them, banish them, shoot them and the landowners may thank God if this year they collect half of their usual income."[8]

By destroying the old economic relations between serf and master the abolition of serfdom introduced the need to reorganize society on new premises. First of all, a new modus vivendi between the masters and their emancipated serfs had to be found. This problem was precariously solved by the enforcement of the new regulations by the executive power of the government. The second problem was

[5] "Pismo I. S. Aksakova v Orlovskuiu derevniu," *Russki arkhiv* (1901), no. 6, p. 297.

[6] I. A., *Sochineniia*, V, 374. The same point of view was shared by Chernyshevski in his "Pisma bez adresa."

[7] "Pismo I. S. Aksakova v Orlovskuiu derevniu," *Russki arkhiv* (1901), no. 6, p. 299.

[8] I. A., *Pisma*, IV, 55 (May 1861).

to reinterpret the role of the gentry in the new social context. As Aksakov himself formulated it: "The peasant question is a gentry question as well."

The great controversy over the future of the gentry began shortly after the gentry of the Moscow province held its first convention after the emancipation. The convention met on January 4, 1862, in Moscow. Several vital questions were on the agenda. First of all, the convention wanted to discuss the new changes to be introduced in local management. This amounted to the discussion of the promised zemstvo institutions. The debates were very lively. One group insisted on giving up their gentry exclusiveness in the management of the zemstvo and having the other estates participate in a common effort for the common good. They were opposed by those who feared that their position was so precarious that the gentry might lose everything with the slightest concession; they wanted an assurance from the government that would guarantee the rights bestowed upon their estate by the Charter of Nobility.[9]

Such a state of affairs was not new in 1862. Demands for the abolition of gentry privileges had been uttered at several gentry assemblies. The most memorable assembly in this respect was the one held by the gentry of the province of Vladimir in January 1860. Protopopov, a local landowner, had declared:

Gentlemen! Nowadays, our aspirations must be inseparable with the needs and the aspirations of all the estates—consequently of the entire state. Let us sacrifice for the sake of the rebirth of our life the arrogant charts, the velvet books, the aristocratic titles, and let us request in exchange for all this proud, vain, and worthless grandeur—a title common to all the estates—that of free citizens, accepting autocracy and the general responsibility of the individual not to administrative arbitrariness but to a free judicial system with a freely elected jury.[10]

At the same assembly, a certain P. Bezobrazov spoke even more poignantly of the gentry apprehensions after the emancipation:

[9] Barsukov, *Pogodin*, XIX, 1–8; see also "Dnevnik Mukhanova," in *Russki Arkhiv* (1897), no. 1, p. 57.
[10] A. Kornilov, *Obshchestvennoe dvizhenie pri Aleksandre* II (Paris, 1905), p. 53, quoting from Khrushchov, D. P. *Materialy dlia istorii uprazdneniia krepostnogo sostoianiia pomeshchichikh krestian v Rossii v tsarstvovanie imperatora Aleksandra II*, 2 vols. (Berlin, 1860–1862), II, 313 et passim—an extremely rare work.

The way our country is governed . . . is well known to all of us. Who among you, gentlemen, has not experienced the tyranny of official arbitrariness and has not been convinced of the crying injustice of our legal system? All this was haunting us at a time when the significance of the gentry was not at stake, when the gentry was considered to be the leading estate and when the gentry, owning material means, could stand up against oppression! What will happen now? Will the new administrative and legal systems be so fair as to protect us and what is left of our property against arbitrariness and duress? What will happen if the gentry are sacrificed to official tyranny together with the people?[11]

The gentry of Vladimir had demanded the following protective measures: (1) the separation of powers; (2) a common administration for all the estates; (3) a zemstvo organization to represent all the estates—responsible only to the courts and not to the government; (4) the government and the police not to infringe upon law; (5) trial by jury; (6) each individual answerable to the courts; (7) every official to be made to answer to the courts without the right to lay the blame on orders from his superiors; (8) new measures to be introduced in order to consolidate credit in Russia.[12]

Similar demands had been made by other assemblies: the St. Petersburg, the Iaroslavl, and the Nizhni-Novgorod assemblies of 1860; the Kharkov assembly of 1861, and finally the Tver assembly of 1862. This last of all assemblies had been followed by governmental repressions—thirteen members were arrested and exiled.[13] One part of society had begun to nurture constitutional dreams. Its views were expressed by the clandestine newspaper *Velikoruss* (the Great-Russian), published by members of the radical intelligentsia. This movement was an abortive affair for it was promptly snuffed out by the government in 1861.[14] All degrees of liberalism on the part of the gentry was opposed by the reactionary nobility. This faction demanded that—in order to safeguard Russia from the combined

[11] Kornilov, pp. 52–53.

[12] *Ibid.,* p. 54.

[13] S. Svatikov, *Obshchestvennoe dvizhenie v Rossii,* 2 vols. (Rostov-on-the-Don, 1905), II, 20–30.

[14] V. I. Burtsev, *Za sto let,* 2 vols. (London, 1897), II, 30–34, for the program of the "Great-Russian." Even more radical were the demands of the writer M. Mikhailov in his address "To the Young Generation" (I, 25–33).

dangers of "red liberalism and bureaucracy"—the tsar should rule
Russia with the help of gentry representatives. Alexander II was
incensed at their oligarchical daydreaming; the authors of the petitions were put under police surveillance or banished like the liberals
of Tver.[15]

In brief, the liberal gentry as well as the reactionary gentry wanted
to receive guarantees from the government in exchange for the
money, prestige, or security they had lost as a result of the emancipation. The former group understood the need for emancipation and
the need to renovate Russia by demanding the necessary liberties.
The latter desired only to preserve their pre-reform status and to
acquire if possible a position comparable to that of the English lords.
The government sternly repudiated both of these groups.

The gentry was arguing at a time when peasant unrest was rife,
when student riots were disturbing the major cities, and when the
Polish rebellion was coming to a head. This period was assessed by
Ivan Aksakov as "an epoch of attempts, of varied strivings, of for-
ward drive and of regression—one cancelling the other—of the
despotism of science and theory over life, of the negation of theory
and science in the name of life, of oppression and liberalism, of conservative progress and destructive conservatism, of servility and
arrogance, of refined civilization and coarse savagery, of light and
darkness, of dirt and splendor." [16]

On January 6, 1862, only two days after the opening of the Moscow gentry assembly, Ivan Aksakov demanded in an editorial that
"the gentry should request permission to abolish itself, in a great
and solemn act before the eyes of Russia." [17] He felt, like the other
Slavophiles, that this step was not only justified but necessary, that
serfdom had become an institution only at the time of Peter the
Great and that it was greatly responsible for class cleavage in Russia. The gentry had descended from the military retinue of the
Kievan princes. The population of ancient Russia had been divided

---

[15] S. S. Tatishchev, *Imperator Aleksandr II—Ego zhizn i tsarstvovanie*, 2 vols.
(St. Petersburg, 1903), I, 363–365.
[16] Barsukov, *Pogodin*, XVI, 313–314.
[17] I. A., *Sochineniia*, V, 218.

between the ordinary people on the one hand and the retainers of the princes on the other. The retainers served the state, whereas the people cultivated the land, traded, and engaged in arts and crafts. This division was carried over into the Muscovy period where there also were two estates: the "people of service" (*sluzhiloe soslovie*) and "the people of the land" (*zemskoe soslovie*). The "land" lived under the jurisdiction and the rules of the communes (*obshchina*); property was owned by the communes and not by the individuals. And, as for the "servicemen," they never lived in communes and always owned personal property. Their activities were not geared to a collective; they were, as Aksakov puts it, of a *personal* nature. Their relations to the state were also "personal" for they received land for their services instead of a salary. The service people were divided into a hierarchy according to their functions and were on duty, whether active or on reserve, all their lives from birth to death.[18]

The most distinctive feature of the Russian gentry is that throughout its history it never developed an aristocracy. The best guarantee against an aristocracy was the peculiar institution of *mestnichestvo*. This word comes from the Russian word *mesto,* which means either place or rank; it may mislead a person by making him believe that the word *mestnichestvo* is the Russian word for hierarchy in the accepted sense of the expression. It was indeed a hierarchy but not founded on a title or a name but rather on the position held by one's ancestors. Thus, a person of the oldest and most illustrious family of Riurik—a pure aristocrat in the western sense of the word —had to yield in rank to a Saltykov or a Buturlin, because the father or grandfather of the latter had held a more important service position in Muscovy than had this Riurikovich's father or grandfather.[19]

The danger of aristocracy reappeared with the reign of Tsar Fedor Alekseevich toward the end of the seventeenth century. He abolished the books in which services were recorded and introduced the "velvet

[18] *Ibid.,* p. 197.
[19] *Ibid.,* pp. 197–198. Dmitri Valuev and Khomiakov among the Slavophiles were interested in the *mestnichestvo.*

books" (*barkhatnyia knigi*), where the emphasis was no longer on the services performed but on genealogy. Aksakov tells us that such an attitude was imported from Poland, that it antagonized Russian historical traditions, and for that reason could not endure. Indeed, a few years later, Peter the Great introduced the table of ranks that made "all aristocracy impossible in Russia." [20] The old families were obligated to serve the state as formerly but they no longer held an exclusive monopoly on service. Furthermore, when he reached a certain rank, a commoner could become a member of the gentry and this privilege was to deal another crushing blow to the aristocratic exclusiveness of the old nobility. Peter the Great did try to differentiate between the old and the new nobility by calling the former *szlachta* but soon they both became known under the single name of *dvoriane* or gentry. The peasants continued to work for their lords of the old or the new nobility; the system was not altered and was essentially a just one.

The greatest disservice rendered to the gentry, ironically enough the most fervently desired by them, was the edict of Peter III "On the Liberties of the Gentry" of 1762, which authorized the gentry to forego their obligation to serve the state. Catherine the Great added in 1785, a "Charter of the Nobility," in which she reaffirmed the privileges granted to the gentry by her late husband and in which she tried to organize the gentry into a privileged estate. The danger of an aristocratic system loomed large but failed to materialize. This would-be aristocracy could not be created along genealogical lines because most of Catherine's favorites were of recent nobility; it could not assume an English character because in England an aristocrat was by birth both obligated and privileged to serve the state. In Russia the obligation of the gentry to serve the state had been cancelled by Peter's edict and Catherine's charter; the exclusive right to serve the state had been taken away previously by Peter the Great.[21]

One of the privileges Catherine granted to the gentry were the titles of hereditary nobility which had not existed before. Yet, it was not possible for the nobility to become a closed caste because any-

[20] *Ibid.*, p. 198. [21] *Ibid.*, pp. 200–201.

one could have access to it through service to the state and as a result of reaching a certain rank.

In the light of this history one wonders why the gentry felt they had a right to become a separate estate. According to Ivan Aksakov, the Russian nobility could be called an estate only from the time of the privileges granted to them by Peter III and Catherine II. Their most substantial and their most exclusive privilege was the right to own serfs and the right to own populated lands. The peasants continued to serve their masters and pay taxes although that was no longer justified; the labor of the peasants was no longer a reward for services to the state. The emancipation of the serfs put an end to serfdom and at the same time an end to the gentry privileges. The Emancipation statute provided that after redemption payments were completed peasants were to have a right to acquire and own land, the merchants also. And as soon as corporal punishment was abolished for the other estates, there would not be any social differences between the gentry and the others as far as rights were concerned. Was there any future for the gentry at all? Ivan Aksakov assigned the gentry, as the most educated class, to the zemstvo: "The disbanded retinue is returning home to the zemstvo bringing into it a new element."[22]

Aksakov took the position that the gentry had lost their former social and historical significance; they should not now lament the loss of their privileges or cling to a past to which there is no return. Addressing them, Aksakov said:

We think that the Russian gentry should first understand the historical development of the gentry institution and realize that further existence of the gentry as an estate (*soslovie*), as it was in the past, is impossible after the great act of February 19, 1861; secondly, they should jettison all their memories, all their fruitless regrets, as well as their pride and exclusiveness and, finally, they should destroy all the barriers that separate them from the people, in the political and in the moral sense, they should also make clear their position vis-à-vis the other estates.[23]

Aksakov continued by pointing out that the initiative belonged to the gentry. Russia was rent by great social contradictions; there

[22] *Ibid.*, p. 202.   [23] *Ibid.*, p. 206.

was no powerful public mind in Russia because it was forgotten
that "there is no other force outside the people and its history."
Russia was being rebuilt on a new foundation, for that reason she
must rediscover the unity of her historical, spiritual, and moral
principles; in other words, Russia must rediscover her *narodnost*
or her personality as a living historical entity. The first step toward
a renovation of Russia must be the abdication of the gentry and the
gentry privileges must be altered and spread to all the other classes
of Russia. This, of course, ought to be preceded by a complete
liquidation of the remnants of serfdom and "a just remuneration
for the losses suffered by the landowners in the incomes of their
estates." [24] Furthermore, the emancipation that put an end to "one
hundred and fifty years of inequity" ought in no way to affect the
economic conditions of the gentry. The demand for the self-abolition
of the gentry as an estate was to have only a social effect, not an
economic one: the landless gentry would become rank-and-file
citizens (*obyvateli*), whereas the landowners would remain as of
old. The "just remuneration" was to help them to maintain themselves in their position.

These were the arguments that Aksakov used against the more
reactionary wing of the gentry. Aksakov was convinced that in a
few years the social distinction of the gentry would not mean anything anymore. And so, the self-abolition of the gentry proposed
by Aksakov would appear to be the *beau geste* that would rehabili-
tate the gentry from the guilt of serfdom. Indeed, he felt that self-
abolition of the gentry as a separate entity would be an act of con-
trition that could redeem the horrible sin of serfdom in the eyes
of the Russians. It would be a first step toward a *rapprochement*
between the estranged parts of Russian society. This latter argument could be supported by the great concern that the Slavophiles
had for mending, or rather bridging, the gap that separated the
upper and the lower strata of the population. The self-abolition of
the gentry would not have obliterated their significance; on the
contrary, Aksakov retained them as landowners and as leaders of

---

[24] *Ibid.,* pp. 208, 216, 218. A detailed exposition of Ivan Aksakov's theory of the
obshchestvo or public mind will be given later in this chapter.

the zemstvo that was about to be created. In brief, Aksakov wanted the ex-gentry to remain the pillar of the renovated Russian state but first they needed to be absolved for their sins in order to write a new page in Russian history.

Aksakov's stand on these questions raised a stormy protest among the gentry at large; as a result, Aksakov acquired many enemies and lost a third of his subscribers. The gentry question started a fierce polemic among Aksakov, Katkov, and Chicherin. The brunt of the fight was assumed by Katkov who shared to a certain extent the ideas of Aksakov but only insofar as the abolition of the gentry as an estate was concerned. Katkov, in his *Sovremennaia Letopis* (Contemporary Chronicle), demanded "the eradication of all barriers between the estates and the replacement of the elections within each estate by the elections of the entire zemstvo." [25] Professor B. Chicherin answered Katkov in *Nashe Vremia* (Our Times). He called the thought of abolishing the gentry "the most current . . . the most commonplace expression of liberalism." He continued by saying that "to imagine that the problem of serfdom could be solved by the statute and that the estate which had existed firmly for many centuries would disappear one fine day is sheer political naïveté." Chicherin accused Katkov of wanting to see the division of Russia into parties—a vertical division, as opposed to the horizontal division of the estates. Katkov retorted that he did not dream of introducing a party system but that he thought that in the future, when Russia was endowed with a wealthy and educated middle class, a struggle among parties would be much more fruitful than the sterile and exhausting struggle between estates; this was the reason why the estates should be abolished. Chicherin argued back by conjuring up the horrible anarchy that would ensue if the time-hallowed estates were destroyed. [26]

Aksakov, who had started the controversy, was delighted at the

[25] Barsukov, *Pogodin*, XIX, 37. Whereas both Katkov and Aksakov wanted the abolition of the gentry, the former wanted all the estates to participate in the zemstvo or to introduce *vsesoslovnost*. Aksakov wanted a segregation of the estates within the zemstvo until a time when the social and psychological barriers would be destroyed. More will be said about this later in regard to the zemstvo question.

[26] *Ibid.*, pp. 37–42.

way Katkov answered Chicherin: "What a limited man this Chicherin! He wants absolutely a *tiers état,* a *noblesse de robe,* and a *noblesse d'épée* . . . Katkov answered him well in the Contemporary Chronicle." [27]

A somewhat different position was assumed by the liberal K. D. Kavelin. In an article entitled, "The Gentry and The Emancipation of the Peasantry," Kavelin stated his belief in "a happy future and a brilliant role" for the gentry. Kavelin, just as Aksakov, realized that gentry privileges were crumbling to pieces, but in contrast to the Slavophile, Kavelin did not believe that the gentry would disappear. In order to preserve itself, the gentry class must not remain static; the emancipation of the serfs brought an equalization of rights between estates, but inasmuch as the gentry would continue to own the bulk of the land it would remain the leading estate. Kavelin devised his social theory of "harmony of class interests." He imagined the people as one organism in which each member of society would occupy a higher or a lower rung of the same ladder; economic interests and the progress of public education would bring together all the estates but the gentry would remain the *primus inter pares* among them.[28] The polemic came to an end when the government announced that all discussions about the future of the gentry were contrary to the views held by the government and were against the spirit of the reforms.

Toward the end of 1862, and the beginning of 1863, Aksakov wrote to Iu. Samarin:

Strange things are happening to our Russian society. It crumbles away, it disappears, it thaws like snow in the spring . . . The gentry, I mean the base for a class-conscious gentry, does not exist anymore. It is dead. One year ago, the gentry could take *en sérieux* their assemblies, get excited, send petitions to the government: at present, as I feel it, the gentry has lost its last faith in itself . . . A certain feeling of impotence and apathy has crept over society at a time when the people acquire

[27] I. A., *Pisma,* IV, 227–228, to Countess Bludova. Pogodin took the side of Chicherin. See Barsukov, *Pogodin,* XIX, 45.

[28] K. D. Kavelin, *Sochineniia,* 4 vols. (St. Petersburg, 1898), II, 109, 111, 126–129. A similar point of view was defended by the Slavophile A. Koshelev in an article called: "What Is The Gentry and What Should It Be?" written in December 1861.

more and more vigor and health. To this state of affairs one should add the financial bankruptcy of the gentry ... A great many gentry emigrate without any special political motivation. Let them go, they are all superfluous people. In the meantime ... a new Russia is growing.[29]

In a series of articles published in *Den,* Aksakov went on to give an image of this emerging new Russia as he hoped to see it in which he developed his theory of *obshchestvo.* This theory is crucially important for an understanding of his position in the sixties, as well as of his leanings toward reaction in his last years. If the proposal to the gentry to abolish itself was aimed against those who nurtured great pretensions for their dispossessed class, the theory of *obshchestvo* was directed against those who dreamed of constitutions and democracy.

2. THE THEORY OF *Obshchestvo*

In the writings of Ivan Aksakov the concept of obshchestvo is always paired with the concept of narod. The narod for Ivan Aksakov did not mean the population of Russia, it had a much narrower sense: "the people is the *common* people, the popular multitudes that lead a direct life and who, like a kernel, are concentrating in their bosom all the future development of their organism." The people is not an active but a potential force. It has, according to Aksakov, all the qualities of the Hegelian acorn: "Indeed, just as the seed contains all the future of the tree with its beauty, its rustling green foliage ... so is the people in the restricted sense of the word keeping in its bosom all the future of its mission." [30]

---

[29] Quoted in V. Garmiza, *Podgotovka zemskoi reformy 1864 goda* (Moscow, 1957), p. 84. Aksakov went as far as to say: "Last year I could raise the question of the self-abolition of the gentry—this year it is impossible to raise the same question . . . the gentry is crumbling so fast that it would be harsh to attack it."

[30] I. A., *Sochineniia,* II, 33. Professor Riasanovsky has pointed out in his book, *Russia and the West in the Teaching of the Slavophiles* (Cambridge, Mass., 1952), pp. 152–156, the distinction that the Slavophiles made between the people and educated society. Konstantin Aksakov wrote: "The public speaks French, the people speaks Russian. The public follows Paris fashions. The people has its Russian customs. The public (at least in its great part) eats meat; the people observes fasts. The public sleeps, the people has already arisen long since and works. The public works (mostly with its feet on the dance floor): the people sleeps or already rises again to work.

The people, according to Aksakov, was not the total sum of all the individuals that composed it. The people was a separate living entity:

The people is not the congregation or the total sum of the individuals that form the people but a live and monolithic spiritual organism living and acting independently from its component parts. The thinking process, the consciousness, the creativity of this organism, its physiological and psychological laws are as mysterious as the mystery of life itself.[31]

One of Aksakov's arguments was the language of a people. He pointed out that philologists might wonder at the wisdom, the logic, the consistency of, say, the Russian language and yet not a single person composing the people had ever thought or worked over the language. The language was polished, improved, and given a personality of its own by the people as one body, regardless of separate individuals. The same could be said, according to Aksakov, of many other manifestations of a people.

The creativity of a people remains unnoticed by the people itself. The people is not self-conscious. Self-consciousness is attained at a higher evolutionary stage of the people, namely in obshchestvo. Aksakov defined obshchestvo as being: "The milieu in which the mental and conscious activity of a certain people takes place. A milieu created by all the spiritual forces of the people. A milieu that is working out the self-consciousness of the people. In other words, obshchestvo is the people in the second stage of its formation or better it is the self-conscious people." [32] This second stage is reached through education but education per se, the acquisition of knowledge does not make the obshchestvo. The literate people, according to Aksakov, do not necessarily constitute obshchestvo or even public opinion because: "Literacy is just the tool for words and may exist when the activity of personal thought does not." The

---

The public despises the people: the people forgives the public . . . The public and the people have their epithets: we call the public honorable, and the people Orthodox." This is quoted on p. 153.

[31] I. A., *Sochineniia*, II, 34.

[32] *Ibid.*, pp. 32–33, 34, 35, 40, 41.

educated man can, however, through his personal experience, grasp the significance and the implication of the people. Education, in a word, is just laying the foundation for the self-knowledge of a people.

Obshchestvo cannot be restricted to one class and it is not based upon class distinction: "Obshchestvo is not created by the upper and middle classes nor by the gentry nor the peasants; obshchestvo is composed only of educated people regardless of their social status." Obshchestvo speaks on behalf of the people while retaining its roots in the people itself, because the individuals compose obshchestvo only if: "they are conscious of themselves as a part of the people, only if they are developing a self-consciousness as a people."[33]

Finally, obshchestvo is seen as a moral force (*nravstvennaia sila*) which speaks on behalf of the people through public opinion. Obshchestvo does not usurp its rights because it keeps intact its ties with the people. In order to manifest itself through the "public mind," obshchestvo must not be hampered—freedom of speech and freedom of the press are conditions *sine qua non* for obshchestvo to exist. But Ivan Aksakov explained at the same time that freedom of expression is not to be misconstrued as a political prerogative as some liberals might think. Such a freedom is but a physiological necessity for obshchestvo just as is the freedom of "eating, drinking, sleeping, breathing, and moving one's hands and legs."[34]

A strong obshchestvo represents the greatest guarantee for a nation against encroachments on their liberties by the government. There can be political institutions devised to safeguard the liberties of the people but without the public mind of obshchestvo these institutions would be inoperative. However, in order to be efficient as the watchdog of the people's interest, obshchestvo must be morally free and apolitical because "without moral and apolitical freedom, without freedom of conscience, public life does not exist—there is no true freedom and political liberties are negligible."[35] Aksakov felt that the best example of a country ruled by obshchestvo rather than by

[33] *Ibid.*, pp. 41, 42.
[34] *Ibid.*, pp. 39–40.
[35] *Ibid.*, pp. 50, 51.

a Parliament was England. In a letter to Countess Bludova, he exclaimed: "Don't you know that England is strong *non par ses lois, mais malgré ses lois*. It is precisely this established force, which makes England strong, that I defend . . ."[36]

Ivan Aksakov warned that: "When the public mind is helpless or nonexistent, the government often creates an imitation of the public mind, as well as an imitation of freedom, an imitation of independence from the government, an imitation of free social activities. In a word, the government tries to create a public mind of its own. Needless to say, all these efforts are vain, because the government, in such cases, strives at the same time to give a direction to the development of society, tries to create and give a base to society in its own spirit, according to the government's aims." According to Aksakov, the state does not represent in any way the consciousness of a people. The state is the form, the exterior shape given by the people to their way of living in an organized entity; its functions are of a purely executive nature: "The state is neither an apostle nor a missionary, it is neither a teacher, a theoretician, nor a propounder of doctrines but it is a judge, a warrior, the enforcer of order and outward decency. Its emblem is the sword, its way is coercion, not conversion; its calling is to safeguard the inner freedom of social development against any attack from outside." Each people creates its own state. The state is the expression of the historical needs of a people. This does not mean that the state is a manageable tool of the people; on the contrary, the state created for defense against enemies started at once to impinge upon the people's way of life and as long as the people would not be conscious of itself and of its personality, or narodnost, there was nothing that could stem the tide of governmental encroachments. The people's only protection would be to evolve obshchestvo, or public conscience, which in its capacity as the articulate part of the people would carry the defense of the people against the trespassing state: "Only obshchestvo acting as the genuine expression of the people may save the people and stop the inward growth of the state."[37]

---

[36] I. A., *Pisma*, IV, 203. The Slavophiles had a great respect for England, which was at the same time a traditional and a progressive country.

[37] I. A., *Sochineniia*, II, 37, 50, 200.

In short, the obshchestvo in Aksakov's sense was to be recruited among all the educated people, regardless of their class origin, who had not broken their spiritual ties with the people and its traditions. The obshchestvo, endowed with full freedom of expression and acting morally, was to reestablish the balance or the harmony between the state and the people. The absence of the obshchestvo would warrant the tyranny of the state. The state would then create an obshchestvo of its own in order to use it as a tool for further advance in the domain of the people. This spurious obshchestvo would stunt the development of the potentialities of a people and would frustrate its mission among the other peoples of the world. Graphically we can visualize Aksakov's scheme as one of three concentric circles. The outer ring represents the state pressing and pushing inward, the inner ring that resists the outer ring is the obshchestvo, whereas the central circle or the core represents the people.

Because Aksakov put such a heavy stress on freedom of expression and on the people it might be possible to misunderstand and to regard him as a fighter for democracy in the accepted sense of the word. This would be a serious error since the enormous emphasis Aksakov placed on the definition of the state as inherently evil and dangerous and the role that the obshchestvo is to play obviate any need for a change of government. Democracy in the European sense of the word is spurious:

> In the West, democracy . . . is striving to give political power to the common people . . . This is theory; in practice, democracy is just the desire of the democrats to take the place of the aristocrats. Actually, democracy is the most uncouth . . . submission to the principle of the state, to the principle of outward material and coercive truth.[38]

The democratic form of government is a fraud inasmuch as all governments are autocratic:

> What are autocracy and unrestricted power? They are part and parcel of every authority in the domain of its function. Without them, authority is no longer authority but a phantom, a fiction . . . The Emperor-demos, the Emperor-Council-of-Ten, the Emperor-Convention, the Emperor-

[38] *Ibid.*, p. 87.

Parliament, the Emperor-Tsar are exactly the same supreme autocratic powers with the difference that in the latter case the power is concentrated in the hands of one person, whereas in the former ones it rests with the popular masses, the crude rabble, or on the educated minority which has never been intelligently defined.[39]

"Democracy," according to Aksakov, "has no place in our (Russia's) life and history." It was justified in the West, however, and here Aksakov used Guizot's theory which claimed that the social history of Europe was conditioned by the Germanic conquests. The struggle between Gauls and Franks continued between the French nobility of Germanic extraction and the French people of Gallic blood. Ivan Aksakov explained:

Democracy in the West has a justified historical sense. It is the expression of the hostility and the struggle between the oppressed conquered peoples and the conquerors-aristocrats. All the European countries are founded on conquests and all their regimes, all the political theories are indicating one great concern: to achieve a mechanical balance between the two contending elements.[40]

Every people has solved its own problem of government according to its own historical needs. The Russian people has opted for the tsar or, in Aksakov's words, for a ruler "endowed with a human soul and a human heart." Democracy is a hoax, for a people never rules itself; if it did, it would cease to be the people "and would become a nation of police agents, governed by a minority called government." The people of any country is apolitical—its ambition is "to be and to live," to lead an unhampered life. Freedom to live is the most important concern of the people; the people does not care whether this freedom wears a Phrygian cap or a crown. Aksakov was sure the Phrygian cap was "the lesser guarantee of freedom, because it speaks in the name of the people and therefore deems itself to be the infallible and supreme instance—it believes itself to be the people." [41] Aksakov's theory was built upon a strong faith in

---

[39] I. A., *Sochineniia*, V, 13.

[40] *Ibid.*, II, 88. See also F. Guizot, *Histoire des origines du gouvernement representatif en Europe*, 2 vols. (Paris, 1851).

[41] I. A., *Sochineniia*, V, 250, 251.

Russian autocracy. Aksakov himself admitted that: "We believe that the idea of true and genuinely Russian autocracy presupposes a complete freedom of the moral and intellectual life in society . . . if this ceased to be it would stop being Russian and would resemble either German absolutism or Asiatic despotism." Aksakov visualized Russia's political situation as the conjunction of two foci of power—the tsar and the people: "It is indispensable to recognize for unalterable truth only one thing: in Russia, there are only two real state powers, only two all-powerful factors—the tsar and the people. It was so in the past, so it is now." [42] This basic Slavophile view was at the core of Aksakov's teachings. The best illustration of these teachings can be found in the letter Aksakov wrote to Alexander von Battenberg in 1881, in which he revealed to the young monarch of Bulgaria the aspirations of the Slavs and those of the Russians in particular. This didactic document is invaluable as a compendium of all the basic pronouncements of Ivan Aksakov on the internal problems of Russia:

The aspirations of the Slavonic races are entirely democratic in the true sense of the word, not in the sense of the revolutionary theories so much in vogue in Europe. The historic mission of the English Tories, of the conservative parties in the West, *die beherrschende Kraft,* as the Germans say, repose among the Slav nations in the popular ranks. It is here and not in the bourgeoisie, in the populations of the towns, in the *soi-disant* cultivated classes, that the government ought to seek its center of gravity. It is the good sense, it is the instinct of the people which ought to regulate the administrative balance and serve as compass in the devious roads that the state has to travel. In Europe it is quite otherwise. The tendency which becomes more and more manifest in the constitutional states of the West is to give a monopoly of power to the class of doctrinaires and theorists, *die Literaten* in Germany. These are they who, in the name of the misleading principle of the "sovereignty of the people," seek to impose on the people the most tyrannical of yokes, to compel it to submit to the despotism of their doctrines, and to direct the helm of the state according to their passing whims and political passions.

[42] *Ibid.,* pp. 12, 22. This is essentially what Konstantin Aksakov also had maintained. Cf. "O vnutrennem sostoianii Rossii" by Konstantin Aksakov, in *Teoria gosudarstva u Slavianofilov—Sbornik statei* (St. Petersburg, 1898), pp. 22–50.

The example of contemporary France is very edifying. It is in the name of the people that a miserable minority of the country, taking advantage of the title of the representatives of the nation, and relying upon a parliamentary majority of some dozens of votes, contrive to outrage legally the religious beliefs of the real popular majority.

The Russian ideal, which is more or less common to all the Slav races, is that of local self-government without political powers, supported and crowned by a central and superior authority, a personal authority, free and untrammelled in the governmental sphere.

Rural autonomy in Russia is so great that the Russian communes resemble little republics, which govern themselves according to their own uses and customs. The people do not want sovereignty, nor do they seek to govern the state; but that which they do desire is a government which inspires them with confidence by its energy, its strength, its disinterestedness, and its national character. The reason why the Russian people know their tsar is because the tsar is not in Russia what the king was formerly in France, *le premier gentilhomme du pays;* he belongs to no party and to no social position, he is above and beyond all, he is the first man of the country, and stands for the people as their own personification. The supreme authority in Russia is neither an apparatus nor a collective body nor a personal and abstract combination, as in constitutional countries. That which the Russian people want is an authority possessing a human heart, a living being whose mind and soul are substituted for the formalism of the bureaucracy and the dead letter of the laws. Before Peter the Great, who introduced into Russia western notions about the relations between authority and the people, the jealousy of power was entirely unknown to Russian sovereigns; they had the good custom of convoking the delegates of the country of all classes of the people to consult with them when they wished to settle questions more or less weighty, or when they wished to secure the sincere support of the whole nation. Although autocrats, they did not believe themselves to be infallible, and they recognized without reserve the necessity for the government to know the thought of the country. These assemblies naturally were only consultative, and only influenced the course of events by their moral force without prejudice to the dignity and the authority of the Tsar. It is that which should be rehabilitated in Russia in a time not far distant.[43]

[43] I. A., *Sochineniia,* I, 403–405. See also O. K. [O. Novikova], *Skobeleff and the Slavonic Cause* (London, 1883), pp. 376–377.

So much can be said for the theory of the obshchestvo. In practice, the situation was disheartening. The educated part of the Russian people, the part that ought to have been the obshchestvo in Aksakov's definition, was completely divorced from the people. Russia was divided into two estranged groups—a Europeanized minority and the bulk of the Russian population who had remained loyal to their historical traditions and to their narodnost. According to Ivan Aksakov, narodnost is to a people (*narod*) what personality is to a person: "Thus the right for the historical existence of a certain people resides in the quality of its personality, or narodnost. Conversely, narodnost conditions the historical development of a people. Just like a man who has reached the point of self-contempt, self-debasement and who is incapable of developing his spirituality so are the peoples who have lost their narodnost and who . . . thereby cease to exist historically." [44] The Slavophiles, and first of all Ivan Aksakov, were the champions of narodnost (*poborniki narodnosti*); therefore, they represented the ideal of obshchestvo as propounded by Aksakov. The theory of obshchestvo was to give weight to the arguments of Ivan Aksakov and his followers.

These two problems—the new role of the gentry and the creation of *obshchestvo*—were to be reintroduced in the polemics that arose on the question of what the zemstvo organization should be and what it should represent in reformed Russia.

3. THE ZEMSTVO

As soon as the government set to work on the emancipation of the serfs, it began to consider a reorganization of local administration. This work was kept secret from 1859 to 1862; then for over one year the zemstvo reforms were debated in the press; finally the *Polozhenie o zemstve* (Statute on the Zemstvo) saw the light in the early days of January 1864. The statute gave the zemstvo jurisdiction over the economic and educational life of the county, as well as the duty to maintain, improve, and promote the public health and the means of communications such as roads and bridges. The work

[44] I. A., *Sochineniia*, II, 245.

of the zemstvo was to be supervised by the government through its provincial administration. In this reform the gentry had not been directly consulted, and the debates in the press and the gentry assemblies did not affect the course of the reform. It appears that the policy of the government was to permit discussion of the issues by the public in order to explore and exhaust the emotions of the interested parties so as to reenter the stage as the judge with the final word. Be this as it may, the polemics that arose on account of the zemstvo reform are interesting inasmuch as they illustrate the mood and the predilections of the Russian gentry in the months following the emancipation of the serfs.

The zemstvo was the nonpolitical administration of the land district or *uezd*. Until the emancipation of the serfs, the administration of the district was the domain of the serf-owning gentry under the vigilant eye of the government. The government by emancipating the serfs by decree frightened the gentry who, for the most part, began to clamor for reforms that would restore their security and preserve them from governmental highhandedness. The zemstvo institution was to serve two special purposes. It was to give the gentry a chance to find a place and to prove themselves in the renovated Russia and, at the same time, to alleviate the state budget by transferring many of its former functions onto the local administrative budgets collected from local taxes.[45]

Ivan Aksakov played a leading part in the polemics of 1862–1863 over the future organization of the zemstvo. At first, his attitude toward the zemstvo was negative if not actually hostile. Aksakov suspected that the zemstvo was to be a mere appendage of the central administration and an intrinsic part of the executive power of the state. He argued: "The zemstvo must not have the right to exile its members to Siberia or send them to jail; it must not trespass the

---

[45] For more details on the zemstvo, see: B. Veselovski, *Istoriia Zemstva za 40 let,* 4 vols. (St. Petersburg, 1909–1911); I. Belokonski, *Zemskoe dvizhenie* (Moscow, 1914); A. Kornilov, *Iz istorii voprosa ob izbiratelnom prave v zemstve* (St. Petersburg, 1906); A. Kizevetter, *Borba za zemstvo pri ego vozniknovenii* (Moscow, 1914); G. Dzhanshiev, "Zemskoe polozhenie 1864 goda," in *Iubeleinyi vestnik* (1892), no. 9, as well as his *Iz epokhi velikikh reform* (St. Petersburg, 1905); and finally, V. Garmiza, *Podgotovka zemskoi reformy 1864 goda* (Moscow, 1957).

boundaries of the governmental domain but it must have the right to voice freely its opinion on the state."[46] The new zemstvo may have to carry out the functions of the obshchestvo. For that, it must not be connected in any way with the state. If it were, the idea of the reform would be defeated and the zemstvo would exist just in order to help the state treasury. Such a future was possible because the Russian obshchestvo was impotent and inarticulate. The zemstvo could, however, become a fine institution, if Russia were to enjoy freedom of expression:

This freedom is more useful and more fecund than any other administrative autonomy; conversely, all the liberal institutions created by the government are not genuine, but lifeless and inconceivable in a silenced society; without freedom of opinion and freedom of speech, society so to speak does not exist and without obshchestvo the people is powerless and the state is a failure.

Aksakov saw in the zemstvo the possibility to recreate the Slavophile concept of the land as opposed to the state. The Slavophiles believed that before Peter the Great Russia had been divided into two halves: the land (zemshchina) and the state (gosudarstvo); these two parts lived side by side, independently and amicably supporting and helping each other. As Aksakov himself declared: "The ancient concept of the zemstvo, the concept of the land opposed to the concept of the state, presupposed a moral, free, and organic force resting on the spiritual unity of all the people and on their common origin, traditions, and basic way of life, as well as on the integrity of the entire people." This integrity was destroyed by the reforms of Peter the Great who dug a deep abyss between the people and the upper classes. The result was that:

The peasants and the gentry represent the East and the West, they are two different civilizations . . . We should remember that these two classes are ruled by different social laws: our people by the laws of communal living and communal landownership, the upper classes by the laws of private property, and their way of life is based on individualism.

[46] All of the quotations from Aksakov in this section come from Sochineniia, V, 209–359, in which he discusses the organization of the zemstvo.

Aksakov desired to see the spiritual and psychological gap between gentry and peasants filled, but was absolutely opposed to any change in the peasants' landownership: the commune was to be preserved at all cost. The first step toward this historical fusion was to be made as soon as the peasants fulfilled their obligations toward their former masters.

While estrangement between the two groups existed, however, the peasants were not to be allowed to commingle with the gentry in the zemstvo assembly; they were to preserve their own peasant self-government. To force them into the zemstvo would be disastrous. The peasant self-autonomy should in no case be destroyed, because the future strength of the zemstvo—and the zemstvo without peasants is not the genuine zemstvo—was to come from the peasantry whose strength lay in the commune and in its *mir*.

Aksakov saw clearly that, although the legal barriers among the various estates were gradually disappearing, the estrangement among the estates would continue for a long time. Neither the peasantry nor the burghers (*meshchiane*) would be active in the zemstvo assemblies for many years. It was the gentry who were called to play the leading role in managing the zemstvo affairs. Aksakov believed that it was up to the gentry to make of the zemstvo either a tool of obshchestvo or to emasculate it and transform it into a sterile body comparable to the gentry assemblies of old. Aksakov felt that the gentry was going through a great crisis; the reforms had removed from under the gentry "the artificial floor on which it stood" and the gentry was either to perish or to redetermine its position in Russia. Aksakov implored the gentry to prove itself to be a civic responsible body; it ought to show its mastery and its knowledge so that all the other estates would recognize in it a champion of their cause. Aksakov's message to the gentry was: "go to your county's backwoods and start your humble work first in the county and later in the province." The new institution of the zemstvo was to be a point of departure for the creation of the melting pot from which the classless or rather estateless society would flow.

Slowly it became clear that the zemstvo faced a great peril from two sides; Aksakov immediately took upon himself to defend it.

The first danger came from the small faction of large estate owners or latifundists and their newspaper *Vest* (News); the second from Katkov and his publications—The *Russki vestnik* (Russian Messenger) and the *Moskovskie vedomosti* (Moscow News). These two parties defended more or less the same point of view but for different reasons. The latifundists demanded that there should be a very high voting qualification in order to participate in the administration of the zemstvo. This qualification was to be expressed in landowner-ship; the amount of land needed in order to be eligible for a position in the zemstvo administration was set at 10,000 *desiatins* (27,000 acres). Katkov wanted the qualification to be counted not in desiatins but in rubles; besides, positions in the zemstvo were to be un-salaried. It is sometimes said that Katkov was at this particular period of time in favor of introducing the western concept of the bourgeoisie and that, furthermore, his scheme would have helped the merchants and industrials who held little or no land at all. Professor B. Chicherin shared the Katkov point of view because he wanted to see the gentry estate preserved.

Aksakov accused the latifundists and Katkov of fostering the creation of a landed aristocracy in the English fashion. His arguments against aristocracy have been already expounded. Aksakov feared that the aristocratic oppression of the countryside would lead to a "democratic outburst" of the people from which "as well as from aristocracy may God preserve us." The role of the gentry should be to recreate the fusion of the Russian people into one united whole. This role was to be moral in its nature; demands for voting qualifications were immoral.

Aksakov's second line of attack was to prove that the institution of a property qualification for voting (*tsenz*) was not Russian, that it had been borrowed from the West, and that it was a remnant of serfdom. Indeed, the right to vote in the gentry assembly had been decided by the number of serfs one owned; after the emancipation, qualification in the zemstvo was to be determined by the amount of land held by a landowner. Aksakov maintained that such a system was outrageous: "Why is a person owning one hundred desiatins considered more capable, more intelligent, and endowed with more qualities for participating in social affairs than the man who possesses only ninety-nine and nine-tenth desiatins?" Aksakov refused to acknowledge a conservative reason for the high voting qualification; it was a byproduct of egoism and material interests of the wealthy. Historically, such a stand was indefensible because the land did not belong to a few individuals but to everybody: the communes as well as the *pomeshchiki* were juridically landowners. Aksakov was very sympathetic to the middle-gentry; later in his life, in 1883, he was to write: "Our middle-gentry has played in Russia in certain respect the same historical role as the *tiers-état* in the West or the middle-class, that is to say only the good part of the role: without rebellions or class-hatred. The middle-gentry, while attracting into its midst and absorbing peoples from the lower classes, might have stopped the formation of a western type of bourgeoisie in Russia in the worst sense of the word." This predilection toward the middle-gentry to which Aksakov himself belonged might have prompted him to oppose the introduction of a high tsenz.

Aksakov argued in the following manner: if the tsenz were high, a minority of wealthy landowners would emerge as the ruling body of the countryside. This minority would be weak against the majority composed of all the lesser landowners who together owned more land than the rich majority. The tsenz-group would thus yield to the majority from the moral and economic points of view. As a result, there would arise a great animosity between the richer and the poorer landowners. In the West, the landed aristocracy may have been needed as a repository of conservatism and stability, because ever-dwindling small properties cannot withstand the adversity of changing times. In Russia, according to Aksakov, the opposite was true. The role of the western aristocracy was played by the people because the people were the largest landowners. Such a situation did not warrant, however, the introduction of a low tsenz. For Aksakov there was no contradiction between the fact that the Russian people were the main conservative force and his refusal to lower the barrier in order to permit the peasants to have an individual participation in the management of their county. The reason was the preservation of the commune. Aksakov feared that a low tsenz might entice some peasants to become landowners: "You are going to lure the best out of the people, who, in turn, would lose their organic vitality in your gentry milieu." This would threaten the monolithism of the commune: "You will create upstarts, *parvenus,* people that are neither fish nor fowl, people that are debauched by the consciousness of their accidental, purely superficial and spurious superiority over their lower, less wealthy brothers." Historically, Russia had evolved two kinds of ownership: the private ownership of the gentry landowners and the collective ownership of the commune. These two types of ownership ought to remain equal in their rights. There should not be any privilege or enticement that would coax people from one type of ownership into the other. According to Aksakov: "It is not freedom if, in order to maintain the commune, you close tightly all the doors and let only one open—the exit from the commune into the class of personal landowners." Thus there should not be any low tsenz, because the tsenz would serve as an incentive for the most clever of the peasants to become landowners. This would drain all the best peasants away from the commune. As a Slavophile, Aksakov did not want to see the disintegration of the commune and as a member of the landed gentry he had no use either for a land aristocracy or for prospective Lopakhins.

In brief, Ivan Aksakov's position on the zemstvo can be summarized in the following manner: the newly-created zemstvo was not the ideal historical zemstvo because the reforms of Peter the Great had created a cleavage between the gentry and the peasants. The genuine zemstvo was inconceivable without the participation of all the estates. The gentry, as the more educated class, were to take the leadership in the zemstvo and bridge the psychological and spiritual gap separating them from the peasants. Aksakov advised the gentry to act "morally" and in the interest of the county: the peasants would then accept them as their champions and not as their foes. In the meantime, the gentry and the peasantry should be separated in the zemstvo assemblies. Landed aristocracy should be

avoided as well as the destruction of the commune; private property
and communal property should coexist without any attempt to
weaken the commune.

4. THE LEGAL REFORMS

On October 1, 1862, the government announced its intention to
replace the old court-system with new institutions previously unknown in Russia. These were justices of the peace, trial by jury,
public trials, and courts of appeal; in addition, the judges were to be
permanently assigned to a given jurisdiction so as to make the new
court independent of the administration. The new regulations received their final form in the *Sudebnye Ustavy* (Legal Statutes)
published in November 1864.

Aksakov had abhorred the old judicial system; it is to him that
the famous words with regard to the old practice belong: "The old
court-system! Hair stands on end and the skin creeps at the mere
recollection of it!" [47] But in spite of his aversion for the old legal
order, Aksakov did not immediately welcome the legal reforms. First
of all, he feared that the new laws and the new procedures would
be a servile copy of the institutions of the West and that the
peculiarities of the Russian people would be disregarded. He urged
a study of Russian common law, similar to English common law,
the origins of which ought to be sought in the peasant communes,
and he was pleased that the new reforms were not extended to the
peasantry, who were to preserve for a time their own judicial system,
in particular their district-courts (*volostnoi sud*):

> We cherish the peasant district-courts, no matter how imperfect they
> may be, because we see in them a token for a future development of
> the people's law (*narodnoe pravo*), of the juridical customs of the
> people. It is our opinion that with the new legal reforms the peasant
> district-courts should not be abolished. On the contrary, they should be
> given greater significance by the grant of jurisdiction over all those who
> live in the district (*volost*), and the district should be permitted to elect
> judges from those who have residence in the district, whoever they hap-
> pen to be.

Aksakov thought he had found a new activity for the gentry; if the

---

[47] Aksakov's views on the legal reforms are found in the *Sochineniia*, V, 536–661.

gentry were the judges of the peasant courts they would gain a certain control over the peasantry and a new significance in the countryside.

In commenting further on the old and the new court systems, Aksakov submitted that the old system was new inasmuch as it had been a part of the reforms of Peter the Great and as such had never been acknowledged by the people.

The recent reforms were just as foreign to the people: "The old *new* is being replaced by the new *new*: both of them because their origins are equally alien to the people." Even trial by jury was fraught with danger:

In regard to trial by jury, we are afraid that this is the only institution which can level out the imperfections of man's justice, an institution of ancient Slavic origin at that, an institution which is a sort of a contradiction, an anomaly against the background of Roman formal law in western continental Europe. We are afraid, we repeat, that this excellent thing will be distorted by an . . . artificial planting in Russia.

Aksakov also protested against attempts to limit jury participation to people with higher education. He pointed out that in England, where trial by jury was represented at its best, the jury was composed of honest people regardless of their social or educational level. And he also felt that the new legal reforms should have been discussed by the gentry assemblies just as the reforms emancipating the serfs had been. Aksakov was displeased by all government highhandedness with respect to reforms.

Aksakov liked the plan for justices of the peace in part: "The form has been given, it is not a bad one; what we need is a content. Life itself will put content into this form; unfortunately, life is given very little freedom." But he fought the law that limited the competence of the justices of the peace. The latter had competence only on claims below five hundred rubles. Aksakov believed that it was up to the contending parties to decide whether they wished to have a particular justice of peace as their judge; the amount involved should not play any role. He was haunted by the fear that a judge might become a tool of the administration, for such a connection would ruin the reforms.

However, in analyzing the new laws and regulations, Aksakov

was irked by the contradictions they contained. The legal reform statute claimed that the new court system was applicable to all classes equally, yet the same statute differentiated between those who were subject to corporal punishment and those who were exempt from it. Aksakov pointed out that two accomplices, equally guilty but belonging to these two different categories, would be tried separately, and that while one might be freed the other could be sentenced, under the existing regulations, to spend two years in Siberia. And he did not think that the reforms should be widely applied in Russia. They first should be tested only in one or two provinces. The mistakes that would become apparent could be eliminated; once perfected, the new system could be safely applied in the rest of Russia.

According to Aksakov, the court must be the expression of "social morality and social conscience"; only in some extreme cases should morality yield to formal law. In the case of the statute, law came first and conscience could be used by judges only in some special instances. Nevertheless, Aksakov demanded that the claims involving peasants and landowners be solved by arbiters of the peace (*mirovye posredniki*) appointed by the government. Aksakov feared that a gentry arbiter would not be fair toward the peasants.

A few years of the new court system seems to have dispelled all the misapprehensions that Aksakov had expressed at first. In 1876, he wrote: "The people, who in songs and sayings for many long centuries have told of the injustice and the crookedness of Russian justice, begin to believe in the possibility of justice. The people are no longer afraid of the courts and of the judges and not only are not afraid of the novelty but protect it in a way by the unanimity of their support." The Russians ought to become convinced of the sturdiness of these reforms so that: "no reactionary would dare to attempt anything against the purity of the principles set at the base of these reforms." The courts should remain free of all pressures. Yet, when two years later, in 1878, the jury acquitted Vera Zasulich for wounding the chief of police Trepov, on account of the extenuating circumstances that prompted her to make an attempt on Trepov's life, Aksakov became indignant over the leniency shown by the court to the woman-terrorist. In spite of his indignation, however,

Aksakov's faith in the new legal system was not destroyed by this incident.

5. FAILURES OF *Den* AND *Moskva*

The success of the *Den* was soon spoiled by two things. First of all, the paper lost a great number of its subscribers as a result of Aksakov's attitude toward the gentry; even worse were the problems created by the censorship. In 1862, the *Den* was suspended for three months for publishing a scathing attack on the Baltic Germans. Herzen suggested to Aksakov that he come to London in order to resume the publication of the *Den* abroad.[48] Aksakov declined the offer. Pogodin took upon himself the task of shielding the *Den*. In a letter to the Minister of Public Education in charge of the censorship, Pogodin wrote:

All the Slavic peoples looked to the *Den* as to their loyal friend, their helper, and the deputy for their cause . . . It was the most sturdy moral link between Russia and the Slavs. The suspension of the *Den* will appear to them as evidence of the lack of interest of the government in their plight at a time when we should cultivate their friendly feelings and have them on our side, just in case.[49]

Aksakov tried to pass the editorship onto F. Chizhov, his associate, but the Minister of Public Education, A. Golovin, forbade Chizhov to work for the *Den*. However, after many attempts and with the help of Anna Tiutcheva, a daughter of the poet Tiutchev and Aksakov's future wife, the paper was reopened in October 1862. Anna Fedorovna Tiutcheva was a lady-in-waiting to the Empress and carried great weight at the Court because of both her connections and her reputation as a very intelligent woman. It is not clear when Aksakov became acquainted with her. It might have been during his last trip to Europe where he met the poet F. Tiutchev in Germany. It is possible also that he met his future wife through Countess Antonina Bludova. This incident with the *Den* was the only major trouble endured by Aksakov, although several of its other issues were seized. One of the chief enemies of the *Den* was

---

[48] Barsukov, *Pogodin*, XIX, 412. Herzen made the same offer to the *Sovremennik* and the *Russkoe Slovo*. See *Vestnik vsemirnoi istorii* (1901), no. 12, p. 112.

[49] Barsukov, *Pogodin*, XIX, 417.

the author of *Oblomov*, I. A. Goncharov, who was at that time a member of the censorship division.[50]

In 1865, Aksakov discontinued the publication of the *Den* in order to rest, and also to get married.[51] Professor B. Chicherin was well acquainted with Aksakov and his wife. He left us the following impressions:

Anna Fedorovna Tiutcheva was a very intelligent and educated woman, endowed with a noble and ardent temperament with somewhat of an irritable character. She loved her husband passionately, although she differed with him on many points. In the first days of their married life, it was difficult to speak to them when they were together. Having lived all her life at the Court, she spoke Russian badly . . . They also differed in their opinions. "What am I to do?" she would sometimes say in despair. "I cannot stand the Slavs and I hate autocracy, whereas he praises the one and the other." But there was one thing that brought them together—a deep piety coupled with a sincere attachment to the Orthodox Church.[52]

Vladimir Solovev confirmed the observations of Chicherin. Anna Tiutcheva disliked the Slavs as well as the Russian people because she felt they were insincere and dishonest. Ivan Aksakov could not argue against his wife. The latter used to tell her husband that his only good qualities were his Tartar blood and his German education.[53]

The next journalistic venture of Ivan Aksakov was the publication of the newspaper *Moskva* (Moscow). *Moskva* appeared only from January 1, 1867 to October 21, 1868, less than twenty-two months altogether. During this short period of time it received nine warnings and was closed three times: the first time for three months, the

[50] "I. A. Goncharov, kak chlen soveta glavnago upravlenia po delam pechati," *Golos Minuvshego* (1916), no. 11, pp. 117–156, and no. 12, pp. 140–179.

[51] The letters of Ivan Aksakov to A. Tiutcheva can be found in I. A., *Pisma*, IV, 101–179. In these letters Aksakov made allusions to some affairs he had with other women. Aksakov married A. Tiutcheva in January 1866. A stillborn child was born to them in October 1867. They had no other children.

[52] *Vospominania B. Chicherina*, 5 vols. (Moscow, 1929–1934), vol. II: *Moskva sorokovykh godov* (1929), pp. 242–243.

[53] V. Solovev, "Iz vospominani—Aksakovy" in *Pisma Vladimira Sergeevicha Soloveva*, E. L. Radlov, ed., 3 vols. (St. Petersburg, 1911), III, 278–282.

second time for four months and the third time for six months. Thus for thirteen months out of twenty-two the newspaper was banned. During these forced interruptions *Moskva* was replaced by the *Moskvich* (The Muscovite) edited by a figurehead but really by Aksakov. According to S. Vengerov, one of Aksakov's earliest biographers, the newspaper *Moskva* was not closed because of a hostile attitude toward the government but because "it was *plus royaliste que le roi.*" During the months it existed the governor-general of Vilno, Muraviev, famous for his reprisals against the Polish rebels, was replaced by General Potapov, whose mission was to appease the Poles. Aksakov opposed any tendencies to placate the Poles on the ground that it constituted a threat to Orthodoxy and to Russian interests. He called this new policy anti-Russian and accused the administration of "curtsying" in front of the Poles. *Moskva* was also vehemently anti-Baltic German. The paper was finally closed down when Aksakov accused the Ministry of the Interior of concealing the fact that in 1868 famine was raging in the northern provinces. The Minister of the Interior, Timashev, ordered its ban. Aksakov fought this decision, but to no avail, and from 1868 to 1880 he was forbidden to write and publish.[54]

As a result of this decision it is possible for the biographer to view Aksakov's career as divided into three parts—the first from 1860 to 1868, the second from 1868 to 1880 and, finally, the last from 1880 to the death of Ivan Aksakov in January 1886. These three periods were so distinct from each other that it would be vain and unnecessary to judge their respective merits. Indeed, in the first period the activity of Ivan Aksakov centered chiefly around the reforms and the Polish uprising. During the second period Aksakov had no newspaper of his own and he was obliged to work as a director of the Second Mutual Credit Bank of Moscow. In these years Aksakov became prominent as the leader and tribune of Pan-Slavism. Finally, the last period of Aksakov's life, perhaps the most tragic of the three, was a time of great disillusionment and of great confusion in the thinking of the aging and ailing Slavophile.

[54] S. Vengerov, *Kritiko-biograficheski slovar russkikh pisatelei i uchenykh,* 6 vols. (St. Petersburg, 1889–1904), I, 330–333.

CHAPTER IV

Nationalities and Nationalism

I. THE POLISH PROBLEM

Although the Polish uprising of 1863 was smaller and less violent than that of 1831, it was perhaps more disturbing and more profoundly felt than the previous rebellion. The uprising occurred at the time when Russia was passing through a crisis, when the reforms of the period and a greater freedom of expression were changing many social habits. The emancipation of the serfs had been followed by peasant *émeutes* in many parts of Russia, as well as by other more or less violent disturbances in St. Petersburg. These events had taken place in 1861 and 1862; the Polish revolt of 1863 added oil to the fire.

The 1831 insurrection had been resolved by the victory of the Russian troops over the Polish armies. In the aftermath Poland lost the right to its own army and government; and became for all practical purposes a part of the Russian empire under a military dictatorship. When Nicholas I died, Alexander II seemed to be intent in preserving this situation but, in fact, he began to grant the rights taken away by his predecessor. In May 1856 an amnesty was granted to the Polish émigrés as well as to the exiles. In the summer of 1857, a medical school was established in Warsaw with the hope that this school would become the nucleus of a future Polish university. The same year permission was granted to Polish landowners to found an Agricultural Society which soon became the center of the Polish right-wing opposition to Russian domination.

As a result of the amnesty many exiles returned from abroad. Many were imbued with a strong nationalist fervor; some had had experience of serving with Garibaldi and contributing to the unification of Italy. They dreamed of a strong and independent Poland which could assume its proper place among the other nations of the world. Why couldn't this happen in Poland since it had been possible for Italy? The more radical of the exiles, who became known as Reds and were affiliated with the Polish Democratic Society, whose headquarters were in London, advocated a military uprising to free Poland from Russia. The Reds were more radical than the Whites (as the Polish landowners affiliated with the Agricultural Society were known). The Reds were for the most part republican in their political outlook—the Whites were artistocratic. At the time of the uprising the Reds were led by General L. Mieroslawski who had served in Italy with a Polish legion.

As so often happens Alexander's actions did not mollify the Poles, but further aroused an ardent patriotism and stimulated a general restlessness. This led to the first important popular demonstration, which took place in Warsaw in June 1860 at a funeral for the widow of a Polish general who had been killed in the 1831 uprising. This demonstration was followed by others in the early days of 1861. Each time the demonstrators were dispersed by the army. Fearing further complications the Russian government hoped to win the affection of the Poles with blandishments. It gave Poland a liberal government headed by Marquis Alexander Wielopolski. The period between April 1861 and June 1863 is known as the Wielopolski era.

Wielopolski's aim was to win the restoration of the Statute of 1815, which had made Poland an autonomous country under the Russian crown. He introduced a series of positive reforms: the Polish University was established; the lot of the peasants and of the Jews was improved. Yet Wielopolski soon provoked the hatred of both the Reds and the Whites. He was jealous of his power: as soon as possible he disbanded the "Red Delegation" or provisional committee composed of Reds with whose help the demagogic Russian administration had hoped to maintain peace and order. And he dealt in the same manner with the Agricultural Society. To show his determination he issued an order to fire on those who demonstrated against his measures. Tension mounted. Wielopolski escaped several murder attempts. The Whites led by Count Zamoyski demanded the restoration of the Polish frontiers of 1772.

Wielopolski then had recourse to the last measure that could possibly have stopped the tide of the insurrection. He ordered the induction into the army of all the young people who were known, because of their alleged lack of political and social stability, to be potential supporters of the revolution. This measure violated the 1859 law, which stipulated that recruitment into the army should be by lot and not by administrative decision. Nonetheless, the Wielopolski's order was put into effect in early January 1863. But the secrecy of the operation had been poorly guarded; the recruiting units came too late. Most of the young people involved fled to the woods, organized guerilla bands, and attacked isolated Russian garrisons. The uprising began in earnest.

However, this insurrection was to be far less effective than that of 1831, because there was no regular Polish army. It was only partisan warfare. The Reds and the Whites could not find a *modus vivendi;* to the great detriment of the insurrection they were hostile to each other. The Russians did not find it difficult to put down the uprising toward the end of 1863, although isolated pockets of resistance continued to exist until the end of 1864. In the western provinces, particularly, the uprising backfired quickly; Polish landowners were promptly routed by a peasant militia composed of Ukrainian, Belorussian, or Russian elements.

Still, the Polish uprising sparked a diplomatic crisis. France, England, and Austria assailed Russia with bellicose diplomatic notes. Once again Russia was threatened by a European coalition, but Russia stood fast; besides, the conditions for a war against Russia were not propitious to the protesting nations. For instance, the Prussian king and Bismark declared their neutrality, while offering secretly, through the embassy of Count Alvensleben, their assistance to Russia, lest the Polish uprising should get out of hand. Prussia needed Russian gratitude for the future. Austria was watching Prussia in apprehension of losing the spoils in the impending Schleswig-Holstein affair; therefore, she did not press the issue of intervention. Moreover, these powers did not want to see Napoleon III emerge as the leader of a European crusade against Russia. As for France, it was too entangled in Mexico to do anything against Russia.

In Russia the uprising and the threat of a hostile coalition channelled Russian public opinion into a single patriotic stream. Many polemics were written about the future of Poland. Contributing to them Aksakov and Katkov became well known for their patriotic eloquence and their strong views on the Polish Question.[1]

In 1861 and 1862, Aksakov spoke of Poland with a paternalistic and often condescending benevolence. The annexation of Poland by Russia was, according to Aksakov, an unavoidable thing: "The existence of Poland in her original form and organization based on principles that manifested themselves in Polish history was, according to all historical probability, no longer possible . . . a historical nemesis had avenged all the injustices committed by Poland against the Russian people in the beginning of the seventeenth century." [2] During the first three partitions of Poland, Russia had acquired lands that were inhabited by Russian peoples, by Ukrainians and Belorussians who were Orthodox and closely related to the Great Russians. This was entirely justifiable. Russia did not wish the end of Poland, and Poland would have disappeared altogether if Alexander I had not demanded the creation of a Polish kingdom under the Russian crown at the Congress of Vienna. The Poles of that time understood this quite well; it was Koscziusko, himself, who called Alexander I "the resuscitator of Poland." What is more, the Russians had never attempted to Russify Poland. The Prussians, however, had ruthlessly Germanized the Poles of Poznan (Posen). Speaking of the policy of the Prussians in Poznan and that of the British in Ireland, Aksakov exclaimed: "We would always lack the evil energy, the harmony of ill will and wicked deeds which are so necessary for success in an immoral action." [3]

The anti-Russian agitation in Poland, however, increased toward the end of 1861 and throughout 1862. Although Aksakov did not really believe it would be possible to come to an amicable understanding with Poland, he still wished that an attempt to reach some sort of *modus vivendi* be made by both parties; Aksakov wanted: "A peaceful and brotherly discussion of mutual rights and relations . . . a clear consciousness of their [Russian and Polish] needs . . . enlightened by an unbiased respect for truth and warmed by mutual

[1] I. A., *Sochineniia*, III, 381.   [2] *Ibid.*, p. 9.   [3] *Ibid.*, pp. 6, 80, 137.

love and tolerance." Yet his true feelings were, in fact, far removed from such sanctimonious sentiments. Aksakov thought that the best way of settling the Polish problem was to rid Russia of the Poles: the Russian troops ought to leave Poland and return to the Russian frontier. The Poles, left to their own devices, would soon succumb because: "Ultramontane Catholic fanaticism, the aristocratic principles of the *szlachta* and exclusive national pride . . . could not be used as a constructive discipline."[4] Aksakov was sure that in a few years Poland would beg Russia to take her back. If the Poles, on the other hand, tried to cross the Russian border and reconquer the western provinces of Russia in order to reestablish the frontiers of 1772, Russia would have the moral right to punish them for their impudence. Aksakov, in spite of all his distaste for Poland, hoped to see the Poles as friends and not as foes: "If the Poles were capable of regenerating themselves, of atoning for their historical errors, and becoming a peace-loving Slavic people, then, of course, the Russian people would be happy to see in them kind and kindred neighbors." Not long before the uprising, Aksakov professed to believe that sooner or later "Slavic Poland would merge with Slavic Russia"—such was the unavoidable course of history.[5]

As far as Aksakov was concerned, Poland was exclusively the territory where the bulk of the population was Polish. Poland was the former Duchy of Warsaw plus the Prussian region of Poznan (Posen) and a small part of Austrian Poland. The ambition of the Poles to see Poland reestablished within its frontiers of 1772, including all the western provinces of Russia and Lithuania was sheer lunacy:

Looking at Kiev one involuntarily thinks that every Pole who makes claim on Kiev in the name of Polish nationality should be placed into an asylum and subjected to a serious medical treatment in keeping with all the rules of science . . . It is also true that almost the entire Polish educated class, that is, the entire Polish *szlachta,* should have been confined to that asylum![6]

[4] *Ibid.,* pp. 10–11. See also I. A., *Pisma,* IV, 209, to Countess Bludova.
[5] I. A., *Sochineniia,* III, 11–12.
[6] I. A., *Sochineniia,* VI, 297.

When the insurrection flared up in January 1863, Aksakov refused emphatically to recognize it as a national movement. The rebellion was only: "the rebellion of one part of the population, mostly from the cities, of the lower *szlachta* and proletarians of all kinds, aroused and led by insane and rabid demagogues." [7]

The majority of the population of Poland was made up of peasants. These peasants were treated little better than chattels by their Polish landowners. The Polish word *bydło,* meaning cattle, also designated the peasantry. Aksakov implored the Russian government to capitalize on the class antagonism existing in the Polish countryside by placating the Polish peasantry with serious reforms and by promising to emancipate them, once and for all, from the thralls of the Polish gentry. The uncommitted peasantry should, at all cost, be enlisted against the rebellious landowners. Aksakov urged the government to hurry before the peasantry was swayed to the side of the rebels. Such a policy would be both humane and expedient, he warned that too quick a shift of the government's support from the gentry to the peasantry was a double-edged sword.

On the one hand, it would be desirable to create a strong and independent Polish peasantry as a counterweight to the seditious *szlachta*; this, according to Aksakov, was "the only political path the government should follow if it wanted to keep Poland." On the other hand, "democratism" introduced as a political device by the power of absolutism was fraught with danger. The normal evolution of social forces was not dangerous but, prompted and instigated by higher authority, these social forces might assume a revolutionary form and flood the state with violence and terror. In such an eventuality, the Russian government would have to interfere once again—this time in order to crush such a new social revolution—and the use of brutal force against a newly-born popular movement would antagonize all the Polish people. On the economic level the Russian government would have to choose between two policies. It could either allow the peasants to seize the land belonging to their lords and stop paying their dues to them or give its support to the rebellious Polish szlachta against the peasantry. In short, Russia would

[7] I. A., *Sochineniia*, III, 23.

have to opt between a *jacquerie* culminating in complete anarchy or lose the support of the peasants by helping the rebels, who were largely landowners. Russia faced a dilemma that she would have to solve one way or the other, even though she was in danger of losing either way.[8]

Aksakov was sure that Russia could crush the rebellion without bothering about the peasantry, but victory, in that case, would not solve the Polish problem. A new dictatorship in Poland would pave the way for another rebellion; liberalism, as introduced by Marquis Wielopolski, had proved to be impotent and insolvent. It would have been suicidal to reintroduce it in the new administration. Thus, Aksakov proposed his own solution to the problem, a solution that would enlist the support of the peasantry and that, at the same time, would neutralize the rambunctiousness of the szlachta. Russia ought to organize the convocation of a Polish *Sejm,* composed not only of gentry, as in the past, but of all the people. This Sejm ought to be modeled after the Slavophiles' idealized version of the Russian Zemski sobor. Such an assembly would be truly representative of the aspirations of the Polish people. By proposing a Polish Sejm, Aksakov propagated his own Slavophile ideas about the Zemski sobor.

Aksakov considered the possibility that demand for secession might be voiced even by the Polish Sejm. Indeed, the Sejm could be foolish or misguided enough to demand complete political freedom for Poland. In that case, anarchy would ensue. Anarchy was in Aksakov's words the only alternative to a union with Russia. The wayward Poles should be punished for their levity: "Let Poland be punished by all the horrors of anarchy" exclaimed Aksakov. Fortunately, anarchy cannot last forever. Aksakov was confident that eventually the "healthy part of the country would overthrow the yoke of the demagogues and appeal again to the Russian emperor, begging him to re-accept Poland under his strong arm." If the Poles persisted in balking at reunion with Russia, Prussia and Austria would not procrastinate with a final partition of Poland. This would be the *finis Poloniae* that Russia had so far prevented but which, according to Aksakov, was long overdue.[9]

[8] *Ibid.,* pp. 29–30.   [9] *Ibid.,* pp. 31, 32, 63–65.

Needless to say, the Russian government did not heed the exhortations of Aksakov. It did not create any Polish Sejm although it may be said that the lot of the Polish peasants was generally improved. Aksakov's views did not change, although he was forced to accept the facts. During the insurrection Aksakov had said:

We have tried different methods of administration in Poland. First there was a thirty-year dictatorship: it did not create any Russian party. Then there was the liberal system of Wielopolski: it proved to be a failure. Why? Because it is impossible to satisfy the legitimate demands of the Poles when these demands are stretching beyond anything which can be offered by the best, the most liberal administration. The Poles want political autonomy—complete independence and secession. The Polish problem remains unsolved and we should constantly expect a new uprising.[10]

After the insurrection was over, Aksakov continued to be pessimistic when he said: "Never and under no circumstances (autonomy or complete freedom) could Russia have peace with the Polish szlachta (the way history has created it) or with Polish Latinity: we can expect peace only from the birth of new social elements and the regeneration of the old."[11] Aksakov's last hope was his faith in the Polish peasantry and in the social changes he expected to occur as a result of the emancipation of the Polish serfs.

Aksakov attracted the attention of the public by his ruthless attacks on all those who professed any sympathy for the Poles. Shortly after the outbreak of the insurrection, Aksakov published in his *Den* the letter of a certain Kasianov from Paris, who flayed Bakunin for his connection with the Polish revolutionaries and for his alleged plan to organize an expedition against the Baltic provinces. Bakunin's maneuver, launched from Sweden and a fantastic enterprise, was aimed at helping the Poles by diverting the Russian army from Poland to the shores of the Baltic sea. Kasianov, of course, was none other than Aksakov himself writing under a pseudonym. In his comments on Kasianov's, or his own letter, Aksakov attacked Herzen for the proclamation he had published in *Kolokol* (The Bell) a proclamation that supported the aims of

[10] *Ibid.*, p. 213.   [11] *Ibid.*, p. 404.

the Polish rebels. Although Herzen was opposed to the unrealistic scheme of Bakunin, he had hopes, at least at the beginning, that the Polish uprising would bring some desired changes in Russia. Nevertheless, he took upon himself to defend Bakunin on the pages of Aksakov's publication. Aksakov published Herzen's reply with a commentary that branded Bakunin and Herzen as traitors to the Russian and Orthodox causes. Aksakov announced emphatically that Herzen had committed political suicide by siding with the enemies of Russia.

Indeed, it was the Polish question that put an end to Aksakov's friendship with Herzen. Before the Polish uprising Aksakov had corresponded with Herzen, occasionally sending him information about various problems in Russia. The tone of their letters was friendly, and Aksakov during his second trip to Europe had visited Herzen in England. Their relations were at their best when Herzen wrote a heartfelt article on the occasion of Konstantin Aksakov's death.[12] The split between the two therefore was painful to both and even after it Aksakov continued to like Herzen. At the end of 1863, fulminating against the young Nihilists, Aksakov exclaimed: "Herzen, in spite of his extremes bordering on crime, in the moral sense stands much higher than those young people whom he for the most part engendered and whom he educated. There is force in him, there is heart, there is a warm interest in the welfare of society, although he understands it quite wrongly. At least, he is not a cosmopolitan."[13]

In the April 1863 issue of *Vremia* (Time) appeared an anonymous article under the title of "The Fateful Question." This article started a veritable chain reaction of patriotic recriminations; it also led to the closure of *Vremia*. The author of this article, who subsequently

---

[12] "I. S. Aksakows Briefe an A. I. Herzen (1857–1861)," in *Konstantin Kawelins und Iwan Turgenjews Sozial-politischer Briefwechsel mit Alexander Iw. Herzen,* Prof. Michail Dragomanow, ed. (Stuttgart, 1894), pp. 163–175. Herzen wrote his article "K. S. Aksakov" in *Kolokol* for January 15, 1861. Herzen's letter to *Den* is in I. A., *Sochineniia,* VII, 443–458. Herzen had published in 1857 in his *Polar Star* the satyric poem of Ivan Aksakov *Prisutstvennyi den v ugolovnoi palate* (A Sitting of the Criminal Court).

[13] I. A., *Sochineniia,* III, 247.

proved to be N. Strakhov, viewed the Russo-Polish contention as a struggle between two opposite principles: between the Russian barbarians on the one hand and the civilized and Europeanized Poles on the other. Strakhov supported his arguments with historical facts. His conclusion was: "The Polish people has the right to feel equal in civilization to all the other European peoples and, consequently, they cannot but look on us as on barbarians." Strakhov went on to urge the Russians to overcome their backwardness, because he felt that as long as Russia remained a barbarian country "the Poles may look at themselves, with all sincerity, as the representatives of civilization and they have a right to interpret their struggle against us as the war of the European spirit against Asiatic barbarism." It was the Poles, according to Strakhov, who should lead the Slavs and not the Russians.[14]

Katkov attacked the author of "The Fateful Question" by calling him a "masked bandit." Strakhov hastened to write an apologetical letter in which he explained his motives. He asserted that his purpose was to shake the Russians out of their torpor and force them to pay attention to culture and to their way of life rather than to dedicate themselves only to "victories and pogroms." Katkov accepted this explanation. He wrote an article in which he attempted to exonerate Strakhov from the accusation of treason to Russia. Katkov called Strakhov a "confused man" but without malice. However, Iuri Samarin and Aksakov did not accept Katkov's point of view. Aksakov was particularly incensed at Strakhov for giving authority to his "calumny" with quotations taken from the writings of Ivan Kireevski. Aksakov argued that Kireevski had indeed mentioned Polish culture but had spoken of it as a thin veneer covering only the upper classes.[15]

But if Katkov incurred the wrath of the Slavophile tribunes, Aksakov could not avoid the thunder of the ultra-patriotic Katkov on the question of Polish independence. As already mentioned, Aksakov believed that: "The political independence of Poland would be more useful for us than even for Poland. We must not

[14] Barsukov, *Pogodin,* XX, 311, 313.
[15] *Ibid.,* pp. 314–322.

bind the future of our social development to the alien and particularistic (*samobytnyi*) development of Polish society. After freeing
Poland from terror and upon returning to her liberty of expression
and of opinion, and after introducing into Poland's civic life a new
element—the Polish peasantry—endowed with all its rights, we
would do well to give Poland full political independence. Poland
should be able to secede from Russia; if not, her union with Russia
would be a voluntary one." [16]

To this Katkov answered:

The enigma of the Polish question, according to Aksakov, resides
in the fact that Poland, at present, is something called a social force
[*obshchestvennost*] and as such is harmful and baneful for Russia. It
must therefore be transformed into something different something called
a political or state entity; then only it will lose its baneful quality. When
Poland becomes such a political force, that is, when Poland is promoted
to a state, then, according to Aksakov, the Polish question will be safely
solved. Aksakov remains deaf to all testimonies and firmly maintains
that the Polish uprising is not the fruit of an intrigue but is a great
popular movement.[17]

Katkov accused Aksakov of accepting the Polish uprising as a
popular uprising although the Polish peasantry did not participate
in it. Aksakov refuted all of these accusations. On the last point
made by Katkov, Aksakov retorted: "*Moskovskie vedomosti* (Moscow News) does not want to acknowledge that the revolt is a popular uprising because the peasants have no part in it . . . During the
one thousand-year history of Poland, the peasantry has not played
any role; it remained passive, it did not participate, it was not the
active part of the people." [18]

Katkov's confusion was understandable because Aksakov juggled
with notions that were if not altogether contradictory, at least incompatible or difficult to synthesize. On the one hand, Aksakov
meant by people the peasantry—as opposed to the educated and
westernized szlachta. These two groups were mutually hostile in

[16] I. A., *Sochineniia*, III, 195, 214.
[17] Barsukov, *Pogodin*, XX, 361–362.
[18] *Ibid.*, p. 363 and I. A., *Sochineniia*, III, 212.

many respects. From this point of view, the insurrection, led and abetted as it was by the szlachta, without the participation of the peasantry, was *not* a popular movement. On the other hand, Aksakov advanced his theory of obshchestvo mentioned in the preceding chapter. This obshchestvo, according to Aksakov, was the educated and socially conscious part of the population as opposed to the uneducated, unconscious, and completely apolitical mass of the people. Obshchestvo was the articulate and the active part of the people; it spoke and acted, therefore, on behalf of the people as a whole. Aksakov called obshchestvo: "the people in the second stage of its formation." In the light of this theory, the people is merely a passive reservoir of potential strength and the raw materials for the future development of a country. To say that the szlachta-led insurrection was popular was in keeping with this theory of obshchestvo; but such a view also clashed with Aksakov's other argument showing that the denationalized szlachta had no right to act on behalf of the peasantry. In brief, Aksakov was not sure himself whether the szlachta had a right to be called obshchestvo or not. It is this moot point in Aksakov's writings that led Katkov and others to wonder about Aksakov's stand. The latter never solved this problem but preferred to use one argument or the other, depending on the problem at any given moment.

A similar ambiguity applies to Aksakov's views on the question of the Polish Sejm and the Zemski sobor. These two assemblies were supposed to be consultative bodies chosen from the entire population, including the peasantry. Such a view constituted a democratic feature in Aksakov's thinking. This democratic ideal, however, was promptly neutralized by his theory of obshchestvo, because the "active, conscious and educated obshchestvo was the natural leader of the "passive, unconscious, and ignorant" narod. Yet how could this ignorant and unconscious people give sound political advice to the tsar? Or was Aksakov's desire for a Zemski sobor an unconscious stratagem devised to enable only the educated classes to have a voice in government? It is not possible to find a clear answer to these questions in Aksakov's writing.

The Russian press debated any and all suggestions for a solution to the Polish problem. One of these suggestions was that proposed by Emile de Girardin, the noted publicist and editor of the Paris newspaper *La Presse*. Girardin was firmly opposed to any secession of Poland from Russia for he believed that if Russia became free and liberal, Poland could profitably merge with her neighbor. The naïve Frenchman believed that "l'absorption de la Pologne par la Russie dans la liberté" was a sure remedy both for the long historical feud between the two contending countries and for the liberalization of the Imperial regime. Be this as it may, however, his proposal was debated in all seriousness in the pages of the Russian press in 1863 and later. Aksakov took a very firm stand against any scheme designed to appease the Poles. He repeated his position: "The Russian people, more than any other in the world, recognizes the right of every nationality to lead its own way of life." [19] But Poland and Russia were antithetically opposed to each other. Poland was a Catholic daughter of the West whereas Russia was Orthodox and belonged to the East. Adopting Girardin's plan would have meant the surrender of Russia to Polish influence because Russia still lacked national self-consciousness. Poland possessed a great and self-conscious social force, or obshchestvennost; Russia lacked a comparably strong voice of public opinion and was therefore at a marked disadvantage. Regretfully or gleefully, it is hard to say, Aksakov added: "We cannot yet sing a duo with Poland, but she is capable of spoiling our solo." The only solution was to give independence to Poland within the boundaries of the former Duchy of Warsaw.

The Polish uprising brought in its wake some diplomatic complications with France, England, and to a lesser extent Austria. Napoleon III, the shrewd, self-appointed champion of the right of self-determination of the people, wanted to convene a European Congress at which he would preside that would settle the Polish problem. Russia declined the invitation as did the others invited. The threats uttered by England and by France had created a war climate in Russia. Aksakov welcomed the possibility of such a conflict: "We shall be at the helm of historical events only when we

[19] I. A., *Sochineniia*, III, 70.

stop refusing warlike challenges, when we meet events half-way, fortified by our own public opinion."[20] Katkov was just as firm in his attitude toward a possible war with the West. The patriotic zeal of the two journalists was appreciated by the authorities. Count Dimitri Bludov, president of the State Council, wanted Katkov and Aksakov promoted to membership in the Imperial Academy of Sciences. The academicians, however, protested very firmly; as a result of recriminations, the candidacies of Katkov and Aksakov were withdrawn and the entire matter forgotten.[21]

2. POLONISM AND CATHOLICISM

The fate of the western provinces of Russia was of far greater moment to Aksakov than was the fate of Poland proper. Under the vague name of "western provinces" (*Zapadnye guberni*) or that of "western region" (*Zapadnyi krai*) the following areas were designated, from north to south: Lithuania, comprising the provinces of Vilno, Kovno, and Grodno; Belorussia, comprising the provinces of Minsk, Vitebsk, and Mogilev; and, before 1842 the Bialystok area, which became in 1842 part of the Grodno province, Volynia, Podolia, and the province of Kiev. The ethnic content of the western provinces could be described as follows: the peasantry was either Ukrainian, Belorussian, or Lithuanian; trade was in the hands of the Jews, who were very numerous in the area; the land belonged for the most part to Polish landowners. It should be noticed that the division by classes of the population in the western region corresponded roughly to the division by nationality and by religion, with the exception of the Lithuanians who were mostly Catholic. On the one hand, there were the dominant but alien Poles and Jews; on the other, the exploited but largely Orthodox and national peasants.

The Poles were a minority in the western provinces, but a minority that was very strong because of economic position and of dominance in the local administration. And because they were a minority, the Poles urgently felt it necessary to render the lower-class popula-

<hr>

[20] *Ibid.*, pp. 67–68.
[21] Barsukov, *Pogodin*, XX, 366. See also A. Nikitenko, *Zapiski i Dnevnik*, 2 vols. (St. Petersburg, 1905), II, 153, entry for December 19, 1863.

tion as harmless and as obedient as possible. The Lithuanians, Belo-russians, and Ukrainians were backward and uncultured peoples as compared to the relatively refined and educated Polish gentry. They were raw material to be shaped in the interest of the ruling minority by the combined efforts of Catholicism and education. This attempt to spread Catholicism and the Polish language was called Polonization; the principle behind Polonization was called Polonism.

Aksakov granted that the Poles were entirely justified in their desires to recreate Poland: "Every people has the moral and un-conditional right to existence and to independent life but this only within the boundaries of its ethnical group: this is true only if the people is conscious of its existence, has faith in itself, wants and is capable to live . . . The Italians have a right to form one Italy . . . and the Poles have a right to strive to unite all the Poles into one Poland." [22] But to claim peoples who are not Poles was "unfair, immoral, and partly based on dubious arguments." By "dubious arguments" Aksakov meant the claim that the Poles made to the western provinces on the grounds that these had belonged to Poland before 1772, the date of the first partition.

Aksakov felt that Russia had been sobered by the two uprisings. It had become aware of the Polish danger in ethnic Poland; but it also ought to take a good look at the western marches and to realize that the danger of Polonism there was more ominous than an open revolt. A revolt can be crushed by force, but what can avail against a slow and insidious poisoning of minds? Aksakov proposed a pro-gram for fighting against the Polonization of the western provinces and suggested a vigorous campaign of Russification.

First of all, the Polish landowners were to be deprived of the right of landownership in Russia. Aksakov did not mean confisca-tion: the Polish landowners would be remunerated for their losses. The first step toward a reconquest of the Polonized area was the destruction of the economic base of the dominant nationality: "Is it possible that foreigners or people who not only do not consider themselves Russian but who also deny the Russian people their

[22] I. A., *Sochineniia*, III, 34.

rights to Russia, to Russian land, that those who do not abide by Russian laws and by the rights of Russian nationality be allowed a share of Russian land?" The land thus obtained by the eviction of the Polish landlords should be populated by Russian landowners and Russian peasants. The government should organize this re-settlement.[23]

Secondly, all Polish officials were to be dismissed and replaced by Russians. These harsh measures were demanded by the very nature of the uprising: "this insurrection is not a rising of a few cut-throats; neither is it the upheaval of sundry disorderly elements which each country has; rather it is a phenomenon which cannot but be supported by every Pole as a Pole . . . with the exception of the peasantry." [24]

Thirdly, the administrative centers of the western provinces ought to be shifted further to the East, to cities that were not Polish strong-holds such as Vilno, Minsk, and Kamenets-Podolsk but to Pskov, Chernigov, Kiev, and Kherson. Russia also ought to improve the quality of her administration in these critical areas, although Aksakov conceded that this was the most arduous part of his pro-gram: "In Russia one may recruit and train as many brave soldiers as one wishes, but all the efforts of the government for more than a century have not succeeded in training honest officials—not even one percent of the needed number!" [25]

In keeping with these ideas Aksakov fervently supported the policy of General Muravev in Vilno. Dictatorship was needed to restore order, and the sequestration of Polish estates was desirable in order to break Polish resistance. Because he was a ruthless dicta-tor who had ordered the seizure of Polish property, General Mura-vev deserved, according to Aksakov, the undying gratitude of the entire non-Polish population of the area under his jurisdiction. When Muravev was dismissed in 1865, Aksakov bitterly assailed his successor General Potapov for undoing the "dictator's" work.[26]

[23] *Ibid.*, pp. 86, 87, 91, 92, 112.
[24] *Ibid.*, p. 211.
[25] *Ibid.*, p. 240.
[26] *Ibid.*, pp. 118, 190, 405, 409, 583. *Moskva* (Moscow) was suspended because of Aksakov's stand against General Potapov.

For Aksakov the measures described above could successfully cope with the Polish ethnic element in the western provinces but certainly not with cultural Polonism. Polonism haunted this western region in the forms of the Catholic Church and of education in the Polish language. The Catholic Church was particularly vicious. Polish priests had led the bands of insurgents. As Aksakov put it: "the Polish and the Papal questions are closely bound together." [27] The worst aspect of Polish history was the penetration in the mid-sixteenth century of the Jesuits, who poisoned "the spirit and the flesh of the Polish people." Poland became the favorite daughter of Rome because she was the line of defense against Orthodoxy and against Muscovite "barbarism." Conversely: "Catholicism has not accidentally, but by virtue of historical and inner circumstances become the inseparable and fundamental element of the Polish political idea, so that the triumph or the defeat of Catholicism is, at the same time, the triumph or the defeat of Polonism and vice versa. He who abjures Latinity abjures at the same time the Polish political Catechism, and he who abjures the Polish political Catechism abjures . . . his close union with the Latin Church." This was the reason, according to Aksakov, why Polish Catholicism must be combatted; French and German Catholics, on the other hand, were not to be feared in Russia because their faith was not a political platform of aggression.[28]

Aksakov went as far as to suggest the introduction of Orthodoxy in the heart of Poland: "We think even that in the Polish kingdom, in the basically Polish areas, the Orthodox mass, the Orthodox service conducted in Polish and a dozen or more married priests of Polish nationality recruited among converted Poles (there is no doubt that they could be found) would have a beneficial effect on the minds of the Polish villagers and would appear to them in a more favorable light than the Latin mass said by celibate Catholic priests!" [29]

Poland was a renegade in the Slavic world, even more so than the Czechs and the Croats, because she not only embraced Catholicism but she also "in her fanatical hatred of Orthodoxy, professed by the

[27] *Ibid.*, pp. 133, 297.   [28] *Ibid.*, pp. 463, 468, 469.   [29] *Ibid.*, p. 475.

majority of the Slavs . . . smothered the feeling and the consciousness of Slavic spiritual communion." Poland became the vanguard of the Roman Germanic world. "There is no more wicked enemy of Slavdom than Papism," said Aksakov "because it contradicts the spiritual nature of the Slavic race." Orthodoxy does not infringe upon the rights of nationalities, but the Catholic Church is "permeated with occidental one-sidedness. It is nothing more than the West, than Rome promoted to *ecumenical* significance and striving toward the mastery of the world and the subjugation of the universe." [30]

The imperialism of Ancient Rome had found its continuation and its expression in the spiritual imperialism of Catholic Rome. Rome is constantly on the move to conquer the rest of the world for the West. This assumption was corroborated, according to Aksakov, by the fact that Rome does not recognize national churches and that the services must be conducted in Latin. The Pope was the autocratic ruler of "a universal spiritual empire," he was the infallible head of the Church, he was deemed to be the vice-Christ. Aksakov pointed out that Catholics were not members of their Church but its subjects. In the Catholic Church the people was rated as *anima vilis* who could not be permitted to read the Holy Scripture and to whom the Eucharist could not be offered in both forms. But the difference between the Orthodox and Catholic Churches went even further. Orthodoxy was a spiritual religion, whereas Catholicism was a practical faith. Catholicism was based exclusively on external truth, on earthly authority and on things far remote from the inner morality or from spiritual life. Catholic Rome was the heir to the old pagan Rome. Ancient Rome was practical and rational. It gave the world the Roman Law, one of the greatest and the most amazing monuments of history. But the heirs to the Roman Law have forgotten the famous words: *summum jus—summa injuria*. They have forgotten that Christianity introduced the new principle of inner truth, a truth not founded on logical assumptions but based on the words of God.

Catholicism had absorbed the spirit and the essence of Roman

[30] I. A., *Sochineniia*, I, 558–559.

Law. This explained why Catholicism, on account of its rational consistency, had such a great appeal for many people. But at the same time rationalism was detrimental to faith. In order to restore its inner equilibrium, therefore, the Catholic Church had to rely on the supremacy and the infallibility of papal authority.

The Latin and Germanic peoples were saturated with Roman Law very early in their history, as well as with its embodiment in the Catholic Church. The Slavs were a different people and their world view was different: "for a Slav in general and for an Orthodox Slav in particular, juridical truth is less important than moral truth. All the strivings of his soul . . . are directed toward the inner truth." [31] The aristocratic element in Catholicism was repugnant to the democratic spirit of the Slavs, a spirit which found its expression in the veche, in the mir and in the obshchina. Any attempt to Catholicize the Slavs was, according to Aksakov, a perversion of the Slavic nature.

In order to defeat Catholicism in the western provinces, full support must be given to the Orthodox brotherhoods existing in those areas. Money should flow to them from all parts of Russia. Pre-Petrine Russia fully understood the significance of the Orthodox brotherhoods. When Tsar Alexis had to surrender to Poland the lands he had acquired in Lithuania and Belorussia, he demanded of Poland the preservation of the rights and freedom of the brotherhoods, centered around their churches. The brotherhoods were needed as a token against denationalization and as a way of educating the young in the tradition of their fathers. The same article was reintroduced in the treaty between Poland and Russia ratified by Sofia in 1686.[32] The Uniate movement should be stopped and no assistance should be given to the Catholic or Jewish religions.[33]

---

[31] *Ibid.*, pp. 559–562. On the Protestants Aksakov wrote to Countess Bludova: "Do you know (as you undoubtedly do) that the Protestant peoples have higher moral standards and live far better than the Catholic and the Orthodox peoples. I cannot disassociate in my mind Protestantism from lush pasture-land and fat cows: their ideal is more attainable and earthier. Yet does this mean that we should cast away Orthodoxy and embrace Protestantism?" in I. A., *Pisma*, IV, 229.

[32] I. A., *Sochineniia*, III, 248, 333–341, 343. Aksakov referred to the *Polnoe Sobranie Zakonov*, II, no. 1186, par. 9.

[33] *Ibid.*, pp. 468, 474.

Secondly, the Orthodox clergy must be given the right—indeed, they must be urged to participate—in local politics and in the administration of the western districts.[34] In the field of education Aksakov suggested that the Polish University of Vilno should be replaced by an Orthodox Academy which would possess the double function of preparing men for the priesthood of offering a higher education for everyone eligible. At all levels the schools should be imbued with a militant Russian spirit.[35]

Aksakov demanded all these measures in order to stop the Polonization of the western region, yet at the same time he felt that they were not sufficient in themselves. The Russian people should become more conscious of its own nationalism, of its national spirit, or narodnost: "The weakness of Russia consists in the fact that its [position] is based on the strength of the bayonets and not on a social force." And Aksakov liked to repeat the words of Talleyrand about the bayonets: "on peut s'y appuyer, on ne peut pas s'y asseoir."[36]

By *narodnost,* Aksakov meant the Great Russian national spirit:

No state should lose sight of the essence of its life and strength, the true source, the cause and the base of its historical existence. It seems to be hardly necessary to say that in the Russian Empire—this essence, this source of life and strength, this seat of constructiveness is Russia, the Russian people, not Poland, the Baltic Provinces, not Bashkiria, no matter how closely associated they may be with Russia.[37]

3. ANTI-SEMITISM

Ivan Aksakov had come into contact with Jews for the first time during his trip to Bessarabia in 1848. Since the reign of Elizabeth, Jews had not been allowed to settle in Great Russia and it is understandable that the young Aksakov should view them as a strange and exotic people. In one of his letters home the twenty-five-year-old Aksakov wrote: "And how beautiful are the Jewesses! Among all the

[34] *Ibid.,* p. 42. It must be remembered that the zemstvos were introduced in the western provinces only in 1911 by Stolypin.
[35] *Ibid.,* pp. 505, 667.
[36] *Ibid.,* pp. 187, 412.
[37] *Ibid.,* pp. 203, 204.

Asiatic faces, their faces are the most humane. There is something dreamy in their features." [38] Nor could Aksakov conceal his admiration for the organizational ability and the talents of the Jews. Yet even at this time, the seeds of anti-Semitism were already present in his mind. Indeed, Aksakov confessed that, in spite of all the qualities of the Jews, he could not "get rid of the idea that every Jew continues to crucify Christ in his mind," an idea that became later a leitmotif of his future anti-Semitic propaganda. [39] But at this time Aksakov explained the unfavorable characteristics of the Jews by blaming the cruel circumstances of their history.

However, when he returned to the South in 1855, Aksakov's tone changed. He began to complain about the squalor in which the Jews lived: "The Jews live in very filthy conditions, they sleep almost fully clothed and under greasy featherbeds. It could be said that the Jews in general are a repugnant people, although very gifted and intelligent." [40] Aksakov's first anti-Semitic articles appeared only in 1862. In fact, four years before, in 1858, Aksakov had protested against an anti-Semitic article in *Illiustratsia,* a journal of that period. Entitled, "The Jews of Western Russia and Their Present Situation," this article grossly insulted and debased the Jews and its appearance called forth a series of protests by all the known literati and publicists of Moscow and St. Petersburg, Ivan Aksakov among them. [41] His conversion to outspoken anti-Semitism was apparently motivated by the discovery of the social and economic situation in the western provinces, which was a direct result of the expulsion of the Jews under Elizabeth, the partitions of Poland, and the restrictive measures introduced under Nicholas I, as well as by the demands for more rights that the Jews made shortly after the emancipation of the serfs.

Aksakov, at first, linked the Jewish problem with the problem of Polonism in the western region: the Poles were both exploiters and

[38] I. A., *Pisma,* II, 18, 19.

[39] *Ibid.,* p. 36.

[40] I. A., *Pisma,* III, 178.

[41] A. Nikitenko, *Zapiski i dnevnik,* 2 vols. (St. Petersburg, 1904), I, 537. See also "Pisma M. E. Saltykova k V. P. Bezobrazovu," in *Golos Minuvshego* (1922), no. 2, p. 139.

invaders of Russian nationality; the Jews were leeches who weakened the population by draining their economic vitality, thus, creating favorable conditions for Polonization.

Aksakov advertised what he considered to be the rapaciousness of Jewish exploitation in forceful, vivid, and virulent terms. The struggle against this exploitation became the key-word of his anti-Jewish propaganda. Aksakov wrote:

One finds in the western provinces a degree of exploitation that cannot be compared to the exploitation of the worker by any factory-owner or landowner. There, [Jewish] exploitation, like a boa, is strangulating the population. It drains all the blood of the people and keeps them fettered in such a horrible bondage that no worker or peasant in Jew-free Russia can have an idea about it. It is an old oppression, an arrogant oppression; its results are important though its character is unbearably petty. It is so much more insulting because the exploiters belong to another race and another creed. But our "liberals" cannot find a word of reproach against these exploiters: their liberalism has evaporated as if by an enchantment, as if it did not exist at all! [42]

He continued by attacking the social taboo imposed by liberal opinion against discussion of the Jewish affairs on the pages of the Russian press:

"The idea of our time," "the liberal idea," "the humane way of thinking" have become in our progressive society a sort of scarecrow frightening away any truly bold criticism. They are a sort of shingle behind which hide willingly all kinds of lies, which often are not only non-liberal and non-humane but, indeed, forcibly disruptive and insulting to the silent masses' right to live and exist. [This silence] is maintained in the interest of a pseudo-oppressed, noisy, and vociferous minority. This despotism of certain ideas, this blind trucking to certain idols is explained by the history of our social growth and, no doubt, possesses its useful side, when the ideas in question are moral. But . . . many good deeds are

---

[42] I. A., *Sochineniia*, III, 723. In this anti-Semitic diatribe Aksakov never mentioned that the majority of the Jews lived in dire poverty and were cruelly exploited not only by the local authorities but also by their richer and more powerful coreligionists. For a firsthand account read, for instance, the memoirs of Paul Axelrod, *Perezhitoe i peredumannoe* (Berlin, 1923). Axelrod, one of the first Russian Marxists, gives a frightening description of the squalid conditions in which the poorer Jews of the western provinces lived.

performed, if not out of conviction, at least through fear, by a certain spiritual cowardice in the face of the awesome ideas of the century. Such a reason, of course, is immoral, unfounded, and seldom fruitful.[43]

To a certain extent, Aksakov was prompted to speak out against the Jews because of the repeated demands that were made in favor of more privileges and rights for them. Aksakov was against giving any priority to the Jews over the Russian Dissenters, who were also hoping to receive more rights. Yet Aksakov had to equivocate. He believed that in the name of Christian precepts, not of civilization, the Jews should be granted more rights under the express condition that such rights would not negate the Christian principles from which they were derived: "Jews could be allowed into many positions, but not to those where Christians would have to submit to their rule or where they could influence the administration and the legislative process of the country . . . We were never the enemies of the Jews. We acknowledge the great gifts of this people and we sincerely lament their going astray."[44] However, it is difficult to imagine a post in the Russian Empire which would not affect Christians unless it was in the administration of Jewish affairs. Aksakov's suggestion might have been sheer hypocrisy or another diplomatic tribute to those "humane and liberal ideas" of his times that he so sincerely detested. But this was written in 1862; soon after, such scruples would not bother him anymore.

Aksakov soon buttressed his argument that the Jews are the economic slave-masters of the Christian population of the western provinces by others of greater and deeper significance. Originally Russia had received the Jews because they had no other place to go and in order to show compassion for human beings, regardless of their creed, since this was in keeping with Christian teaching. The Jews should know this and be grateful. They must remember that they are guests and that they should not claim any rights: "The hosts may receive and even cater to guests, however unwanted they are, but they cannot give them their seats and grant full power to those who advocate the overturn of all order in the house: they

[43] I. A., *Sochineniia*, III, 687.
[44] *Ibid.*, p. 693.

cannot give them the right to command and run the house." But Aksakov also described the Jewish problem as consisting in a search for a *modus vivendi* with a nationality "that finds its justification in the negation of Christianity ... If the Jews recanted their religious beliefs and acknowledged in Christ the true Messiah, no Jewish problem would exist." Those who were not with Christianity were against it. The Jews were a hostile element to be conquered or destroyed.[45]

Aksakov spoke also of collusion between the Catholic clergy of Poland and the Jews because of the mutual esteem once displayed by the Great Rabbi and the Archbishop of Warsaw. Aksakov wrote that:

> It would have been a thousand times more honest and moral if the Catholics and the Jews came to each other and said: "We repudiate Christ and his commandments and we repudiate the Talmud and our expectation of the Messiah; we merge together in the name of our human calling!" ... But as long as they do not say this and continue officially to adhere, respectively, to the teachings of Christ and to the Jewish teachings, they offer an ugly example of base lying, hypocrisy, and disrespect for their callings as well as contempt towards people who profess their faith sincerely.[46]

Sincerity of faith meant for Aksakov intolerance and aggression against any other religion; tolerance and friendship between people professing different creeds was suspect in his eyes.

Anticipating a possible accusation of prejudice, Aksakov set out to prove that the Jewish faith was the most prejudiced in existence. Christianity was the logical culmination of Judaism; thus Judaism "found its explanation and justification only in Christianity." Contemporary Judaism was for Aksakov: "the embodiment of a historical period that had outlived itself, it is a superseded and petrified moment in the universal spiritual evolution. Any attempt on the part of Judaism to have a further historical life is tantamount to the negation of everything that came after it; Judaism is the negation of the evolution of mankind. The Jew is an anachronism, but

---

[45] *Ibid.*, pp. 690, 699, 729.
[46] *Ibid.*, p. 691.

an anachronism unwilling to reconcile itself with its destiny and pretending to have contemporary significance. At the same time, if this anachronism had contemporary significance, it would exclude anything existing now, everything that is the logical result of the past." Unwilling to reconcile himself with two thousand years of history "a Jewish believer continues to crucify Christ in his mind and to fight inwardly with rage for the lost right of spiritual leadership against him, who came to cancel the Law by carrying it out himself." [47]

Nor were the Jews who had abandoned Judaism without joining Christianity a source of consolation to Aksakov, for, as he said of them: "they cease to be Jews without breaking away from Jewry; while at the same time, since they do not become Christians, they are something in between; they are moral and intellectual amphibiae. They are what the 'progressive' Jews call: (those who) join universal human civilization." Such Jews were dangerous for any society:

A Jew who abjures the faith of his forefathers and who wants, at the same time, to remain outside Christianity is not only a man beyond the pale of the moral law that should govern his inner world and his relations to society; he stands outside of the social principles and the conditions on which our contemporary society is founded and by which it is governed . . . When you hear of a Mohammedan, Jewish, or Buddhist society, you know the moral law by which these societies are ruled and you understand that the members of these societies feel morally secure within the boundaries of their acknowledged laws. But, as soon as a man recommends himself not as a subject to a moral and religious law but as a member of universal civilization, you will not fail to ask him the following question: what is the common code of moral rights and obligations of this civilization which puts itself above religion as a dogma and as a way of life?" [48]

By rejecting Christianity the Jews had rejected European civilization because European culture was inseparable from Christianity: "You must understand Christianity if you want to understand

---

[47] *Ibid.*, pp. 700–702. "A Jew," said Khomiakov in his "Historical Notes," "after Christ's coming, is no more than a living nonsense, which has no reasonable excuse for existence; he therefore has no meaning in history."

[48] *Ibid.*, pp. 702, 705, 706.

Dante, Schiller, Goethe with his Faust, Raphael, Shakespeare and so on." By refusing to acknowledge Christianity, the Jews denied the achievements of European culture: "It is clear to anyone that from a Jew you cannot obtain either a Goethe or a Schiller or a Shakespeare but possibly only a Heine or a Börne." [49]

Aksakov was distressed to see the prevailing misconception that pictured the Jews as underprivileged citizens in Russia. According to Aksakov, the Jews were perhaps the most privileged nationality in Russia. The Jews formed a state within a state; they lived in Jewish communities, which were protected by the laws of the Russian Empire. These laws also protected the Jewish religion, because a Jew who wanted to become a Christian could do so only after receiving a written authorization from the Jewish administration of his *kahal,* or community, an authorization he was not very likely to receive. Fulminating against the "criminal complicity" of the Russian administration, Aksakov cried out: "We should not be speaking of the emancipation of the Jews but rather of the emancipation of the Russians from the Jews . . . Involuntarily, one shudders at the sight of Russia held captive by the Jews and asks oneself: where are we? In Russia or actually in Jewish Palestine, as the Western provinces are nicknamed from times long forgotten." [50]

As we know, the career of Ivan Aksakov as a publicist was interrupted from 1868 to 1880. During these years his interest in the Jewish question did not die, in spite of the momentous events in the Balkans and in Russia. In 1878, in a letter to a friend, Aksakov commented on the content of the anti-Semitic "Diary of Warsaw" (*Varshavski Dnevnik*) published by Prince N. Golitsyn:

The work of Prince N. N. Golitsyn is truly remarkable; yet it is impossible to adopt his point of view, although I do not admit at all any indifference in matters of faith even from the governmental point of view. I do not see the point of printing a list of crimes committed by the Jews in the fifteenth, sixteenth, and seventeenth centuries. Did he do it in order to prove that there exists a sect of infanticides? The task is to prove its existence right now. To unmask the Talmud—that is another

[49] *Ibid.,* p. 707.
[50] *Ibid.,* pp. 708, 712.

thing. Invite the Jews to abjure the Talmud and encourage their return to pure Mosaism! To stir hatred gets us nowhere; at least, the enumeration of the crimes produces a painful impression which is, I would say, detrimental to the journal.[51]

Anti-Talmudism was to be a new aspect of Aksakov's anti-Semitic campaign.

Aksakov was allowed finally to resume his journalistic activity in 1880, shortly before a wave of pogroms swept through southern Russia in the wake of Alexander II's assassination. Following this event, Russia lived through a period of great tension. This tension found its release in a series of pogroms committed by the population of the southwestern provinces against the Jews. This violence produced a painful impression both at home and abroad. The pogroms were condemned on the pages of the press, and not necessarily of the liberal press only. Aksakov, on the contrary, defended the cause of those who had perpetrated abuses against the Jewish population. He explained that the pogroms were directed against Jewry in general and not against individuals. As if the massacred Jews were to appreciate the difference! Aksakov argued that the pogroms were not prompted by the lust of looting but by the desire to cast off the yoke of Jewish oppression:

The man who has visited so much as once our southern and western border provinces, where Jews live unhampered, and who has seen with his own eyes the oppression of the local Russian population by Jewry (we have been there many times) will know that the popular movement is not only natural but even quite unsurprising.[52]

The underlying reason for the pogroms was just and no one, if he considered that there were as many casualties on one side as on the other, should complain particularly. Aksakov warned the public that the Jews had adopted a new stratagem: having accumulated a great amount of wealth through the exploitation of the Christians, they now paraded as conservatives, as a bulwark against

[51] "Pisma I. S. Aksakova k V. F. Putsykovichu," with introduction by S. O. Iakobson in *Na Chuzhoi Storone* (Berlin, 1924), no. 5, p. 148.
[52] I. A., *Sochineniia*, III, 719.

anarchism and socialism. They tried to represent the pogroms as socialist or anarchist outbursts hoping thereby to gain the sympathy of the government. Aksakov replied to this that, if Jews had lost property, the Ministry of Finance should reimburse their losses but that, at the same time, Russia should do something in order to get rid of the Jews. The legend that the Jews were cramped for space must also be disproved. The Jews were allowed to live in twenty-five provinces, yet they chose to remain in those regions where they could exploit their victims. As a proof of this contention, Aksakov cited the case of the 14,000 Jews who fled Russia shortly after the pogroms but who returned to their old homes when calm was restored, many of them from the United States. Aksakov furnished the explanation: Jews were parasites who lived where they could exist at somebody else's expense. The verdict was: "Jewish predatoriness is a national quality." [53]

According to Aksakov, the Jewish commune, or *kahal,* was the most faithful expression of this predatoriness. Aksakov supported his allegations by citing the revelations of a certain Brafman, a Jew converted to Russian orthodoxy, who had published in 1869 a two-volume work called "The Book of the Kahal" (Kniga Kagala). (A second edition was published in 1871.) "This book," said Aksakov, "should be the point of departure and the cornerstone for all reflexions on the Jewish question in Russia." [54] Aksakov took great pains to advertise this book by quoting it in his many articles devoted to the kahal system.

The jurisdiction of the kahal, according to Brafman, was based on a "Talmudic" rule which claimed supposedly that: "The property of those who profess another religion is free. Whoever takes it first becomes the owner." In other words, according to Brafman, the

[53] *Ibid.,* pp. 717, 724, 789–790.

[54] I. A., *Sochineniia,* III, 765. For more information on this case, see S. M. Dubnow, *History of the Jews in Russia and Poland,* 3 vols. (Philadelphia, 1918), II, 187–190, 194. Jacob Brafman (1825–1879) was, according to Dubnow, a Jewish draftdodger, who, having taken offense at his Jewish community's draftboard, decided to malign it and offered his services to anti-Semitic government officials. "The Book of the Kahal" was a collection of Brafman's statements, revealing the "anti-social character of organized Jewry." See also L. Greenberg, *The Jews in Russia* (New Haven, 1944), pp. 93–96, 111.

entire area—property as well as people—around a kahal "belonged" to the kahal.

This "ownership" served as the foundation for a special set of relations between the Jews of the same kahal. The kahal sold the right of exploitation, as if it were a "concession," to its members. The right to exploit or "own" a Christian was called *maarufia* or *meropia*. The right to the property of the Christians was called *hazakah*. The contract between the individual and his kahal was known as *hakhlat*.

A Jew who had a meropia from his kahal was the master of a certain Christian; no other Jew was allowed to interfere with this exploiter-exploited relationship. The same applied in the case of hazakah. The kahal offered to the contracting party legal advice and protection against anyone who tried to upset the contract. If a Jew transgressed by poaching on some other Jew's preserves, a secret Jewish tribunal called *Beth Din* tried and punished the wayward Jew. This Beth Din could even carry out death sentences. If a Christian misbehaved towards his "master," the kahal punished him with *kherem*. The kherem was a sort of excommunication. No Jew was allowed to have any business with the excommunicated; it meant that the landowner of the peasant could be ruined or starved by the imposition of kherem because trade was in the hands of the Jews. A Jew who tried to break the kherem would then be tried by the stern Beth Din.[55]

Before proceeding any further, it is interesting to note the technique used by Aksakov in his anti-Semitic propaganda. Aksakov constantly used many Hebrew words, which he did not understand in their historical and Talmudic contexts, in order to create an atmosphere of fright and suspicion before the foreign, the strange, and the unexplained. Indeed, these Hebrew words were made to sound like magical incantations belonging to dark and evil forces, which threatened the non-Jews with a mysterious danger. Also, the repeated use of Hebrew words in the writings of Aksakov gave a pseudo-scholarly authenticity to his anti-Semitic arguments. But to return to our narrative.

It is by this set of arrangements, which Brafman attributed to

[55] I. A., *Sochineniia*, III, 749–750.

Jewish society, that Aksakov explained the reluctance of the Jews to leave their kahals and go to the twenty-five provinces in which they were allowed to settle. This fact also explained the futility of settling the Jews on land. Each time such an attempt was made, the Jews, instead of working, rented out their land to the peasants, embroiling more and more the local population in their "dishonest" schemes. Demanding the emancipation of the Russian people from the Jews, Aksakov exclaimed:

The Russian kulak is a rare and exceptional phenomenon, but in the Jews one finds an entire corporation, an entire and solid organization of kulaks—millions of them, solidary among themselves and helping each other. Their profession, their calling boils down to being kulaks, and to exploiting the Christian population. The remarkable thing is that our socialists are vituperating against the rule of capital . . . but they are silent on the Jewish question, although the hateful idea of capital never found a better impersonation . . . than in Jewry! [56]

As is clear, the possibility exists that Aksakov wanted to deflect revolutionary agitation into anti-Semitic channels. If this supposition were proved correct, then the scapegoat view of anti-Semitism would have found a new illustration and a new confirmation.

Every student of modern anti-Semitism knows of the "Protocols of the Wise Men of Zion," also known as the "Protocols of the Elders of Zion." This document was supposedly fabricated by the Russian police at about the time of the revolution of 1905. [57] It purported to prove that the Jews were striving for the conquest of the

[56] *Ibid.*, pp. 744, 768, 788.

[57] There is a general consensus of opinions that the Protocols were fabricated under the aegis of the Russian police. The authorship of the Protocols is attributed either to General Rachkovsky, the Russian police chief in Paris or to a certain Sergei Nilus, the writer of the mystical and apocalyptical Russian treatise: "The Great in the Little: The Coming of Anti-Christ and the Rule of Satan on Earth." The content of the Protocols has been partly borrowed from a little-known work of a certain Maurice Joly, *Dialogue aux Enfers entre Montesquieu et Machiavel* (Brussels, 1864), directed against Napoleon III. For more information see: Herman Bernstein, *The Truth about the "Protocols of Zion"* (New York, 1935); John S. Curtiss, *An Appraisal of the Protocols of Zion* (1942); Benjamin Segel, *The Protocols of the Elders of Zion: The Greatest Lie in History* (New York, 1934); Philip Graves' three articles in *The Times* (London) of August 16, 17, and 18, 1921, published separately under the title *The Truth about the Protocols: A Literary Forgery* (London, 1922) and Hugo Valentin, *Anti-Semitism* (New York, 1936), pp. 165–183.

world and its transformation into a Jewish empire. There is little doubt that this document was devised with the intention of linking revolutions with Jewry so that the latent anti-Semitism of the Christians might became an asset against revolutionary agitation. Few people know, however, that the Protocols were to a certain extent a repetition of the publication of an allegedly "secret letter" of Adolphe Crémieux, president of the Alliance Israélite Universelle, to members at large, a letter which was first published in France in the *Antisemitique,* later in Germany in the *Deutsche Volkszeitung: Organ für soziale Reform,* and finally in Russia in Aksakov's *Rus.* This anti-Semitic hoax was by its purport and intention the precursor of the most notorious Protocols, published a quarter of a century later and, as such, it was an important step in the history of anti-Semitism. Since it was Ivan Aksakov who first published and annotated Crémieux's letter for his countrymen, his role in the growth of anti-Semitic ideas in Russia is thus clearly established. Lastly, the publication of this letter in Russia, after it appeared in France and Germany, would show that many anti-Semitic ideas travelled eastward rather than westward. This point is valuable in mitigating the opinion of those who have tried to link Nazism to the heritage of Russian anti-Semitism. One such thinker, Heiden wrote:

It would be too much to call the Nazi foreign policy that was now inaugurated a Tsarist policy. Nonetheless, its spiritual sources were actually in the Russia of the Tsars, in the world of the Black Hundred and of the "True Russian People." These Russian émigrés, when obliged to leave their native soil and become nomadic and homeless, brought their idea, their hopes, and their hatred to Central and Western Europe. The gloomy, bloodthirsty Russian anti-Semitism infected the quieter German type. Merezhkovski preached horror of the Bolshevist anti-Christ; the protocols of the Wise men of Zion were eagerly read in Germany.[58]

If this is so, history once more indulged in an ironic billiard game: Russian anti-Semitism, encouraged by the authority of the *Deutsche*

---

[58] K. Heiden, *The New Inquisition,* translated by Heinz Nordon (New York, 1939), pp. 41–42. Peter Viereck in his *Metapolitics* (New York, 1941) also speaks of the Russian influence on the Nazi movement. The point of view that suggests that Russian anti-Semitism was strongly colored by German anti-Semitism was advanced by S. M. Dubnow, in his *History of the Jews in Russia and Poland,* already cited.

Volkszeitung, eventually came to influence the German National Socialist Party!

The aim of Aksakov's writings was to establish that the Jewish Ideal was nothing else than the negation of the Christian Idea. Basing himself on the "Crémieux document," he linked the negation of Christianity to the Jews' alleged desire to dominate abhorred Christianity:

Because the Semitic idea has been brewed up from the principle of negation, the world imperialism (*miroderzhavstvo*) of the Jews (which is undoubtedly on the march) is expressed—for it cannot express itself in any other way—by the gradual spiritual sapping of the foundations of the existing Christian world and, outwardly, by the material advantages that the Jews have over the Christians through their use of the most sinful, the most immoral force—the *force of money,* in other words, *the force of exploitation.*[59]

The Jews, moreover, were a cosmopolitan tribe. Aksakov explained that although the Jews took the nationality of the country in which they lived, they did not cease to be Jewish. Jewish religion was not so much a spiritual force but rather a racial and nationalistic cult. All Jews were first and foremost citizens of world Jewry; only secondly, and for material advantages exclusively, were they citizens of the countries in which they lived. The Jews, therefore, were dangerous to those countries. They carried their spirit of negation into literature, art, the stock market, and so on. Aksakov viewed with alarm and concern the gains that the Jews had made in Germany and the Habsburg Empire. The formation of German anti-Semitic groups was welcomed by him as "the awakening of German society," for Jewry was, and here Aksakov quoted Iu. Samarin, "foncièrement hostile à un ordre moral et social chrétiennement constitué." [60]

The evidence for this allegation could be found, said Aksakov, in the existence, in Paris, of the *Alliance Israélite Universelle.* Formed in 1864, it was "the government of the Jewish universal republic." As a proof of this worldwide conspiracy, Aksakov quoted from the so-called Crémieux letter:

[59] I. A., *Sochineniia,* III, 730.
[60] *Ibid.,* pp. 731, 733.

We have no compatriots; we have only religious followers. Our nationality is the religion of our fathers. We do not acknowledge any other nationality . . . Only Jewry represents a religious and political truth . . . The Jew will not become the friend of a Christian or a Moslem until the beacon of the faith of Israel shines everywhere . . . The Christian Church is our eternal enemy. Every day will see the nets of Israel spread over the earth and the holy prophecy of our books will come true: there will be a time when Jerusalem becomes the temple for all peoples . . . The day when all the riches of the earth belong to the Jews is nearing . . .[61]

When the Jews in Russia protested against the publication of the Crémieux document, Aksakov asked them why did not the Jews of France and Germany sue the *L'Antisemitique* and the *Deutsche Volkszeitung* for slander, since Crémieux's letter had also appeared on their pages: this would have been the best way to vindicate themselves, but, according to Aksakov, the Jews preferred not to do it. Moreover, he, Aksakov, could find nothing in this letter which he did not know before: the letter was a reflection of the Jewish religion and no more. Aksakov could not understand all the fuss made about this letter, especially in view of the fact that a certain Gordon had written in the Jewish journal *Ha-Shahar* (The Dawn) in 1871, the following lines: "Would the Messiah find among you useful people when he comes, in order to restore our life as in the past? Would he find among you a finance minister, a military man, or scholars, or statesmen capable to represent Him at the courts of foreign potentates . . . and indispensable for His Kingdom?"[62] Aksakov also tried to match many of the statements of the "Crémieux document" with quotations taken out of context from articles of the *Russki Evrei* (Russian Jew), which, as could be expected, railed against Aksakov and his ideas.

Aksakov also made fun of the liberal *Vestnik Evropy* (European Courier), which had proposed that it would be a fine thing if Russians intermarried with the Jews. The rebuttal came from the "Russian Jew" itself, which stated that the Jews did not want to intermarry because they did not want to lose their identity as Jews.

[61] *Ibid.*, pp. 751, 819–821.
[62] *Ibid.*, pp. 830–837, quotation from p. 840.

To intermarry with non-Jews would have meant the end of the national existence of the Jews, it would have been the suicide of the Jewish race.[63]

Finally, Aksakov advocated the revision of Russian laws pertaining to the Jews. First of all, Jewish peculiarism should not be protected. In making this recommendation Aksakov had in view the statute of November 13, 1844, which ordered the creation of Jewish schools and gymnasia, and also the statute of March 24, 1873, which permitted the creation of teachers' colleges for Jews; he was particularly displeased at the fact that the Talmud was mandatory in the curriculi of these schools. Aksakov, who claimed that the Talmud was the root of the Jewish evil, professed his sympathy towards the Karaim Tartars who were of non-Talmudist Jewish faith.[64] Otherwise, Aksakov could not suggest any practical solution to the Jewish problem he helped to create.

This study of the anti-Semitism of Ivan Aksakov is important because it describes anti-Semitism of the "fathers" of those sons who formed the ranks of the Black Hundred and of the Retinue of the Archangel Michael in the last years of imperial Russia. A younger contemporary of Aksakov, Vladimir Solovev had sensed the danger of ultra-nationalism. Nationalism as a cult was bound to degenerate into violence and savagery. Solovev distinguished three stages in this process:

The worship of one's own people as the preeminent bearer of universal truth; then the worship of this people as an elemental force, irrespective of universal truth; finally the worship of those national limitations and anomalies which separate the people from civilized mankind, that is, the worship of one's own people with a direct negation of the very idea of universal truth—these are the three consecutive phases of our nationalism represented by the Slavophiles, Katkov, and the new obscurantists, re-

[63] *Ibid.*, p. 797.

[64] *Ibid.*, pp. 801, 814–815. It seems obvious that Aksakov's knowledge of the Talmud came from anti-Semitic tracts. It is possible that Aksakov used as a reference "The Talmud and the Jews," published in 1879, by a certain Hippolyte Lutostanski. The latter was a defrocked and renegade Catholic priest from Vilno, who, upon embracing Orthodoxy, earned a living by vilifying the Jews and their religious practices.

spectively. The first were purely fantastic in their doctrine, the second was a realist with fantasy, the last finally are realists without any fantasy, but also without any shame.

And Solovev concluded: "The worship of the virtue of the people, the worship of the might of the people, the worship of the savagery of the people—these are the three descending steps of our pseudo-patriotic thought." [65] In this respect, Aksakov is a good example. He proved his nationalism by molesting the Jews and other minorities and he was a precursor of those, who in the twentieth century, made savagery the center of their patriotic cult.

4. OTHER NATIONALITIES

Russia was a large multinational empire. The rise of nationalism throughout Europe in the nineteenth century affected to a certain extent the nationalities which lived on the periphery of European Russia. Among them were the Ukrainians and the Baltic peoples. The policy of Aksakov here was consistent with his views on Polonism. He defended the rights of the minorities against the cultural and economic encroachments of the non-Russians—the Poles and the Jews in the western provinces, and the Germans in the Baltic lands—but he fought equally against the nationalism of these minorities because such a tendency threatened the integrity of the Russian empire and his dreams of a Slavic millenium.

While Aksakov struggled with the Polish and Jewish "problems," Iuri Samarin, who had spent several years in Riga, took upon himself to attack and censure the Baltic Germans. Samarin wrote a large work on the borderlands of Russia, chiefly on the Baltic provinces. He published his books in Europe, in Berlin and in Prague, because he could not do so in Russia, where the Baltic Germans enjoyed a privileged position at the Court and in the administration. Aksakov's contribution to the discussion of the "Baltic problem" consisted in advertizing Samarin's books in Russia and placing his articles in the journals that he, Aksakov, published.

[65] V. S. Solovev, *Sobranie sochineni*, V, 185, as quoted in Nicholas Riasanovsky, *Russia and the West in the Teaching of the Slavophiles* (Cambridge, Mass., 1952), p. 197. Solovev's conclusion is found on p. 241 of *Sobranie sochineni*, vol. V.

In his comments on the work of Samarin, Aksakov accused the Baltic Germans of disregarding the Russian nation and of forgetting that the government in Russia was and should be Russian rather than a supranational institution. In many respects, Aksakov concluded, the Baltic Germans were similar to the Jews: "The Jews, like the Germans, do not acknowledge the existence in Russia of a Russian nationality and doubt (for the Germans it is a question that they settled negatively long ago) whether the Russians were really the masters in the Russian land." [66] Russia was to blame for making of the Baltic provinces a "rococo museum" where social injustices were preserved. Aksakov sided with the downtrodden Letts and Ests, demanding their emancipation from the tutelage of a neo-medieval and feudal German nobility. The conspiracy of the Baltic nobility in collusion with Germany against Russia was conspicuous and should be fought by leaning on the non-German local population.

As regards the Balts' northern neighbor, Finland, on the other hand, Aksakov expressed only positive sentiments. He presented this country as a paragon of civic virtues that should be emulated by all. It was a land where the people were "satisfied and happy, where society was not contaminated by lies or by fantastic and unrealizable strivings, where the young generation was not a sickly miscarriage or weak, irritable and nervous as a prematurely born child, and where the social environment was free, so to speak, of the miasmata of the hospital and the graveyard.[67] Aksakov implored the "honest, sober and healthy Finnish people" to care for the Russian population in Finland. As for the Finnish Sejm, it was a living proof that Russia did not intend to Russify anyone.

It is possible that Finland did not present a threat in the eyes of Aksakov because the Finns had no distinct culture of their own or, at least, not the progressive type of culture characteristic of the Germans and the Poles. Furthermore, the Finns lived among Finns and did not wield any power over non-Finnish peoples. It can be

[66] I. A., *Sochineniia*, VI, 8. See the first 167 pages of this volume for Aksakov's treatment of the Baltic problem.
[67] I. A., *Sochineniia*, III, 215.

argued also that Aksakov chose Finland as a pet minority in order
to be able to prove that he was against any Russification of the
borderland peoples. Indeed, his attitude toward the Ukrainian cultural and political revival was quite different from his attitude
toward the Finns.

Aksakov was disturbed by the emergence of Ukrainian nationalism
or, as it was then called, Ukrainophilism. From the historical point
of view it may not be possible to say exactly when this trend started,
but it is probable that Ukrainophilism had existed since the seventeenth century. It became stronger as the encroachments of the
Great Russians increased, particularly when serfdom was introduced
by decree in 1783 and when the Ukrainian leaders were replaced by
officials of the Imperial Government. The beginning of the nineteenth century witnessed a strong upsurge of Ukrainian self-consciousness: Kotliarevski wrote his Ukrainian *Aeneid* and Bantysh-
Kamenski revived the history of Ukraine's martial past. And the
cultural revival never really stopped, although it slacked down considerably in the eighties, at least in the Russian Ukraine; the center
of agitation was transferred from Kiev to Lemberg (Lvov) in
Austrian Galicia.

An illustration for Ukrainophilism in the middle of the nineteenth
century can be found in the ill-starred Brotherhood of Cyril and
Methodius, in which the Ukrainian bard T. Shevchenko and the
historian and novelist Kostomarov played an important role. This
Brotherhood, created in 1846 and disbanded by the Gendarmes in
1848, was representative of a romantic type of Ukrainian nationalism.
Later Ukrainophilism manifested itself under the guise of separatism
or of federalism within a renovated, constitutional Russia. In the late
seventies and in the eighties, the leader of such expression of
Ukrainophilism was Professor M. Dragomanov. Although Aksakov
was somewhat interested in this movement, he was not a specialist
on Ukrainian matters, and wrote very little on the subject.

Aksakov loved the Ukraine as a country but disliked its inhabitants. Aksakov was sure that the Ukrainians were not the descendants
of the Kievan Russians but of those people who settled in the
Ukrainian steppes during the centuries that followed the fall of Kiev,

and who were of mixed racial stock, although predominantly Slavs. As a proof of this view, he advanced the arguments that the steam bath so necessary to the Kievans of yore was totally unknown to the Ukrainians and that the *byliny,* or Kievan *chansons de geste,* were sung only in Great Russia.[68] He protested against the introduction on a large scale of the Ukrainian literary language; following the opinion of Khomiakov, he welcomed the development of the local vernacular solely for religious purposes. By this means, Orthodox preaching would gain strength against Polonism and against the Uniate Church. Aksakov, furthermore, asserted that Gogol became famous only because he wrote in Russian. Despite these views, however, Aksakov disapproved any coercive measures against the revival of the Ukrainian language, for "every lie, as we said more than once, must be given full freedom to commit suicide. All the falsehood of this Ukrainomania would soon become so incongruous that it will disintegrate. Only the genuine (Russian) essence will remain." [69] The Ukrainophiles were nothing but "willing and conscious traitors to the Russian cause" because they "served the Polish rebellion." [70] Aksakov and Kostomarov clashed on this subject. Aksakov maintained that the rise of Ukrainophilism was a monstrous absurdity because there existed already a Great-Russian state, a beautiful Great-Russian language and a rich literature. These were infinitely superior to anything that the Ukrainians could ever dream of attaining. Kostomarov, on the other hand, claimed that Russia had stunted the normal development of the Ukraine throughout its history and asserted that, if the Ukraine should enjoy unhampered freedom of culture, it would certainly contribute in every respect to world culture.[71]

The growth of Ukrainian nationalism in Galicia in the second half of the nineteenth century was another source of worry for Aksakov. Aksakov had high hopes for Galicia as a force in the future development of Slavdom. He believed that the Orthodox Galicians who

---

[68] "Iz perepiski I. S. Aksakova s N. M. Pavlovym o drevnei russkoi istorii," *Russki Arkhiv* (1887), no. 8, pp. 486, 491.

[69] Barsukov, *Pogodin,* XX, 334.

[70] I. A., *Sochineniia,* I, 493.

[71] Barsukov, *Pogodin,* XX, 348–353, and I. A., *Pisma,* IV, 257–268.

were mistreated by the Poles and the Austrians would be easily swayed to the Russian side. Furthermore, a pro-Russian Galicia would have been strategically very convenient for containing the Austrians and the Poles. But Aksakov's hopes were now crumbling to pieces. Galicia became a center of Ukrainian nationalism which was allowed and even sometimes encouraged by the Habsburg government. Aksakov thought that Galicia was succumbing to the Ukrainophilism imported from the Russian Ukraine and consequently the Ukrainophiles took all the blame for this turn of events.[72]

In the case of all the border peoples, for Aksakov the antidote to separatism was the assimilation of the national minorities by the Great-Russian element. This assimilation should never, according to Aksakov, be carried out by force because force seldom was effective. History showed many examples of assimilation of strong conquerors by weak conquered peoples. Yet true assimilation could only be the outcome of a strong feeling of narodnost. Narodnost is to a people what personality is to a man. The man or the people with a strong personality always win over those who have a weaker personality. The personality of a people was also the moral strength of this people. In order to assimilate the border peoples and fight separatism, each and every Russian should work to remedy the causes that weaken the *narodnost* of the Great-Russian nation. Nevertheless, despite these general recommendations, Aksakov did not advance any suggestion on how to build a strong personality for a people, nor did he attempt to indicate a way to achieve the much-vaunted moral integrity that would attract and absorb the multinational elements of Russia into a united Great-Russia.

Aksakov's belief in the peaceful assimilation of national minorities within the Empire did not prevent him from claiming in addition those lands outside Russia's present frontiers that once had belonged to Russian princes. Aksakov wrote that: "There is no doubt that Russia would have (if she chose) historical and ethnic reasons to restore the boundaries of the Crown of St. Vladimir and reunite to Russia the Russian tribes in Hungary, Bukovina and Galicia." In

[72] I. A., *Pisma*, IV, 85–86.

Central Asia also, Russia had a *mission civilisatrice* to fulfill because there "the interest of Russia and the interests of the vanquished peoples give full freedom for Russia's policy—a Christian and civilizing policy—which sows with one hand the seeds of the true teaching while with the other it consolidates the firm base of a social order and of private enterprise that was lacking in these large and fertile lands which needed management." [73]

Ivan Aksakov's views on the nationality problem were not very clearly defined. Aksakov advocated an ambiguous policy which at first glance was almost metaphysical, but which also encouraged crass imperialism in the name of some "superior truth" or some abstract historical reasons. The problem of nationality constitutes an important part of Aksakov's ideas. His pan-Slavist ideas will be discussed in the next chapter.

[73] I. A., *Sochineniia*, I, 206, 425.

CHAPTER V

The Pan-Slavist

Among the older Slavophiles, only A. S. Khomiakov had been interested in the Slavs outside of Russia. For him the concept of Slavdom had a special meaning—it was Russia and her spiritual brood, not as it was, but as it would be in the future. It also meant a world opposed to the West and united by the call of the blood and by a common Orthodox faith. Slavdom was the magic word that conjured up all the longings and wishes of the Slavophiles to see an Orthodox culture flourish on the grave of the western world. Ivan Aksakov was the spiritual heir of Khomiakov. During his lifetime there were great changes in the Balkans and he became the leader of all the Russians who wanted to see the liberation of the Slavs from the yoke of the foreigners.

It is possible to treat Aksakov's pan-Slavist ideology as a single and separate subject because he held it consistently for nearly thirty years. Special attention must be paid to the years of his presidency of the Slavic Benevolent Committee, for they were crucial in the history of the Balkans. Indeed, Aksakov replaced Pogodin as president of the Slavic Committee in 1875, and held this post until 1878, the year in which the Committee was closed. Finally, Aksakov's political analysis of the Slavic states must be followed chronologically.

It seems as though Aksakov was always fascinated by the Slavs. In a letter to his family written in 1844 the young Aksakov was proud to report that he had made a collection among his colleagues in Astrakhan for the construction of Orthodox churches in predominantly Catholic Dalmatia and Moslem Herzegovina.[1] But the first evidence that he was thinking seriously along pan-Slavic lines is to be found in the "confession" he submitted to Nicholas after his arrest in 1849. At first, Aksakov had believed that the Habsburg

[1] I. A., *Pisma*, I, 192.

Empire could become a Slavic Empire. In the memorandum sub-mitted to Nicholas I, Aksakov wrote:

In respect to my brother Gregory's opinion that Austria could become a Slavic monarchy, I can say that I held the same point of view because the German elements of the Empire have decayed and the latter would have collapsed long ago, if it were not for the support of the Slavs. I now think that that would have been very sad because the emergence near Russia of a self-styled and powerful Slavic monarchy would attract all those South Slavic peoples we are now repulsing and because it would deprive Russia of its significance: to be the only vessel of Orthodoxy and Slavic principles on earth.[2]

Many years later, Aksakov repudiated the idea of Slavic political supremacy within the Habsburg Empire. In 1865 Aksakov wrote:

It is possible to meet the Magyar *honveds* by lining against them Slavs in German uniforms, but as soon as we do not deal with coarse and impersonal material strength but with spiritual principles . . . the All-Slav idea dissolves into thin air like a ghost. The only remaining things are the tribal elements—Czechs, Croats, Serbs, etc., of which there is none capable of offering the inner spiritual force which would give Austria a new political definition that would place the Slavs above the Magyars.[3]

The Slavs of the Habsburg Empire did not have: "a common Slavic language that would unite them and a Slavic political principle," besides: "The lessons of history, it seems, should have taught them that they have nothing to hope from Austria and that dreams of a Slavic confederation prepared on German leaven are impossible and sinful dreams."[4] But in 1849, if Aksakov knew that Russia should be "the only vessel" of Orthodoxy and Slavdom—a principle that became the basic tenet of his teachings—he was equally aware of the difficulties his program would have to face in the future. In the same memorandum, Aksakov submitted:

[2] I. A., *Pisma,* II, 159–160, and M. Sukhomlinov: "I. S. Aksakov v sorokovykh godakh," *Istoricheski Vestnik* (1888), no. 2, p. 343.

[3] I. A., *Sochineniia,* I, 47.

[4] *Ibid.,* p. 137.

We do not believe in pan-Slavism, in the first place, because such an endeavor would demand a unity of faith among the Slavic peoples: the Catholicism of Bohemia and Poland is hostile and alien to as well as unmixable with the Orthodoxy of the other Slavs; secondly, because all the separate elements of the Slavic nations would (inevitably) amalgamate and lose themselves in a stronger, more purposeful and more powerful element—in the Russian element; thirdly, a great part of the Slavic peoples are contaminated by the influence of a shallow western liberalism which is repugnant to and which will never be accepted by the Russian people.[5]

The danger of western liberalism, the schism existing between the Orthodox and the Catholic Slavs, and the historical mission of Russia later became the three central themes in Aksakov's writings on pan-Slavism.

The reign of Nicholas I was not propitious for writing on Slavic problems; as a consequence, the two issues of the ill-fated *Moskovski sbornik* of 1852–1853, of which Ivan Aksakov was editor, did not contain any important material on the Slavic question. The debacle in the Crimea and the death of Nicholas were responsible for a change in the views of the Russian government and of the Russian public on those Slavic nations held in subjugation by common enemies: the Turks and the craven Austrians. It should be remembered that "ungrateful" Austria was blamed for the unfavorable turn taken by the war because she forbade the Russians to cross the Danube in order to strike at the heart of the Ottoman Empire. Had the Russians trespassed, Austria threatened to join the coalition. Professor Pogodin, an ardent pan-Slavist, sent a letter to the tsar urging him to use the restive Slavs against the Ottoman and Habsburg Empires, but Nicholas was adamant and stubborn in his legitimism; he would not consent to become the abettor of revolting subjects against their God-appointed sovereigns. With the death of Nicholas, the dismissal of Nesselrode, and the burning wound of Sebastopol, the allegiance to the spirit of the Holy Alliance was severed. The Turks and the Austrians were so odious to the Russians that all Russian sympathies gradually came to be directed toward

[5] I. A., *Pisma*, II, 160; M. Sukhomlinov, "I. S. Aksakov v sorokovykh godakh," p. 343.

potential allies—the Slavs of the Ottoman and Habsburg Empires.

The *Russkaia beseda* (the Russian Colloquium)—published from 1856 to 1860, and edited by Ivan Aksakov after 1858—had articles dealing with the Slavs in every issue. These articles were more of a historical than a political nature. Furthermore, since the "Russian Colloquium" was published at great intervals, its scope was necessarily limited.[6] Nevertheless, Aksakov wished to make the "Colloquium" a beacon for the Slavic world. In a letter to Prince Cherkasski, Aksakov explained his aspirations: "This (Slavic) question must be made as popular as possible. It must be taken out of the field of archeology and brought to life endowed with political significance. In a word, the "Colloquium" should be a political center for the Slavs and a real prime-mover."[7] Aksakov wanted to create a Slavic bureau as a branch of the "Russian Colloquium"; this bureau was to be a cultural center through which the solidarity of the Slavic world could be organized. When Koshelev, the owner of the journal, decided to suspend the publication, Aksakov entreated him to continue the "Colloquium" because it was an important Slavic organ. He failed to convince Koshelev and the "Colloquium" was discontinued in 1860, when Aksakov was abroad with his ailing brother Konstantin. In the last issue of 1859, an issue that Aksakov believed to be the final one, he wrote:

We have succeeded in extricating the Slavic question from the realm of archeological interest and in bringing it into the realm of a living, active sympathy; thus we have brought to life an intellectual movement in the circle of our literary Slavic brethren . . . We are happy to have succeeded apparently in dispelling misconceptions such as existed among us, as well as among the other Slavs concerning Russian pan-Slavism and in convincing our brethren that our sympathy is alien to any encroachment on their independent development. The recognition of the right of every Slavic nationality to an independent way of life has always been the slogan of Russian Slavophilism.[8]

[6] M. Petrovich, *The Emergence of Russian Panslavism, 1856–1870* (New York, 1956), pp. 111–112.

[7] O. Trubetskaia, *Materialy dlia biografii kn. V. A. Cherkasskago* (Moscow, 1901), p. 124. Aksakov's letter of July 17, 1858, to Cherkasski as quoted in Petrovich, p. 113.

[8] Ivan S. Aksakov, "Zakliuchitelnoe slovo," *Russkaia Beseda* (1859), no. 6, pp. VI–VII, as quoted in Petrovich, p. 114.

As soon as Aksakov was released in mid-1858 from the ban that
prevented him from writing and editing under his own name, he
took up the editorship of the "Colloquium" and started to think
of publishing a weekly newspaper that would reach more people
than an unwieldy and almost academic journal like the "Colloquium." (Aksakov had been forbidden to publish by a punitive
sanction of the Censorship for the second issue of the *Moskovski
sbornik* in 1853.) This new newspaper was to be the *Parus* (the
Sail), of which we have already had occasion to speak. In a letter
to Vladimir Lamanski, a beginning Slavic scholar at that time,
Aksakov said: "At present you and I have no ground under our feet
in our sympathy for the Slavs, that is, the Slavic question does not
extend to the core of the people, it is alien to them. One of the *Parus'*
tasks, among other things, will be to popularize the Slavic question
as much as possible." [9] Aksakov thought he would be encouraged
in his quest by the Chief of the Asiatic Department of the Ministry
for Foreign Affairs, Egor Petrovich Kovalevski, and by a relaxation
of the censorship in matters related to foreign policy.[10] He was to be
strongly jolted out of his illusions when the *Parus* was closed down
after the second number, because it contained four articles that were
considered to be outrageously objectionable by the Censorship. Three
of these articles dealt with domestic affairs—censorship, serfdom,
and laws affecting city dwellers. The fourth article, the most "dangerous," had in fact been written by Pogodin. It was called "The Past
Year in Russian Life" and set forth an evaluation of Russia's position among the other Slavic peoples of the world. Pogodin's conclusion was that: "For the sake of the balance of Europe, ten million
Slavs must groan, suffer, and agonize under the yoke of the most
savage despotism, the most unbridled fanaticism and the most des-
perate ignorance." Speaking in particular of the Habsburg Slavs,
Pogodin drew the following picture:

[9] "Perepiska dvukh slavianofilov," *Russkaia Mysl* (September 1916), p. 3. In the
same letter Aksakov wrote: "We recognize every nationality and we assert that the
policy of the Russian people is the complete recognition of the originality of every
other people capable to be original. It is true, we are not the government but
Russia . . ." (p. 2).
[10] Barsukov, *Pogodin*, XVI, 306, and I. A., *Pisma*, IV, 2.

In Austria there are five million Germans and twenty million Slavs who are alien to the former in language, creed, and history and who cannot tolerate the former, but rather hope against hope for a chance to free themselves. Austria cannot sleep a single peaceful night at home without making fast all her doors, without tightly closing all the windows, without posting sentries everywhere, without surrounding herself with all kinds of guards—and it is this Austria, if you please, which feels an invincible vocation to gather into her arms ten million more Slavs in the East who are even more alien to herself. And Russia, which includes sixty million Slavs, kinsmen of the Austrian and Turkish Slavs, is told, in the words of the German publicists: mind your own affairs and do not even think of turning your eyes toward the East! Such is the role which the benevolent Germans relinquish to Russia. What is Russia itself doing in the arena of European politics? She keeps silent. [11]

Although these lines did not belong to Ivan Aksakov, they are significant because they reflect Aksakov's own view on the question. He not only permitted this article to appear in his paper; he also edited it, making in it some unauthorized alterations—a fact that led to a temporary estrangement between Pogodin and Aksakov. Later, with the publication of the *Den,* Aksakov would sound the same appeal for Russian interference in the Slavic affairs.

After the *Parus* fiasco, Aksakov left Russia for his second trip to Europe. This time he went to the Slavic lands visiting Bohemia, Croatia, and Serbia. Furthermore, in preparation for his trip he became acquainted by letter with the important personalities of the Slavic world; he also studied Serbo-Croatian.

His trip to the Balkans exceeded all his expectations. Ironically enough, he received the warmest welcome in Catholic Croatia, where he was dined, wined, and cheered in the most exuberant fashion. Aksakov was more than pleased with this reception, although he was also alarmed at the success achieved by the Catholic champions of the Slavic cause, namely the bishops Juraj Strossmeyer and Franjo Rački. Serbia also enchanted him: "My impression of Serbia is an impression of youth, freshness and vitality," he noted in his letters. [12] In Belgrade, Aksakov delivered to the Serbs, "The

[11] Barsukov, *Pogodin,* XVI, 331–332, 450, as quoted in Petrovich, p. 118.

[12] I. A., *Pisma,* III, 434, 453–459, 473. See also his letters from the Slavic lands on

Address to the Serbs," a document in which the Slavophiles warned their Slavic brethren not to succumb to the enticements of the West.[13] Aksakov explained the purport of the address in the following manner: "There is nothing political about it. The aim of the address is to present to the Serbs our bitter experience while it is not too late so that they will not repeat our errors." [14] Unfortunately for the Slavophiles, the Serbs, or at least the Serbian press, gave the address a cold welcome; it seemed to be very untimely because the Balkans enjoyed at that moment a relatively peaceful life.[15]

The death of Khomiakov and the presence of Aksakov in the capital of the Habsburg Empire in October of 1860, resulted in a demonstration of Slavic solidarity. Ivan Aksakov, accompanied by his brother Konstantin, asked the Rev. Raevski, the chaplain of the Russian Embassy, to have a mass said in the memory of Khomiakov. At the appointed time the church was filled with representatives of the Slavs of the Habsburg Empire, who started to recite by heart many of Khomiakov's poems. For fear of a diplomatic incident the Russian ambassador, Knorring, reprimanded Father Raevski; the personnel of the embassy was strictly forbidden to attend the service. It appears that the Russian government made all possible efforts not to antagonize Austria by cultivating the sympathies of the Slavs; even the pro-Russian Serbian publication the *Srpski Dnevnik* was banned in Russia.

On his return to Russia, Ivan Aksakov began to petition for permission to publish the newspaper *Den*. Permission was granted and, although Aksakov realized that internal development in Russia

---

pp. 349–512, and his diary of the trip in the appendix to the third volume of his letters on pp. 107–153.

[13] A. S. Khomiakov, "K Serbam, Poslanie iz Moskvy," *Polnoe Sobranie Sochineni,* 8 vols. (Moscow, 1900), I, 377–408. See also the text of the address in *Russki Arkhiv* (1876), no. 3, pp. 104–127. In English, see P. K. Christoff, *An Introduction to Nineteenth-Century Russian Slavophilism: A Study in Ideas,* vol. I: *A. S. Khomiakov* (Gravenhage, Mouton, 1961).

[14] "Pismo I. S. Aksakova grafine A. D. Bludovoi—1860 g.," *Russki Arkhiv* (1915), no. 6, pp. 130–132.

[15] A. Pogodin, "Imperator Aleksandr II i ego vremia v otsenke serbskago obshchest-vennago mnenia, shestidesiatye gody," *Zapiski russkogo nauchnago instituta v Belgrade* (Belgrade, 1936), p. 17.

demanded more immediate attention, he dedicated a section of his newspaper to Slavic affairs. As public interest in the Slavs gained momentum with time and events, the tone of Aksakov's articles and speeches mounted apace; soon many other Russian newspapers began to be interested in the Slavs. In a few years, the Slavic question had become the issue of the day.

The need for pan-Slavic solidarity was explained by Aksakov in Slavophile terms. Europe was rent by two hostile principles: the West and the East or the Romano-Germanic world and the Slavic Orthodox world. Aksakov wrote: "It is time to understand that the hatred, often instinctive, of the West toward the Slavic Orthodox world stems from other deeply hidden causes: these causes are the antagonism of two opposed principles of enlightenment and the jealousy of a senescent world toward a new world to whom the future belongs." [16] Russia was the most powerful and the most advanced member of the Slavic family, it was therefore her duty and moral obligation to rescue the other Slavs: "To emancipate the Slavic peoples from material and spiritual oppression and bestow upon them the gift of an independent spiritual and even political life under the powerful wings of the Russian eagle is the historical calling, the moral right and the obligation of Russia." [17] Aksakov warned his readers that the leading intelligentsia of the Slavs needed the support of Russia and of the Russian public opinion by means of the Russian press. If this support was lacking, they would gradually desert Russia for the West in search of help and moral comfort. This shift of direction would be tantamount to a suicide, for the western peoples were "the enemies of the Slav world from times immemorial." The aim and purpose of the Slav section of *Den*—and Aksakov hoped that his example would be emulated—was to utter to the Slavs: "... a lively and friendly word, a word that, while arousing and promoting in them the feeling of Slavic national consciousness,

[16] I. A., *Sochineniia*, I, 5.

[17] *Ibid.*, p. 6. Aksakov arrogated to himself and his paper the right to be the only authority in Slavic affairs. When Hilferding, a Slavicist of renown, published a few of his articles in another newspaper, Aksakov became very angry at him. For Aksakov's monopolistic views on Slavic affairs see "Iz perepiski A. F. Gilferdinga s I. S. Aksakovym," *Golos Minuvshego* (1916), no. 2, pp. 201–208.

would at the same time strengthen their spiritual tie with Russia, *without whom their own self-styled development and success is unthinkable and impossible.* Let the Slavs not forget this!" [18]

On Aksakov's lips the puzzling expression "Slavic national consciousness" meant the gravitation toward Russia of all the Slavic peoples. If the Slavic nations were not to be attracted by Russia, they most certainly would be drawn toward the West. Much later, in the early eighties, Aksakov explained his views in a more direct fashion:

Every Bulgarian, be he conservative or liberal, who is capable of intriguing against Russia, or of plotting even a semblance of insult to her honor and dignity, is for sure a scoundrel to the marrow of his bones and a traitor to his people because he pushes it into the Austrian nets. This is an axiom.[19]

At the same time, it was Russia's moral obligation to help the Slavs because: "They need us and we do not need them: they expect from us spiritual and material help, as well as liberation from Turkish, Greek, or German yokes. The Russian people, on the other hand, can do without them [the Balkan Slavs] in solving its own internal problems." This condescending remark is not entirely true, however, for Aksakov expected a great reward for Russia. He believed that the crusade for the liberation of the downtrodden Slavs would bring in its wake a national regeneration of Russia: "The Russian national self-consciousness will become stronger and grow firmer as it realizes its spiritual unity with the Slavic world and when it no longer feels alone in its war against its internal enemies—the common enemies of Slavdom—the renegades of Russian nationality." [20] This statement is crucial for understanding the motivations of Ivan Aksakov. In a letter to Princess E. Cherkasski written in 1875, Aksakov admitted that the aim of his life was the destruction of the social barriers existing in Russia: "We have contributed in our life, as much as we could, to the destruction of legal and juridical differentiations (between social groups), the rest is just a matter of time." [21]

---

[18] I. A., *Sochineniia*, I, 9.   [19] *Ibid.*, p. 533.   [20] *Ibid.*, pp. 9, 14.
[21] I. Kozmenko, "Perepiska I. S. Aksakova s kn. V. A. Cherkasskim (1875–1878)," *Slavianski Sbornik* (Moscow, 1948), p. 140.

Like the other Slavophiles Aksakov believed that a historical mission awaited Russia, but that, in order to fulfill it, Russia must first become morally and socially monolithic. The reforms of Peter had fragmented Russia into incompatible groups, this inner dissension was the disease and the curse that prevented Russia from taking her deserved position in the world. To bring together the Russian people was the first step toward the Russian millenium.

We have already seen how Aksakov campaigned against gentry privileges and how he supported all the reforms that tended toward the equality of the citizens in the state; his infatuation with the merchant class belongs to the same category of thinking. The merchant class, which had emerged from the peasantry, was to become the link between the people and the upper classes. Aksakov knew that equality would not necessarily bring harmony, since the memories of times past were still lingering in the heads of the former serfs. Nonetheless, he thought that a lofty, moral, and Christian deed (a *podvig*), in which everybody, both peasant and nobleman, would participate could begin to cement the crevices existing in Russian society. Such a lofty ideal was at hand: the liberation of the Slavic brethren was the sacrifice that Russia should offer in order to gain staunchness and cohesion. The mortar that would have been used for cementing the disjointed blocks of the Russian people was to be prepared with the sweat and blood shed by all the Russians for a holy cause. It is tempting to view the pan-Slavic crusade of Ivan Aksakov as a redemptive sacrifice. From war and death a new life was to arise, a life without the taint of the past. Aksakov did not offer any advice as to how this future Slavdom would operate and what should be its organization. It is possible that he also wanted to see the formation of satellite states, standing between Russia and the West, but there seems to be no doubt that his most important goal was to fuse the Russian people into one monolithic and homogenous body.

Until the Polish insurrection and the protests of the Catholic world against the reprisals in Poland, Aksakov avoided making any distinction between the Orthodox and the Catholic Slavs. In 1862, Aksakov, together with Pogodin and others, was one of the organizers of the commemoration of the long-forgotten "Enlighteners of the Slavs"—Sts. Cyril and Methodius. The first service held in Russia in honor of the two saints was to be, according to Aksakov, "the token of the future spiritual reunion of all the Slavs and the link that would join the scattered brethren." [22] Although these were the ultimate pan-Slav hopes of Ivan Aksakov, his own image of Slavdom rested on somewhat particularistic foundations.

Specifically, Aksakov's creed rested on the following three principles: Orthodoxy; an unquestioned faith that Russia was "the only vessel of Orthodoxy and Slavic principles on earth"; and a mystical belief that the Russian popular spirit, or *narodnost,* would flourish only when the other Slavs could thrive freely. In Chapter IV we presented Aksakov's ideas on the role of the Catholic Church in the great battle of East and West. It may be recalled that his central point was the conviction that the behavior of a nation or of a state was conditioned by the religious beliefs of that nation or state and, therefore, that the differences between the historical development of the Orthodox, Catholic, and Protestant states were due primarily to the differences between these three faiths.[23] The Eastern Question, or the clash of various national interests in the Balkans, Aksakov thus interpreted as a clash between the Catholic and Orthodox worlds.[24]

Judging Slavdom in this light, Aksakov divided the Slavs into four groups: first of all, Russia, which was the spiritual Mecca of all the Slavs; the Orthodox Slavs; the Catholic Slavs, who were led astray by Catholicism, such as the Czechs and the Croats; and finally the Poles, who were lost to Slavdom because Catholicism had sunk too deeply into Polish minds. A Catholic Slav was a contradiction. Poland was beyond redemption, but there was still hope for the other Catholic Slavs. Whereas, Poland "absorbed Latinity in her flesh, blood and soul" and, at the same time, repudiated her Slavic fraternal ties by becoming the vanguard army of the Latin West

[22] I. A., *Sochineniia,* I, 13.

[23] *Ibid.,* pp. 96–97.

[24] See Chapter III; "We and They" in N. Riasanovsky, *Russia and the West in the Teaching of the Slavophiles* (Cambridge, Mass., 1952), pp. 60–69.

against the Orthodox Slavic world, the other Catholic Slavs had preserved "their Slavic souls"; they were alien to any "Latin fanaticism" and, *mirabile dictu,* they continued "in one way or another, consciously or unconsciously, to harbor Orthodox traditions." [25]

Seeing and sensing the awakening of Slavic consciousness among the Czechs and the Croats, Aksakov believed that these two peoples were ready to forget that they had been Catholic for one thousand years. For Aksakov, nationalism could not be divorced from religion because religion was the very content of nationalism; pan-Slavic nationalism therefore, meant Orthodoxy. According to Aksakov, John Hus was an Orthodox martyr and a national hero, and the cult of John Hus would return the Czechs to the Orthodox faith: "Hear ye, Czechs!" wrote Aksakov, "The Council of Constance did not part . . . the pyre of Hus is not dead; it continues to burn, but this time not only in Constance but in Prague proper. Who is feeding the fire? For God's sake put the fire out under the stake of Hus!" [26] As for the peoples of Croatia and Dalmatia, they deeply revered the Orthodox faith of their forebears and had preserved in some parishes the old Glagolitic alphabet; this reverence for the past filled Aksakov with great hope for the future. Again and again, Aksakov exhorted these Slavs to return to Orthodoxy:

Now or never, if the Slavs want to remain Slavs and not only that but also free their Slavic souls from the chains of spiritual bondage which subject them to the destiny of the Latin world, they must answer the question posed to them by current history; they must give a definite and undodging answer; they must repudiate Rome and its deeds officially and publicly without compromise and detours . . . Choose then, Czechs, Moravians, Croats, Slovaks and Slovenes! Do you wish together with Western Europe to procrastinate by making deals and compromises between atheism and superstition? Do you wish to be mired together with Europe in the impassable bog of spiritual contradictions . . . or do you prefer to take the wide spiritual road of Orthodox truth that is followed by sixty millions of your Slav brethren, the road followed once by your ancestors? Do you want Christ or the pope as the head of the Church? [27]

[25] I. A., *Sochineniia,* I, 176.
[26] *Ibid.,* pp. 96–98, 100, 314–315.
[27] *Ibid.,* pp. 177–178. It is pertinent to note that Aksakov was on the *qui vive.*

Aksakov assigned the most crucial role in the Balkans to the Serbian people, in whom he perceived all the traits of the legendary heroes, or *junaks*. It is also possible that this predilection was dictated by the fact that the Serbs were the most strategically located for delivering blows both to Austria and to the Ottoman Empire. This view, however, lasted only until the defeat of the Serbs and the volunteers of General Cherniaev at Alexinatz in 1876, and was completely dispelled when King Milan turned to Austria in 1882.

While it lasted, Aksakov's faith in the Serbs was not placed in their intelligentsia, which was oriented chiefly to the West, but in the Serbian people. In a letter to his friend, the Rev. Raevski, Aksakov declared: "In Serbia all the strength is in the people, and our consul should rely absolutely on the people and its representatives. Only this direction can give us power in Serbia, can give power to our policy. This is the only lever we have and one which, in spite of all their efforts, neither Napoleon nor Franz-Joseph could acquire."[28] Convinced of the correctness of his views, Aksakov wrote in 1862:

It is toward Serbia that the eyes of all the Slavic peoples who are smarting under the Turkish yoke are now turned; it is toward Serbia that all the aspirations of the Bulgars and the Bosnians are directed; it is from her that help is expected by the battle-weary Herzegovinians and the Montenegrins. If Serbia only lifted the standard of insurrection, the Slavs of Turkey would rise as a single man. Indeed, of all the Slavic peoples it is the Serbs who can unite most easily, and if the hopes of the other Slavs may still seem to be unrealizable political dreams, the definitive liberation of the Serbian people does not belong to the realm of fancy![29]

Shortly after the publication of the papal edict of infallibility in 1870, an event that created a certain discontent among the Czechs, Aksakov raised the money for the erection of an Orthodox church in Prague. This gesture was explained by Aksakov in the following manner: "Should it be explained that the return of the Czechs to Orthodoxy would have an enormous significance not only as far as the progress of truth is concerned but for Russia proper, not only in the religious sense but in the political sense as well?" See "K voprosy o slavianskom edinenie (Pismo I. S. Aksakova o propagande pravoslaviia v Chekhi)," *Istoricheski Vestnik*, 45:775–777 (September 1891).

[28] I. A., *Pisma*, IV, 52. See also I. A., *Sochineniia*, I, 23.
[29] I. A., *Sochineniia*, I, 22.

During his lifetime Aksakov was punished for his infatuation with the Serbian people with the agony of disillusionment that is inflicted upon every idealist whose views are his hopes and reality his despair. His only escape was to hold onto the notion that the people were not responsible for the dastardly deeds of their government or their intelligentsia. Each time that Aksakov was disappointed by Serbia he would lay the blame on the government, which instead of toiling for Slavdom was poisoning its own people with forced Westernization: "All this [adoption of European models] from our point of view, was premature and has weakened Serbia considerably; it has sapped the former wild force inherent in the popular self-expression of the Serbs, but it did not give and could not give her in exchange the strength of a correctly and firmly organized state."[30] Even the Serbian *Skupshtina,* or Assembly, which, according to Aksakov, was a Slavic institution like the Veche or the Zemski sobor, was being infiltrated by regulations that threatened to transform it into a pitiful parody of a European parliament. In 1881, Aksakov evoked the evolution of the Serbs in the following bitter and sarcastic lines:

They jumped directly from their epic time and from their bucolic age into the civilization of our century. They acquired at once an "intelligentsia" by sending about five swineherds to study philosophy from Hegel (it is a fact) and they instituted Courts of Appeal and of Cassation (valuing, of course, their foreign names); after that they established a totally European constitution.[31]

The Polish insurrection caused great embarrassment for Aksakov as well as for the other pan-Slavs. They were forced to explain to the Slavs that Russia was their well-wisher at a time when the Russian army was dealing ruthlessly with a sister Slavic country. Aksakov's confusion must have been great because he did not try to solve this conflict until more than a year after the beginning of the uprising. In 1864, Aksakov wrote:

Between the interests of Russia in Poland (correctly understood) and the interests of Russia in the East, there is essentially no contradiction

[30] *Ibid.,* p. 23.
[31] *Ibid.,* p. 325.

and there should not appear any incongruity such as the German and perhaps also certain Russian political publicists have imagined. We are convinced that the correct settlement of the Eastern Question conditions the correct solution of the Polish Question and vice versa.[32]

As a further proof that Russia was not trying to Russify Poland, but that, on the contrary, she was aiming to protect the Polish nation, Aksakov cited the emancipation of three and a half million Polish peasants from the bondage of a westernized szlachta. The conduct of Russia in Poland was thus beneficial to the cause of Slavdom. Aksakov admitted that the Polish question was a difficult one but he thought that it should be settled between Russia and Poland without the interference of either Prussia, Austria, or France.

This latter stand was taken by Aksakov in view of his apprehension of a rapprochement between Russia and Prussia, which indeed happened and resulted in the agreement between Alexander II and Count C. Alvensleben, the Prussian emissary of Bismark. Aksakov feared that the Russian government would try to use Prussia in order to coerce Austria to break away from a possible coalition against Russia, formed by France, England, and the Habsburg Empire. This commitment to Prussia and Austria would lead Russia into another Holy Alliance which, according to Aksakov, had kept Russia ensnared in the toils of Central European diplomacy for over thirty years. Russia should not be bound by any alliances, she must be free to have her own national policy:

Thanks to the idea of the Holy Alliance we have forgotten that the interests of Russia are opposed to those of Austria, that our strength, our significance in Europe must rest chiefly on the sympathies for us of the Slavic peoples who are now under the domination of the Austrians and of the Turks, that Austria is the wickedest foe of the liberation of the Slavs even from the Turkish yoke, and that as a consequence any cordial alliance with Austrian power would only consolidate this yoke and turn away from us the friendship of our coracial and for the most part coreligious brethren, our natural allies.[33]

Aksakov was equally alarmed by the policy of Napoleon III, who arrogated to himself the role that belonged to Russia, namely, that

[32] I. A., *Sochineniia*, I, 33.   [33] *Ibid.*, p. 29.

of championing the liberation of the Slavic nations, and who at the same time sowed insidiously the seeds of a "cosmopolitan revolution." As a result, by not helping the Slavs, Russia pushed them into the arms of France and England. Another cause of Aksakov's alarm was the penetration of Bulgaria by the Jesuits, who were sent by the West because European leaders knew that "the betrayal of Orthodoxy has as a consequence the betrayal of *narodnost*." Orthodoxy and Slavic self-consciousness must go together; the Greeks were Orthodox, but they were just as bad as the Austrians and the Turks; they oppressed the Slavs by means of "Turkish jails, Turkish executioners and Turkish arbitrariness." [34]

As for the Slavs within the Habsburg Empire, Aksakov believed that their future was grim. Since there were fifteen million Slavic subjects in the Empire, their number was a threat to the German and Magyar elements. Aksakov sensed the inevitability of an *Ausgleich* long before it happened in 1867. The idea of a Habsburg federation, cherished by the Czechs in particular, was not a viable solution because the Slovaks would refuse to be absorbed by the Czechs and thus be separated from their brothers living in Hungary. Still, though the Slavic problem existed in the Habsburg Empire, the real crisis was not yet in sight for: "The Slavs so far are the most docile subjects of Austria. The best armies of Austria are Slavic, no one has served the German banner of Austria with such zeal as the Croats and the Galician peasants. It is hard to admit it, yet one cannot hide the truth: among the Austrian Serbs there are a great many generals and not a single martyr for the cause of nationality." There was no harmony among the Slavs; they were split between Catholicism and Orthodoxy, they belonged to groups speaking different languages, and they were attached to political systems that were alien to their spirit. If the Slavs wanted to form a harmonious system, they should gravitate around Russia, because Russia "was the natural and genuine center of attraction for the entire Slavic world." [35]

At first glance, the idea of Slavdom in the writings of Ivan Aksakov may appear elusive. Indeed, Aksakov, departing from the

[34] *Ibid.*, pp. 39, 41.   [35] *Ibid.*, pp. 46, 149.

all-inclusive idea of Slavdom, ejected the Poles as renegades without a chance of redemption and tolerated the other Catholic Slavs, only so far as to give them one chance of readmission—that of conversion to Orthodoxy. Such a double amputation left Slavdom reduced to the Serbians and the Bulgars. Yet, Aksakov raised these exclusive standards still further by proclaiming that all the Slavs should have Russia as their center of attraction; when Serbia first and Bulgaria shortly after her turned their backs on Russia, the Slavdom of Ivan Aksakov was virtually reduced to Montenegro. As Alexander III once said in a toast: "I drink to the only ally of Russia—Montenegro." In this respect, Aksakov and the tsar shared the same point of view.

Nevertheless, it is possible to understand this virtual negation by Ivan Aksakov of any meaningful idea of Slavdom. Aksakov strove with all his might toward an imaginary Slavdom endowed with imaginary virtues; in fact, however, he contributed to the political emancipation of the Slavs on terms that denied his ideal. This political emancipation was propitious for the penetration of western ideas and, by the same token, for the defeat of Aksakov's most cherished hopes for the golden future of Slavdom. Aksakov belonged to the type of thinkers about whom Karl Mannheim so aptly said:

Their thinking is incapable of correctly diagnosing an existing condition of society. They are not at all concerned with what really exists; rather in their thinking they already seek to change the situation that exists. Their thought is never a diagnosis of the situation; it can be used only as a direction for action. In the utopian mentality, the collective unconscious, guided by wishful representation and the will to action, hides certain aspects of reality. It turns its back on everything which would shake its belief or paralyse its desire to change things.[36]

Aksakov was such a man. He had a utopian vision of what Russia and Slavdom should be. And, because his dream was the motivation and the purpose of his life and of his actions, Aksakov protected it jealously from anything that could threaten or dissipate it. From the point of view of his subjectivity, the glorious vision of a re-

[36] K. Mannheim, *Ideology and Utopia: An Introduction to the Sociology of Knowledge* (London, 1949), p. 36.

generated Russia and of a spiritually united Slavdom was more real to Aksakov than objective reality itself. Thus, it can be explained why Aksakov was the champion of narodnost without narod and of pan-Slavism without Slavs.

Indeed, a meticulous study of the writings of Ivan Aksakov yields two frustrating conclusions: first of all, the people or narod is not conscious of its national and cultural identity or narodnost, and secondly, the Slavic peoples are not conscious of their common cultural and historical destiny. In both cases, the "real" Russian people and the "real" Slavs fall short of the "ideal" standards set for them in Aksakov's utopia. This statement does not contradict by any means the observation that Aksakov was the foremost pan-Slavist of his time. Slavdom was an essential ingredient in his aggressive drive for a moral and social purification of Russia.

Under such conditions the absence of any concrete suggestion for the reorganization of the future Slavic world seems quite in order. The absence of constructive ideas in Aksakov's articles became particularly conspicuous during the days of the Slavic Ethnic Exhibition, held in Moscow in 1867, an exhibition that Aksakov helped to organize.[37] It is true that Aksakov's coverage of the Slavic gathering was interrupted by a ban imposed by the censorship on the newspaper *Moskva* (Moscow) and that he could publish only two editorials dealing with the great issue of the day. Therefore, he limited himself to repeating that: "The Slavic world is unthinkable without Russia, all the strength of the Slavs is in Russia, all of Russia's strength is in her Slavism." This assertion was to be taken as the point of departure, as an axiom that would determine the future, which, according to Aksakov, would take care of everything: "We repeat, if Russia would only develop in herself a Slavic consciousness, the rest would come by itself."[38] The duty of Russia was "to realize the Slavic brotherhood on earth and call all the brothers

[37] For full details on the exhibition, see S. A. Nikitin, "Slavianskie sezdy shestidesiatykh godov XIX veka," in *Slavianski Sbornik: Slavianski vopros i russkoe obshchestvo v 1867–1878 godakh*. N. M. Druzhinin, ed. (Moscow, 1948), pp. 16–92. It is curious to note that of the seventy guests from the Slavic lands only eleven were Orthodox, the rest Catholic (p. 71).

[38] I. A., *Sochineniia*, I, 153, 154.

to freedom and to life." [39] Aksakov's newspaper was neither interested in the creation of an all-Slav language nor in a Slavic federation of states, nor did it wish the annexation of the Slavic lands by Russia. This lack of concern for the real conditions in the small Slavic countries goes far toward explaining why Aksakov refused to attend a Slav Congress held the following year in Prague.

However, if the years 1868–1880 were not propitious for Aksakov's activities as a journalist, they did not affect his work for the Slavic cause. It must be remembered that Aksakov was forbidden to publish or edit any newspaper during this twelve-year period. From 1858 to 1875, he was the treasurer and the secretary of the Moscow Slavic Benevolent Committee. This Committee was founded in 1858 for the purpose of helping the population of the oppressed Slavic countries and especially for building them churches and schools. [40] In 1875 the president of the Committee, Professor Pogodin, died; Aksakov became his successor. He remained in this position until the Committee's demise in 1878. It is precisely these years, from 1875 to 1878, that were the most crucial and decisive in the history of the Balkan Slavs; by the same token they also marked the high peak of Aksakov's fame and influence on the public opinion of Russia.

The spark that ignited the Russo-Turkish war of 1877–1878 was struck by the insurrection of Herzegovina in 1875. At first, Aksakov could not believe that the time had come for the Slavs to free themselves from Turkish domination. In a letter to Princess E. Cherkasskaia he wrote: "I must admit that I am very concerned and disturbed by the Slavic movement in Turkey, which has developed so far only in Herzegovina. I do not have the slightest doubt that all this is Austria's doing, that Austria, under the cover of her friendship with Russia, is trying to take over the East." [41] Aksakov was

[39] S. A. Nikitin, p. 59.

[40] For more details, see S. Nikitin, "Vozniknovenie Moskovskogo Slavianskogo Komiteta," in *Voprosy Istorii* (August 1947), no. 8, pp. 50–65, and A. Georgevski: "Moskovski Slavianski Blagotvoritelnyi Komitet i ego sudba," in *Zapiski istoriko-filologicheskogo fakulteta* [Vladivostok], I, sect. I (1919). See also Petrovich, pp. 129–152.

[41] "Perepiska I. S. Akaskova s kn. V. A. Cherkasskim," *Slavianski sbornik* (Moscow, 1948), p. 152.

certain that Russia was being cheated again by the alliance of the three emperors, as she had been cheated in the past by the Holy Alliance. Two months later, nevertheless, he was organizing a collection for the Herzegovinian cause, promising to "ring the bell" across Russia. The Russian government, however, forbade any collection for the insurgents, yet allowed money to be gathered for those who suffered from Turkish reprisals. Aksakov was distressed at these limitations for he believed that he could obtain more money for the support of the insurrection or for weapons than for "medicine and maize." His views proved to be correct in the three years that followed.[42]

General Cherniaev and his newspaper *Russki mir* (Russian World) were instrumental in gaining the favor of Russian public opinion for more vigorous support of the Herzegovinian insurrection. He suggested the formation of a Russian corps of volunteers that he himself was ready to command. In order not to lose any time, he further proposed to set out immediately with only ten officers and fifty soldiers. These men would carry with them weapons and ammunitions for five hundred insurgents. Aksakov staunchly supported the project of this would-be Russian Garibaldi. He promised to take charge himself of the financial aspect of the expedition. The collection of funds, however, at first proved to be very difficult: the Moscow merchants neither trusted nor approved of the quixotic projects of Cherniaev and Aksakov. In the meantime, pan-Slavist sentiments were spreading, and soon the entire Russian press, with the exclusion of most of the leftist publications, began to clamor for the support of the insurrection. In November of 1875, five months after the beginning of the uprising, Aksakov could write: "The money for the collection flows in, in a steady stream, and despite the paucity of funds, the absence of interest from the government, and its diplomatic stand on the entire matter."[43] The

---

[42] S. Nikitin, "Russkoe obshchestvo i natsionalno-osvoboditelnaia borba iuzhnykh slavian v 1875–1876 gg.," in *Obshchestvenno-politicheskie i kulturnye sviazi narodov SSSR i Iugoslavii* (Moscow, 1957), p. 11.

[43] *Ibid.*, p. 26. By that time, Aksakov no longer managed the only center for the collection of clothes and money; similar centers were created in Paris and Geneva. The Russian Red Cross sent a detachment to Dubrovnik.

money gathered by the Moscow Slavic Benevolent Committee in coordination with the St. Petersburg Committee was sent to a certain G. Veselitski-Bozhidarovich, a Russian of Serbian ancestry who bought rifles and ammunitions for the insurgents. The Soviet historian Nikitin has stated: "There is no doubt that Russian funds were the basic source of support for the Herzegovinians." [44] If so, the importance of the part played by Aksakov needs no elaboration.

The Herzegovinian uprising was followed by two abortive Bulgarian insurrections in the fall of 1875 and the spring of 1876. The spread of anti-Turkish unrest in the Balkans forced the intervention of Serbia on behalf of her rebellious brothers. Before taking this final step, however, the Serbian government needed to secure a loan in order to finance the war. A certain Protich was sent by the Serbian government to Russia to investigate the possibilities for a war loan. Aksakov received Protich, instructed him and gave him letters of recommendation to the right persons in St. Petersburg; moreover, since the wife of Ivan Aksakov was a former lady-in-waiting with connections at the court, she introduced Protich to the empress and to the heir, the future Alexander III. The latter and his mother, the empress, were in favor of a more drastic approach to the Balkan situation than was the government. Through their intercession public subscription for a loan was authorized by the tsar. Aksakov managed this loan and, although the subscriptions were not as numerous as it was hoped, it gave him an opportunity to affirm himself as a public leader.[45]

The war between Serbia and the Ottoman Empire began toward the end of June 1876. General Cherniaev left for Serbia at the head of a small group of volunteers. Ivan Aksakov armed and equipped the more than two thousand men who served at one time or another under Cherniaev. As the president of the Moscow Slavic Benevolent Committee, he proved to be a good organizer, a great fund raiser, and an excellent propagandist. In a speech to the Slavic Committee

[44] *Ibid.*, pp. 29, 31. Veselitski-Bozhidarovich wrote: "The donations from France were discontinued in January 1876; those from Switzerland in April; in June England ceased to send help. Russia alone remains faithful to the hapless Slavs" (p. 30). A total of 360,000 rubles were collected in Russia for the Bosnians and Herzegovinians.
[45] *Ibid.*, p. 46.

Aksakov pointed out that the Slavic crusade was supported by the people: "Two-thirds of all the donations were made by the poor, the overburdened simple folk."[46] In another place in April 1876, he repeated that: "much money was sent by Russia, but the contributions were made chiefly by people who were not rich, even by paupers. From the wealthy gentry (the Bobrinskis, the Sheremetevs, the Demidovs) and from the Imperial palaces the contribution has been quite modest until now." With the funds thus raised, Aksakov took upon himself the recruitment of volunteers for military and medical duties.[47]

The failure of the two Bulgarian uprisings made Aksakov lose patience with the Bulgarian patriots. Disappointed, he concentrated his efforts on Serbia and the Cherniaev expedition. Nonetheless, he did not believe in Cherniaev's fantasies of liberating the Slavs with the support of public opinion and a handful of mercenaries; rather Aksakov felt that support of Serbia's war action would serve primarily to create a favorable climate for Russia's intervention against the Turks. As he wrote to Cherniaev:

Serbia cannot stand at the helm of Russian society and in no way should Russian public opinion trail behind Serbia. The Serbs have not yet grown to such a point. Only the Russian stock, or rather only Russia, has a political future. The other peoples could exist only in a close association with Russia in a form not yet determined by history. Our task is to liberate them and give them an opportunity to live and grow; it is our task to take away their national egoisms, which are detrimental to the common Slavic idea.

The Slavic question could be answered only by Russia "in its integrity, as a state, with the government at its head." The emancipation of the Slavs should not be allowed to occur independently of Russia; in another letter to Cherniaev, Aksakov wrote: "by equipping and sending you to Serbia, and by supplying you later with volunteers, I had in mind provoking the official participation of Russia. Never have I believed in the possibility of solving the [present] problem

[46] I. A., *Sochineniia*, I, 28.
[47] S. Nikitin, "Russkoe obshchestvo," pp. 55, 62.

by the actions of the committees alone. You cannot do practical things with lyricism." [48]

In the meantime, Alexander II received reports from the police informing him that public rumor called him "a foreigner in the pay of the Germans" for not intervening in favor of the revolted Slavs. Prompted on the one hand by the prowar faction at the court, which centered around the heir apparent, and on the other hand by the nature of a survey of public opinion that he had requested, the tsar ordered on November 1, 1876, the recall of all military personnel on leave of absence.[49] Russia's entry into the war, it should be remembered, was not declared until around the middle of April (old style); yet it is significant that in September 1876, or a little more than a month before the tsar's order to recall the absentees, Aksakov had sent on a mission to Livadia a certain A. Porokhovsh- chikov. The latter was given the task of convincing the tsar of the urgent necessity of war against the Turks. It appears that the mission of Porokhovshchikov was rewarded with success. Before leaving the Crimean residence of the tsar, Porokhovshchikov wired Aksakov the following message: "Complete confidence. The situation is secure. Infinite joy." [50] Alexander II, on his return journey to St. Petersburg, stopped in Moscow and delivered a strong speech promis- ing support to the Slavs.[51] The Moscow Slavophiles and the pan- Slavists were elated. The Moscow city duma, in which these groups had a majority, presented an address to the tsar. This address was composed by Ivan Aksakov and declared: "May thou know, Lord Sovereign, that there has never been a tsar stronger than art thou

[48] *Ibid.*, pp. 71–72.

[49] See a very good account of Russian public opinion on the eve of the war in T. Snytko "Iz istorii narodnogo dvizheniia v Rossii v podderzhku borby iuzhnykh slavian za svoiu nezavisimost v 1875–1876 gg.," in *Obshchestvenno-politicheskie i kulturnye sviazi narodov SSSR i Iugoslavii* (Moscow, 1957), pp. 78–106.

[50] A. Porokhovshchikov, "Iz zapisok moskovskago starozhila," *Istoricheski Vestnik* 67:539–554 (1897). Count Ignatiev, the author of the treaty of San Stefano, ascribed a major importance to this visit in deciding the subsequent course of events. See "Zapiski Grafa N. P. Ignatieva," *ibid.*, 136:446–449 (1914). See also *Dnevnik D. A. Miliutina*, 4 vols. (1947–1950), II, 83–86.

[51] S. Tatishchev, *Imperator Aleksandr II, ego zhizn i tsarstvovanie*, 2 ed., 2 vols. (St. Petersburg, 1911), II, 310.

in this moment of solidarity and unity with thy people. The hour has struck and the harvest is ripe. Tsar-Liberator, be the liberator of our brethren." But the tsar, possibly because of the coming winter, hesitated to take any decision. The address of the Moscow duma was severely censured as being loaded with "Slavophile ideas and subtle democratic innuendoes."[52]

In spite of this setback, Aksakov persevered in his demands for war. In a speech pronounced at a meeting of the Moscow Slavic Benevolent Committee, he commented on the words of the tsar in a rather direct fashion:

These words of the tsar were not the result of an accidental and personal whim of a ruler. They expressed the intuition of the historical spirit. The tsar spoke as the heir of the tsar, as the heir of Ivan III who took from the Paleologi the emblem of Byzantium and combined it with the emblem of Muscovy; he spoke as the heir of Peter and Catherine, as the crowned keeper of the traditions of the times bygone and of an uninterrupted historical heritage. There can be no repudiation of his words, for their repudiation would mean that the Russian people would abdicate its calling and its existence, signing its own death warrant.[53]

And in the spring of 1877, Aksakov wrote still another address to the tsar urging him to liberate the Slavs.[54]

Finally, in the month of April 1877, Russia declared war on Turkey. And although this war was forced by considerations other than the jingoist mood of the public, many were those, including Ivan Aksakov, who were certain that this war was the work of the public opinion. Speaking on this occasion Aksakov said:

This war is needed for the spirit of Russia; this war is for the faith of Christ; this war is for the liberation of the enslaved and oppressed Slav brethren; this war is just; this war is an act of great and holy heroism; this war was entrusted to Holy Russia by the Lord. Behold how she goes forth, exultant, to the bloody feast, professing loudly and boldly the name of God to the great astonishment of the wisemen of the century.[55]

[52] K. Pushkarevich, "Balkanskie slaviane i russkie 'osvoboditeli,'" *Trudy Instituta Slavianovedeniia ANSSSR* (1934), II, 209.

[53] I. A., *Sochineniia*, I, 238.

[54] "Perepiska I. S. Aksakova s kn. V. A. Cherkasskim (1875–1878)," *Slavianski sbornik* (1948), p. 165.   [55] I. A., *Sochineniia*, I, 252.

Aksakov actively supported the war effort by arming and equipping the companies of Bulgarian volunteers that the Russian War Ministry formed among Bulgarian exiles and later from the Bulgarian population. Thus the Slavic Committees, which at first supported the Serbs, shifted their aid onto the Bulgarians soon after the defeat of the Serbian army at Alexinatz, in the fall of 1876.[56]

The war with Turkey was difficult and harsh. The Russian army reached the outskirts of Constantinople in January 1878 after a bloody winter campaign in the Balkan mountains. The Turks capitulated and signed the treaty of San Stefano on February 19, 1878. This treaty provided for a Greater Bulgaria under the protection of Russia. But Austria and Britain were alarmed to see Russia so close to the Dardanelles and they demanded that the Bulgarian problem be submitted to a European Congress. Given a lack of allies Russia had no choice but to acquiesce; the congress was held in Berlin in June 1878. It wiped out many of the gains that Russia had made by the treaty of San Stefano. This humiliation of Russia created a great resentment among the public. At the same time, moreover, terrorism reappeared with an increased vigor. During the Balkan uprisings and the Russo-Turkish war, Russian society became, perhaps for the first time, very active. Through donations, volunteering or work in the committees society participated in the war against the Turks. Even many Populists became favorably inclined toward the liberation of the Slavs. The Congress of Berlin marked a great anticlimax in the enthusiasm of Russian society. One faction of the Populists thought that this discontent could be fanned by terrorist actions against members of the government who had betrayed Russia. Although the rise of terrorism had only an indirect connection with the outcome of the Congress of Berlin, Aksakov was convinced that the humiliation suffered by Russia at Berlin was the cause of and the reason for this terrorism. Russia's defeat at the Congress of Berlin and terrorism frustrated the hopes that Aksakov had at the beginning of the Russo-Turkish war.

[56] I. Kozmenko, "Iz istorii bolgarskogo opolcheniia (1876–1877)," *Slavianski sbornik* (1948), pp. 121–139, and also by the same author, "Russkoe obshchestvo i aprelskoe bolgarskoe vosstanie 1876 goda," in *Voprosy istorii* (1947), no. 5, pp. 95–108.

Aksakov's nerves were strained and his hopes shattered. In a bitter polemic he denounced the Russian government for its treasonable passivity. Speaking of Russia he bewailed: "The western powers, with Germany in the van, are impudently plucking your laurels and offer you instead a fool's cap with jingles, and you obediently, almost with a feeling of gratitude, receive it on your lowered, martyred head!" The Congress of Berlin was "a conspiracy against the Russian people, a conspiracy carried out with the participation of the representatives of Russia." Aksakov could not believe that the tsar, this cornerstone of the Slavophile utopia, could be among the traitors: "Could we possibly believe that all that was sanctioned by the Highest Executive Power? Never!" [57] Such were his conclusions. The guilty ones were the bureaucrats: it was they who had betrayed Russia in order to please the West that they so willingly aped.

This diatribe against the Congress of Berlin and the Russian bureaucratic government was published by a certain Putsykovich in his newspaper *Grazhdanin* (The Citizen). It received great publicity. The government reacted very swiftly. Aksakov was exiled to his estate in Varvarino, the Moscow Committee was closed down, and the other Committees of Kiev, Odessa, and St. Petersburg became tools of the Ministry for Foreign Affairs. Ironically enough, it was in exile that Aksakov was informed that a Bulgarian constituency had advanced his name for the candidacy to the throne of the new state.[58]

Aksakov remained silent for two years. In 1880, he obtained permission to publish his own newspaper. As before he found the money among the merchants to whom he promised a section in his newspaper for voicing their economic needs and grievances but from whom he exacted the condition that his editorial policy would remain independent of them. The new publication was called *Rus,* the old name for Russia. It was to be Aksakov's last contribution to Russian journalism.

In his writing for *Rus,* Aksakov continued to show interest in

---

[57] I. A., *Sochineniia*, I, 299, 303, 304.

[58] "Pisma I. S. Aksakova k V. F. Putsykovichu," *Na chuzhoi storone* (Berlin-Prague, 1924), no. 5, p. 131.

the Slavs, particularly in the Bulgars among whom Russian influence
was strong. Aksakov persevered in writing about Slavdom and the
Russian mission even after the incident of 1883, when Alexander
of Battenberg chased his Russian ministers and advisers from the
country, but he was dissatisfied with Russian policy vis-à-vis Bulgaria. He bewailed the Constitution of Tyrnovo that the Russian
army had brought in its trunks and he begged the Bulgarian people
not to form political parties: "Russia took a great sin upon her soul
by forcing a constitution on the Bulgarian people." [59] The constitution introduced the concept of parties in a people among which class
distinctions were almost nonexistent. The Russian-made constitution
threatened to destroy a social order that Aksakov wanted for Russia.
When in 1881, Alexander of Battenberg abrogated the constitution,
Aksakov was full of praise for the Bulgarian monarch in whom he
saw a man who "quite rightly understands and defines the relations
of his country toward our fatherland." [60] Then in 1883, Aksakov's
attitude changed radically; he called the Bulgarian prince: "a former
officer of the Prussian army and the son of a former *Leutnant-
Feldmarschall* of the Austrian army, who was promoted by the
grace of the Russian tsar to the rank of Prince of Bulgaria." [61] This
change was due, as mentioned above, to the diplomatic crisis which
arose between Russia and Bulgaria in the same year: Alexander of
Bulgaria became displeased when two of his Russian advisers were
recalled without any warning; he retaliated by evicting all the Russian officers who were training the Bulgarian army. This gesture
was interpreted by the Russian government as an insult to Russia.

In 1885, finally, Alexander of Bulgaria endorsed the reunion of
Bulgaria with Eastern Rumelia. Challenged, the Serbs, aided by the
Austrians, invaded Bulgaria, but were defeated by the Bulgarian
army. At this juncture Aksakov was furious at the governments of
both Serbia and Bulgaria, at King Milan no less than at Alexander—
at the former for being a mercenary of the Habsburgs, and at the
latter for embarking on an adventure which degenerated into a
fratricidal war. Aksakov saw a solution to this problem in "a personal union" of Bulgaria with Russia, or in a polity which "would
deprive the Bulgarian authorities of the possibility to have *their own*

[59] I. A., *Sochineniia*, I, 456.   [60] *Ibid.*, p. 450.   [61] *Ibid.*, p. 549.

policy, independent of Russian policy, and of luring the Bulgarian people, for whose liberation the Russians have spilt their blood, into needless and perilous adventures . . ." [62] But instead, much to Aksakov's sorrow, the governments of Serbia and Bulgaria continued to gravitate toward the West.

Aksakov's ideas on the Slavs can be described succinctly as having a double objective. His long-range objective was the creation of an Orthodox East, where Russia would be the center of a new world culture. But in order to reach this universal recognition Russia had to regenerate herself morally and socially. The barriers existing among the estates and their divergent world views had to be eradicated: Russia had to become a country with a unified population united by the common spirit of popular self-expression or *narodnost;* and this latter goal was Aksakov's short-range objective. But he sensed that the destruction of juridical barriers was not sufficient to amalgamate the fragmented Russian society. As a matter of fact, Aksakov was painfully aware that Russian society was becoming a class society under the impact of a growing social mobility and industrialization. Another point of great importance, it seems, was that the tempo of these social changes was faster than any ideological solution that Aksakov could have offered. He might have wanted, therefore, to find a solution to the problem by taking it out of the confines of the Russian empire. It seems that Aksakov believed that his aim would be achieved if he could unite all of Russia in a common sacrifice for a lofty and Christian cause. This sacrifice was a holy war for the liberation of the Slavs.

The absence of any definite constructive ideas for the future organization of Slavdom seems to indicate that Russia was Aksakov's greatest concern. In this respect, the Congress of Berlin was the major crisis in the life of Ivan Aksakov. Indeed, he feared most of all a loss of Russia's prestige for this would have had sad repercussions in the country. This also meant that the faith of the people in the tsar would be shaken and also that the dreams of unity which were at the center of Aksakov's utopia were in danger. It is perhaps in this fact that we should look for the meaning of Aksakov's nationalism.

[62] *Ibid.,* p. 757.

CHAPTER VI

The Last Years

In 1880 General M. T. Loris-Melikov replaced Count D. A. Tolstoi as Minister of the Interior. Loris-Melikov's appointment marked a change in the policy of the government. The stringent restrictions that had fettered society under his predecessors were relaxed and his ministry, which lasted one year, came to be known as "the dictatorship of the heart." The new "thaw," however, came to an abrupt end with the assassination of Alexander II; Loris-Melikov had to resign.

Ivan Aksakov took advantage of the relaxation of the censorship. Toward the end of 1880 he asked for and received permission to publish again. His new publication, *Rus* was at first a weekly newspaper, although as time passed, it became only a biweekly. It was not published more often because there were only a small number of subscribers and Aksakov was in poor health. After his death, one of his closest collaborators recollected:

From the second year of the publication of *Rus,* it became obvious that those who, together with Aksakov, looked harshly and soberly upon Russian society were few. The public, unaccustomed to plain and serious Russian thinking, awaited from *Rus* an effective struggle with the existing state of affairs, the same bold and passionate struggle which had been the trademark of *Moskva* and *Moskvich*. People became disillusioned. Aksakov, in spite of his low opinion of the conservatives in power, did not declare a war on them. Whether this was right or not, let us not judge now, but it is nevertheless certain that this was one of the causes which were responsible for the lack of success of *Rus,* even among those who were capable of feeling with their heart and listening to a true Russian message. When he [Aksakov] decided to break, not his alliance—there was never such a thing between Aksakov and the conservatives—but, let us say politely, his diplomatic relations, when Aksakov rose again as an offended tribune, only then did his influence and the success of his newspaper increase tenfold. But this was almost on the eve of his death![1]

The shame and mortification experienced by Aksakov as a result of the Congress of Berlin were soon compounded by the brutal killing of the tsar. In fact these shocks may have been partly responsible for the severe heart condition that he developed at the end of his life. In these years Aksakov was a sad and disillusioned man. In a letter written in 1884 he confessed to a friend:

I do not have the key to our contemporary life. The long routine of everyday life has set in. This is probably demanded by history. An inner process, a process I cannot yet grasp is taking place. It will certainly require a new breed of people—not militant and fiery champions, preachers, pamphleteers, or awakeners . . . but plain workers with sober, practical, and routine messages. So it appears to me at least. It seems that I should stop speaking, sit back, and watch.[2]

And shortly before his death, Aksakov wrote to A. S. Suvorin, the publisher and owner of *Novoe vremia* (New Times): "The historical economy demands, it seems, the existence, for a certain time, of an era of mediocrity—a process of digestion that should not be disturbed by the actions of talented personalities."[3]

Yet when Aksakov began the publication of *Rus,* he had hoped that his fight against what he disliked in Russia would be justifiable and fruitful. In another letter to a friend he displayed this mood and described the purpose of his new publication:

I took up the publication of the newspaper [*Rus*] only in order to *fight.* The task of the newspaper is to struggle against the false political liberalism of our contemporary society as well as against the antinational and materialistic movement which is the trademark of our "intelligentsia." All around us in the "cultural" section of society revolutionary and negative elements are swarming. It is because of this situation that the newspaper [*Rus*] becomes willy-nilly a tribune . . . One

[1] Quoted by S. Vengerov in his *Kritiko-biograficheski slovar russkikh pisatelei i uchenykh* (St. Petersburg, 1889), I, 341–342.

[2] I. A., *Pisma,* IV, 288.

[3] Quoted by B. P. Kozmin, *Russkaia zhurnalistika 70-kh i 80-kh godov XIX veka* (Moscow, 1948), p. 43.

must speak differently to the people who use revolvers and dynamite.[4]

This was written in 1881; by 1884 Aksakov had already discovered that no one wanted to accept his challenge or even to take him seriously.

We must bear in mind Aksakov's poor health and repeated disappointments when we come to study his last years and to judge his political allegiance to conservatism—as he understood it. We must remember that in his definition the government was just as liberal and just as "antinational" as the intelligentsia of Russia. Indeed, he felt that the government had betrayed Russia by accepting the decisions of the Congress of Berlin and by forcing a constitution on Bulgaria. And he went even further; he saw a direct connection between "bureaucratic liberalism" and its sequel, the rise of terrorism. The constitutional demands which were voiced in the first three years of the eighties, mostly by people in governmental circles, confirmed his suspicion. At the end, Aksakov could no longer believe that the redemption and salvation of Russia would be the work of the peasantry. Furthermore, the appearance of bourgeois elements filled him with anxiety. He warned that "a typical bourgeois force . . . is seeping in. Together with it, an entirely new class of people of so-called "liberal professions" is being formed and they pose already in the quality of *homo novus*. They openly declare war on every historical tradition and, by the same token, on those, who, as cruel fate dictated, are of gentry extraction."[5] His ideas about education illustrate best the changes in his views in these last years.

I. EDUCATION

Aksakov was vitally interested in the educational system. He wanted to see the Russian people educated in a way that would bring them closer to the Slavophile ideal. He believed that education in Russia had been built upon the wrong foundations. Properly speaking, the young were not educated in Russia but were instead

---

[4] L. Bukhgeim, *Pisma I. S. Aksakova, N. P. Barsukova, etc . . . k bibliografu S. I. Ponamarevu* (Moscow, 1915), p. 141.

[5] I. A., *Sochineniia*, V, 547. Aksakov called these: "careerists possessed by ambition and lust for power, whose profession was to advance and open for themselves a road toward 'influential position' " (p. 548).

rigorously trained for positions in the civil service. In 1864 Aksakov wrote: "Freedom of education is incompatible with the mandatory nature of the [hierarchy of bureaucratic] ranks, it is inconceivable under the existing fourteen-rank system." Education must be unhampered and free from the fetters of the Table of Ranks. Abolishing bureaucratic incentives would encourage the creation of private schools adapted to the needs of their charges rather than to those of the bureaucracy. And such a change would do away in part with the sharp differences in the educational levels of the Russian population. In the meantime, the educational system, as it existed, was responsible for the growth of two groups of people—of the officials (*chinovniki*) and of the Nihilists.[6] The former were those whose ambition was fulfilled in the ranks of the administrative apparatus, the latter were all those who either could not or would not accept the bureaucracy as the only purpose of their education.

Aksakov deplored the lack of schools that could cater to all social strata. Merchants, for instance, were afraid to send their sons to get an education because what they would receive in Russia invariably made them useless for working in business. Aksakov welcomed the reform embodied in the law of November 19, 1864, which introduced the bifurcation of secondary education. The new law created two types of gymnasia—the classical gymnasia and the "Real-gymnasia." The classical gymnasia, as their title indicates, were to give primary emphasis to classical studies and languages; they were to be preparatory schools for admission to the universities. The "Real-gymnasia" were to be more practical with an emphasis on mathematics and sciences; they were to be the first step toward such specialized schools as those of engineering and mining and so forth. Aksakov liked the "Real-gymnasia" because "they appeared to be independent institutions rather than preparatory schools for the university. Let the sons of the poorer merchants, artisans, and small landowners receive the opportunity of getting an education which, while sufficient, will not estrange them from their callings in life." [7]

[6] I. A., *Sochineniia*, 690, 693.

[7] *Ibid.*, p. 702. Aksakov urged the study of French and German in the classical gymnasia because these two languages would help the pupils to get acquainted with the treasures of western thought (p. 704).

But by this, Aksakov did not mean that the classical gymnasia and the universities ought to be available to the rich and the privileged only. He wanted to encourage anyone interested in a university education to enter a classical gymnasia and from there to gain admission to a university of his choice. He felt that higher education had to be obtained freely and not be forced upon anyone by the promise of a more or less alluring position in the administration.

Aksakov wrote that school education, in order to be beneficial and fruitful to the individual as well as to society, must express the needs and aspirations of society. In Russia, however, there existed an unfortunate chasm between the educational system and the civilization of the country. Aksakov believed that education, when divorced from or incommensurate with the cultural and intellectual level of the greater part of the country, was no longer beneficial and might even be detrimental to the nation. He compared Russia with the land of the Hottentots whose inhabitants might fancy a university of their own, staffed with professors imported from Heidelberg, Jena, or Göttingen, but where such an institution could never achieve any laudable results because it would be altogether incompatible with the needs and the culture of the Hottentots.[8]

Khomiakov had warned earlier:

If school education is in direct contradiction with the previous so-called preparatory education, it cannot fulfill the expectations [placed in it] as far as usefulness is concerned. It becomes even noxious. All of man's soul, his thoughts, his feelings are split in two. His inner vital integrity disappears. His emasculated mind does not produce anything in the realm of knowledge. Sensitivity, stunned and killed, withers away. This man is, so to speak, uprooted from the soil in which he grew. He becomes a stranger in his own country. The Petrine revolution had such a result. One can explain this error by conditions that were prevalent in the times of Peter, but to repeat constantly the same error would be unforgivable.[9]

Aksakov hoped to see a completely autonomous and independent educational system. Each community, each class of people was to create a school that would answer its needs. Echoing Khomiakov,

[8] I. A., *Sochineniia*, II, 191–192.
[9] Quoted by Aksakov, *ibid.*, p. 193.

Aksakov wanted the schools to be located among the people and not in distant cities where parents could not supervise and guide their children. The state with its purely coercive function was not to have any say in the realm of the mind. Any encroachment of the state in the domain of education was bound to have catastrophic results.[10] But, unfortunately, the state in Russia had its tentacles in every aspect of life. It gave education a single purpose—that of preparing an army of *chinovniki* "without either creative or moral strength." Those who refused to follow this road often left school as Nihilists. The Nihilists were the antithesis of officialdom, their credo was "the negation of everything official in all fields. Nihilism is a disease but not an independent one, it is an illness created by the medicine. This is why Nihilism thrives particularly in our public institutions and is weak in home education." [11]

Although Aksakov wished to see the eradication of all social barriers, he was nonetheless strongly against the introduction of a mandatory system of primary education. Such a measure, he claimed, might be desirable for Prussian children but not for Russian boys and girls. Instead of building many schools, Russia should have a few good ones. These good schools could serve as models for future schools which would at last provide all Russian children with the kind of education they needed. Besides, to speak of a mandatory school system for all was sheer wishful thinking because no zemstvo in Russia was rich enough to afford schools and teachers for such a program.[12] Aksakov feared the effects of primary education on the people since education meant perforce westernization. He was painfully aware that there could not be such a thing as a self-styled Russian or Slavic education. He unwillingly pointed out that the issue of education was a *cul de sac* for the Slavophile ideas of an independent Slavic culture. He was forced to admit that an educated peasant would cease to belong to the people because he would become a European.

In one word—in a Russian popular school, the pupil (more or less the East) not only absorbs knowledge but also the West. Though this state of

[10] *Ibid.*, pp. 198, 203.   [11] *Ibid.*, p. 205.   [12] I. A., *Sochineniia*, IV, 711–721.

affairs is at present unavoidable, it is still the duty of the school to ease and to render harmless this encounter of the East with the West. The school must free itself as much as possible of anything foreign and Russify the sciences and civilization or at least strip them of their foreign trappings.[13]

Aksakov was full of dark premonitions about the future of primary education because most of the teachers, he felt sure, were great admirers of all things western and as such were noxious to the Russian cause. However, their attitudes could be offset by giving a good upbringing (*vospitanie*) to the pupils in addition to their formal education. Indeed, without a good upbringing "the acquisition of knowledge would be the downfall of the pupil while the integrity of the peoples' way of life would be shaken. By opening the door toward civilization with all its enticements, the school could become a perfidious trap for the people, where, instead of the bread for which they stretch their hands, they would find only a stone." In the last years of his life, Aksakov thought that good upbringing could be provided only by the Church and Christianity. Thus, he wished to see every church in Russia with a parish school; he even wished to put the already existing lay schools under the supervision of priests. Aksakov admonished the schools "to bind the peasant closer to the Church, which was and is for the people the repository of all higher moral precepts, of saintly emotions and lofty esthetic delights." He finished by advocating the total fusion of primary education with the parish school system.[14]

Aksakov thought that socially church education would have a most rewarding result, since he as well as Khomiakov and Samarin, believed that equality existed only within the Church. All the peasants could not receive a university education, but a religious education could make them feel that they were, as Samarin put it, a part of the "great organism of love," where they could enjoy equality on a sublime level and where they could enjoy true brotherhood. Aksakov wrote that within the Church the young peasants could learn the essentials of "brotherhood—the spiritual principle of Chris-

[13] *Ibid.*, p. 746. A bit of advice that was carried out under Stalin!
[14] *Ibid.*, pp. 731, 734-750.

tian equality, under which there may licitly and freely exist differences of titles, positions, and ranks." [15] In 1884 Aksakov added: "religion solves all contradictions, it renders harmless all knowledge." [16] And so it happened that toward the end of his life Aksakov embraced the views of his brother Konstantin on education, views that he had so cruelly reviled some thirty or forty years before. Furthermore, having all his life crusaded against governmental interference in education, he was now ready to accept the authority of the Holy Synod, which was for all practical purposes a branch of the administration.

Aksakov's views on the education of the people, in the last years of his life, may be called reactionary because he wanted to prevent social mobility for the lower classes of the nation. A narrow church education and the preservation at all cost of the peasant commune, not because of Slavophile ideals but because it was useful as an institution to check or slow down the growth of the proletariat, was indeed a point of view that any reactionary of that time could have endorsed.[17] His anti-Semitism and his Great-Russian chauvinism also indict Aksakov as a champion of reaction. Moreover, his nationalism had acquired a strong imperialist flavor in the years following the Russo-Turkish war. He not only claimed the "frontiers of St. Vladimir in the West"—Galicia and Ruthenia—but he also demanded that the Black Sea should become a Russian sea and that Russia should keep pushing her borders beyond Transcaucasia along the coast of Asia Minor until "we [the Russians] ride the Straits which are our natural frontiers." [18]

Nevertheless, although Aksakov had many apprehensions about the Russian people, he was not able to side with the government. He accused the administration of all the ills that had befallen Russia, namely, the capitulation at the Congress of Berlin and the rise of terrorism. He saw a direct connection between the diplomatic fiasco and the political assassinations and his tirades against liberalism

[15] I. A., *Sochineniia*, II, 88.

[16] I. A., *Sochineniia*, IV, 744.

[17] For Aksakov's views on the peasant question in the last years of his life, see I. A., *Sochineniia*, V, 417–598.

[18] I. A., *Sochineniia*, II, 787.

irritated even the most patient of his friends. Koshelev, for instance, reproached Aksakov for distorting Slavophilism. Among other things, Koshelev wrote:

Neither Khomiakov, nor Kireevski, nor your brother ever insulted liberalism. In the *Russkaia beseda* (Russian Colloquium) there was not a single word in that sense. We were fighting then against the westernizers and they do not exist anymore. To speak now against any kind of representation, to resent the fact that the censorship is too liberal and to throw sly stones at Loris-Melikov is just horrible! I think, my dear Ivan Sergeevich, that if Khomiakov were alive, he would rather approve our way of action than yours and agree with us.[19]

Yet, in spite of all his reactionary inclinations, Aksakov continued to defend freedom of speech, trial by jury, and autonomy for the Church and other institutions. Shortly before his death, he was given a warning by the censorship because he "commented on current events in a tone incompatible with genuine patriotism." He published the warning in *Rus* as required by law but in the next issue he answered the warning by accusing the Ministry of the Interior of being unpatriotic! This took place in December 1885. A few days after this incident, Aksakov went to the Crimea for a rest. It was too late. On January 27, 1886, he died of heart failure.[20]

2. THE ATTEMPT AT A ZEMSKI SOBOR

The most striking feature of Russian life in the years 1880–1883 was undoubtedly the constitutional fervor that pervaded governmental circles and a portion of Russian society. A great number of constitutional projects were suggested. Of these, especially the project of Loris-Melikov, the minister of the interior and the favorite of Alexander II, was believed to be the harbinger of a constitutional regime. In fact, however, this project had nothing constitutional about it; rather it was a first step toward cooperation between repre-

[19] "Pisma A. I. Kosheleva k I. S. Aksakovu (1881–1883)," *Istoricheski sbornik; o minuvshem* (St. Petersburg, 1909), p. 410.
[20] S. Vengerov, *Kritiko-biograficheski slovar russkikh pisatelei i uchenykh* (St. Petersburg, 1889), p. 342.

sentatives of the nation and the government. The anticlimax came with the assassination of Alexander II, who had signed Loris-Melikov's project only hours before he fell under the bombs of the terrorists.

The beginning of a new reign and the resignation of Loris-Melikov did not discourage those who imagined that a constitutional monarchy might solve Russia's problems. These men argued that if the monarchy were sanctioned by the people the terrorists of the *Narodnaia volia* would have had no authority for committing their dastardly deeds. The champions of a constitution were not discouraged even when Alexander III announced, in his manifesto of April 29, 1881, that he intended to rule autocratically. On the contrary, the ministry of Count N. P. Ignatiev, which lasted from early May 1881 to May 31, 1882, saw many constitutional projects.

The Holy Brotherhood (*Sviashchennaia druzhina*)—a secret society composed of aristocrats at the Court and formed for the purpose of fighting terrorism—became the center of a constitutional movement.[21] Even some of the grand dukes were not adverse to a constitution; the Grand Duke Aleksei Aleksandrovich assured Aksakov's wife that: "No matter what your husband says, Russia, sooner or later, will have to adopt a constitution." And Count A. A. Bobrinski, who was one of the leaders of the Holy Brotherhood and a member of the tsar's entourage, remarked in his diary: "A constitution or at least (some form of) popular representation is, it seems, the means of defense that is indicated by Providence itself."[22]

Similar beliefs were voiced by various persons belonging to other

[21] S. Lukashevich, "The Holy Brotherhood: 1881–1883," *The American Slavic and East European Review* 18:491–509 (December 1959). See also: "Konstitutsionnye proekty nachala 80-kh godov XIX veka," *Krasnyi Arkhiv* 31:118–143 (1928). Also I. D. Shishmanov, "Konstitutsionnaia zapiska gr. P. Shuvalova," *Vestnik Evropy* (1913), no. 8, pp. 136–166, and by the same author "O roli Grafa P. P. Shuvalova v konstitutsionnom dvizhenii 80 gg.," *ibid.* (1914), nos. 1 and 2, pp. 197–221 and 183–191, respectively.

[22] See A. F. Tiutcheva, *Pri dvore dvukh imperatorov,* 2 vols. (1928–1929), II, 123, and A. A. Bobrinski, "Vospominaniia A. A. Bobrinskago," *Katorga i ssylka* 76:73–120 (1931).

political camps. The Slavophile Koshelev, for instance, wrote in his brochure published in 1882 and entitled, "What Then Should We Do?" (*Chto zhe nam delat?*):

We are disturbed by Nihilism but this plague has affected the body of Russia only externally and that because of other ailments from which we really suffer. Guarantee our personal way of life, realize local self-government in keeping with the idea of him who gave it to us, give the opportunity to the Russian land to express, through its trusted members, its opinion on its needs and advantages in the conduct of its affairs. Let the Russians enjoy the right that is enjoyed by the citizens of the entire enlightened world—the right to express freely and responsibly their opinions and feelings—and there will not be any Nihilism and, what is even more important, there will not be many of the other ailments which are exhausting us, stunting us and killing us.[23]

Boris Chicherin said almost the same thing in a public address in 1882, when he was elected mayor of Moscow: "The time will come when the government itself, seeing in us not the elements of ferment but a defense of order, will feel the need to broaden the narrow area of local self-government and to bring the public into the general structure of the Russian state." [24] But all those who dreamed of a constitution had to reckon with implacable enemies. Among these were Pobedonostsev and Count D. A. Tolstoi at Court, and Katkov and Aksakov, among others, in the press.

Aksakov welcomed with all his heart the manifesto of April 29, 1881; yet at the same time he must have realized that there was nothing exceptionally new about autocracy in Russia and that re-affirming it in the existing circumstances meant further encroachments by the bureaucracy on the life of the Russian people. Still, he believed that a Zemski sobor would obviate the danger of constitutionalism and the fear of an all-powerful bureaucracy. In January 1882 Aksakov wrote to Ignatiev:

There is a solution capable of putting to shame all the constitutions of the world, something that is broader and more liberal than these con-

[23] Quoted in N. Knorring, *General M. D. Skobelev,* 2 vols. (Paris, 1939–1940), II, 185.
[24] Quoted in George Fischer, *Russian Liberalism from Gentry to Intelligentsia* (Cambridge, Mass., 1958), pp. 19–20.

stitutions but which at the same time will keep Russia on her historical, political, and national basis. This way out is the Zemski sobor with direct elections by the peasants, landowners, merchants, and clergy. The coronation is a good excuse. The presence of a thousand representatives from the peasantry would dispel, without any other means of coercion, all the constitutional dreams and would serve to assert in front of all the people and all the world the autocratic power in its genuine historical sense. Just as wax melts on contact with fire, so all foreign, liberal, aristocratic, nihilistic and other such intentions will melt on contact with the people.[25]

In order to make this idea materialize, Aksakov sent to Ignatiev a specialist on the history of the Zemski sobor, a certain P. D. Golokhvastov, whose mission was to draft a project of a Zemski sobor as well as that of a manifesto which would announce it.

Golokhvastov appears to have been a rather peculiar individual. He had been a justice of the peace, a factory manager, and a land-owner. He had written articles for the *Russki arkhiv* (the Russian Archive) and contributed to Aksakov's *Rus*. But what is most note-worthy is that he was completely absorbed, not to say obsessed, by the study of the history of the Zemski sobor and by the elaboration of plans for a future Zemski sobor, the convocation of which, accord-ing to Golokhvastov, was ineluctable. He was convinced beyond the slightest doubt that the Zemski sobor ought to be restored in Russia, because it was the only alternative to anarchy. When in 1879 the terrorists of the *Narodnaia volia* attempted but failed to blow up the emperor's train, Golokhvastov wrote quickly to Pobedonostsev, begging him to explain to the tsar that "without the people . . . it is impossible to cope with these seditious trouble-makers as well as with the other disorders of our land." [26] Thus, in the spring of 1882, Golokhvastov reappeared as Ignatiev's consultant on the Zemski sobor and as Aksakov's agent.[27]

[25] P. A. Zaionchkovski, "Popytka sozyva zemskogo sobora i padenie ministerstva N. P. Ignatieva," in *Istoriia SSSR* (1960), no. 5, p. 130.

[26] S. Svatikov, "Proekty narodnago predstavitelstva v Rossii v 1882 g.," *Golos Minuvshego* (1913), no. 7, p. 243.

[27] "Perepiska P. D. Golokhvastova s I. S. Aksakovym o Zemskom Sobore," *Russki Arkhiv* (1913), I, 93–111 and 181–204.

In this affair Aksakov kept in the background and worked in the greatest secrecy. It is possible that he did not want to experience another humiliating defeat as he had in 1870. At that time, on the occasion of the emperor's unilateral breach of the Treaty of Paris, Aksakov had written an address to Alexander II in which he expressed, in the name of the Moscow City Duma, a wish to see more trust between the tsar and his people. This address was returned to the sender because it was allegedly replete with "democratic insinuations." Hurt by this rebuff, Aksakov had written a letter to Pobedonostsev in which he complained about the lack of understanding and the misinterpretation of his words by the officials of the government.[28] Indeed, A. Molchanov, a friend of Aksakov, records in his memoirs that Aksakov henceforth was afraid to mention overtly anything in favor of a Zemski sobor lest it should be interpreted again as a demand for a constitution.[29]

However, much to Aksakov's despair, Ignatiev procrastinated. In one of his letters to Golokhvastov, Aksakov wrote: "I am not happily thrilled but very seriously disturbed by the magnitude of the enterprise. This is the last chance. Should it fail, should it turn out to be a fiasco, there would not be any peaceful salvation [for Russia]."[30] Soon after this, Golokhvastov began to suspect that, were the project of the Zemski sobor to be accepted, Ignatiev wanted to receive the post of prime-minister. This proved to be true. Ignatiev, in order to appeal to the tsar, wanted to pass off the project of Golokhvastov and Aksakov as his own. For this purpose, Ignatiev had copied the long document by hand and kept it ready until he could show it to the tsar. It is generally agreed among historians that Ignatiev was a pathological liar and a deceiver. E. M. Feoktistov, who knew Ignatiev, gives us a most eloquent characterization of his penchant for lying: "Who in Russia did not know this sad feature of his [Ignatiev's] character, namely, a reckless and insatiable inclination for lying? He lied because it was demanded by his nature. He was

[28] "Moskovski adres Aleksandru II v 1870 g.," *Krasnyi Arkhiv* 31:144–154 (1928).
[29] A. Molchanov, "Vospominaniia ob I. S. Aksakove," *Istoricheski Vestnik* (1886), no. 8, p. 373.
[30] "Perepiska P. D. Golokhvastova s I. S. Aksakovym," *Russki Arkhiv* (1913), I, 102.

a clever Figaro, a master at all sorts of intrigues with no regard for the means he used." [31]

The secret of these intrigues for a Zemski sobor, however, was poorly guarded. Pobedonostsev, who knew Golokhvastov, immediately suspected Aksakov to be masterminding the whole affair. He wrote several letters to the tsar in which he warned that: "it [a Zemski sobor] will be a revolution, the end of government, and the end of Russia." [32] The tsar followed the advice of Pobedonostsev— Ignatiev was forced to resign. The new minister of the interior was Count D. A. Tolstoi, a reactionary to the core, who swiftly put an end to any talk of representative government. He even prevailed upon the tsar to disband the Holy Brotherhood. Indeed, it can be said that it was only following the resignation of Count Ignatiev that reaction began in the reign of Alexander III.

When Aksakov was informed that his plan had failed, he exclaimed in sorrow: "Pobedonostsev and Katkov will ruin Russia ... In Russia Katkov and the insane Pobedonostsev are running the show." [33] In proposing a Zemski sobor Aksakov did not want to limit the power of the emperor. On the contrary, he had always maintained that the Zemski sobor was "a free act of autocratic power, it was the prerogative of the autocratic power, it was a natural result of the autocratic power of the tsar." [34] Aksakov wanted to render any constitutional movement impossible in Russia, and he thought the Zemski sobor to be the best stratagem against this western disease. In 1861, at the beginning of his career as an independent journalist, Aksakov had written to V. I. Lamanski:

[31] E. M. Feoktistov, *Za kulisami politiki i literatury* (Leningrad, 1929), p. 199. Feoktistov was chief of the Central Bureau for the Press (*Glavnoe upravlenie po delam pechati*). This project of a manifesto summoning the Zemski sobor, written in Ignatiev's own hand, was published in *K. P. Pobedonostsev i ego korrespondenty* (Moscow-Petrograd, 1923), pp. 261–263.

[32] *Pisma Pobedonostseva k Aleksandru III,* 2 vols. (Moscow, 1925), I, 379–383. Quotation from p. 379. P. A. Zaionchkovski in his already-cited articles believes that Ignatiev showed the project to the tsar who gave it to Pobedonostsev for perusal. See *Istoriia SSSR* (1960), no. 5, p. 136.

[33] "Perepiska P. D. Golokhvastova s I. S. Aksakovym," *Russki Arkhiv* (1913), I, 188.

[34] I. A., *Sochineniia,* V, 90.

I am convinced that Russia will be rejuvenated, if not by revolution (God forbid!), then only by the Zemski sobor. This Zemski sobor must be such that the main role in it will be played by the Russian people and that it will represent the majority of the people. In order to prevent the possibility that the Zemski sobor might be transformed into an ugly Parliament or into an even uglier National Assembly, it is necessary to clear the ground, to destroy the miasmata and the stench of our society. I would like to propagate gradually the idea of a true Russian Zemski sobor and at the same time to sap the faith of our society in vacuous liberalism and to destroy its taste for revolutionary tragicomedies.[35]

3. SKOBELEV AND THE GERMAN PERIL

It has already been pointed out in the preceding chapter that Aksakov felt disillusioned by the political turn of events in the Balkans. How could it have been otherwise? He was personally responsible for helping the political emancipation of the Balkan Slavs and he was therefore instrumental in creating the first favorable conditions for the westernization of their countries. Yet, he never gave up his hopes altogether. He continued to dream of recreating the same pan-Slavic enthusiasm that had swept Russia in the years 1876–1879. In later life, however, Aksakov, a little disappointed in the Slavs, preferred to stress the evil of Austria and the dishonesty of Germany and to claim that the Slavs would perish under the Germanic onslaught if Russia did not stand firmly against it. At this point, accordingly, it is necessary to say a few words about Aksakov's friendship with General Mikhail Dmitrievich Skobelev.

General Skobelev (1843–1882) was an outstanding Russian military man, who had distinguished himself during the Russo-Turkish war and had defeated the Turcomans at Akhal-Teke, in 1881. For these exploits he was hailed as a hero, especially in 1881–1882, the last two years of his life and the peak of his popularity. Alexander III disliked the dashing general just as much as his father, Alexander II, had liked him. Skobelev took umbrage at this disfavor; temperamental and outspoken, he publicly accused the administration of

[35] "Perepiska dvukh slavianofilov—V. I. Lamanski i I. S. Aksakov," *Russkaia Mysl* (December 1916), p. 101.

selling Russia to the Germans and he avenged himself further by overtly professing his preference for a consultative type of government. Such statements uttered by a national hero were bound to create turmoil.

Aksakov became acquainted with Skobelev, on the latter's initiative, in early January 1882. Skobelev's reasons were, as he himself said to Aksakov's wife:

I came to see your husband because I must speak to him. The times we are living in now are serious. When, last year, we took the oath of loyalty to autocracy at the enthronement of the [new] emperor, we did it in the hope, or rather with the firm conviction, that the new reign would open a new era of national policy and that the government would not sell to Germany the interests of Russia. What has happened since? We find ourselves on the same slippery road on the eve of sacrificing to Prussia and Austria Russian interests in the Slavic lands.[36]

Aksakov tried to caution and calm the exasperated general. Yet, according to N. N. Knorring—the most recent biographer of General Skobelev—Aksakov helped the general to work out all the points of the two speeches that the latter gave in St. Petersburg and Paris in the days following their interview.[37]

Although the contents of the two speeches were almost the same, the one Skobelev delivered in Paris was much stronger than the one he made in the Russian capital. In the Paris speech Skobelev addressed some French students, but his carefully planned diatribe was aimed at a much larger and more important audience. Among many other things Skobelev said:

If you want me to name this intruder, this imposter, this intriguer, this enemy who is so dangerous for Russia and the Slavs, I shall do it. It is the author of *Drang nach Osten,* you know him well—it is Germany. I repeat and I beg you not to forget it. The enemy is Germany. The struggle between Slavs and Teutons is unavoidable. It is even very near. It will be a long, bloody, and horrible battle, but I am convinced that the Slavs will have the last words.[38]

[36] A. F. Tiutcheva, *Pri dvore dvukh imperatorov,* II, 230.
[37] N. N. Knorring, *General M. D. Skobelev,* II, 222–234.
[38] *Ibid.,* p. 231.

This speech created a most unpleasant impression in Germany as well as in Russian bureaucratic circles. Aksakov published its content in *Rus,* although without comment. He nurtured great hopes for the future of Skobelev. Aksakov once said to his friend Molchanov: "There is no doubt that Skobelev will have a great role to play in Russian history . . . It is difficult to say whether this role will be good or bad, but it will be a great role in any case."[39]

While sojourning in France Skobelev had established a friendship with Gambetta, with whom he discussed the virtues of a Franco-Russian alliance in the struggle against the German menace. Mme Juliette Adam, the mistress and friend of Gambetta, visited Russia shortly after Skobelev's trip to Paris. Aksakov had a long conversation with her, but its topic and its purpose have remained a mystery. It can be said in general that it is not clear what exactly Aksakov expected of Skobelev and Gambetta.

This episode of Russian *boulangisme* lasted less than half a year. Skobelev died unexpectedly on June 25, 1882, while having a gay time with a German courtesan in Moscow. His death occurred on the eve of an important visit to Aksakov. In the same year Gambetta and the *revenchard* General Chanzy died in France. These three deaths, occurring within a few months of each other, forced Jules Grevy to exclaim: "Is it possible that Germany has signed a pact with death?" Indeed, it was rumored that the three enemies of Germany were poisoned secretly by the German cloak and dagger service. Aksakov also subscribed to this point of view.

As a footnote to the Skobelev-Aksakov relations, it is pertinent to remark that the two patriots did not think of the same Germans when they spoke of the German danger. In an article dedicated to Skobelev and Gambetta, after their deaths, Aksakov claimed that Skobelev meant the Austrians when he spoke of the German danger.[40] In fact, Skobelev never made any distinction between Austria and Germany because he knew that in case of war Russia would

[39] A. Molchanov, "Vospominaniia ob I. S. Aksakove," *Istoricheski Vestnik* (1886), no. 8, p. 379.

[40] I. A., *Sochineniia,* VII, 678–688. Aksakov rather disliked Gambetta for his political beliefs. See other articles on Skobelev in I. A., *Sochineniia,* V, 654–675.

have to reckon with the two of them, and Germany represented by far the greater military danger. Aksakov gave a personal slant to Skobelev's words in order to harness the memory of the defunct hero more effectively to the cause of pan-Slavism in the Balkan-Danubian area.

4. SLAVOPHILISM AND POPULISM

It is also pertinent in this chapter to raise the interesting question of the similarity between Slavophilism and Populism. The two movements were indeed based on a belief in the people and in the virtues of the peasant commune; otherwise, their aims and methods were altogether different. Nonetheless, there are several scholars who saw in Slavophilism the precursor of the Populist movement in Russia. Among them, M. Gershenzon called Petr Kireevski "the founder of our modern narodnik movement." [41] Berdyaev too declared that: "The Slavophiles were the first narodniki among us; they were narodniki on a religious basis." [42] V. Bogucharski went even further when he cited the Slavophiles as the main source of inspiration for the Populist thinkers. He even quoted Ivan Aksakov in order to support his allegations.[43]

Aksakov's views on *Populism* were very close to those later expressed by Berdyaev. In a letter written in 1883 to some students Aksakov accused the narodniki of stealing the basic Slavophile idea: "The journal *Russkoe bogatstvo* (Russian Wealth) and its party always attack the Slavophiles, although they have borrowed from them everything that is original and sensible in their own movement . . . One can see that the narodniki are very close to us and yet an abyss separates them from the Slavophiles. Slavophilism is

---

[41] M. Gershenzon, *Istoricheskie zapiski* (Berlin, 1923), p. 118 as quoted by N. Riasanovsky, *Russia and the West in the Teaching of the Slavophiles* (Cambridge, Mass., 1952), p. 190. See also M. Malia, *Alexander Herzen and the Birth of Russian Socialism, 1812–1855* (Cambridge, Mass., 1961), ch. xii: "The Slavophiles and Nationalism," pp. 278–312.

[42] N. Berdyaev, *The Russian Idea* (London, 1947), p. 41.

[43] V. Bogucharski, *Aktivnoe narodnichestvo semidesiatykh godov* (Moscow, 1912), pp. 10–24. A much more moderate view is taken by E. Kolosov, "M. A. Bakunin i N. K. Mikhailovskii v narodnichestve," in *Golos Minuvshego* (1913), no. 5, pp. 61–89.

unthinkable without religion and without Christian ideals." [44] This statement made a clear distinction between a philosophy based on religious thought and an ideology founded on social ideals. In fact, however, the Slavophilism of Ivan Aksakov was perhaps just as alien to the old Slavophilism as was Populism itself. This view will be discussed in the last and final part of this chapter.

5. A FINAL APPRAISAL

The sudden death of Ivan Aksakov in 1886 stirred Russia, which had been accustomed, for nearly three decades, to the turbulence of the Slavophile journalist and the pan-Slavic crusader. Vengerov recalled: "When the Kireevskiis and Khomiakov died, their coffins were followed by a few dozens of people, and their works are barely read even in our own days—a time of comparatively strong diffusion of Slavophile ideas. But the remains of Ivan Aksakov were followed by more than one hundred thousand people and his articles were read by all literate Russia." [45] Indeed, his widow received almost two hundred telegrams from all over Russia and from many foreign countries. Among these expressions of sympathy, there were telegrams written by Alexander III, all the Grand Dukes, Prince Nicholas of Montenegro, the Serbian Metropolitan Mihailo, the Bulgarian Metropolitans Kliment and Gerasim, the Bulgarian statesman Karavelov, Count Ignatiev, Count Miliutin and Pobedonostsev, as well as by universities, zemstvos, and learned societies.

Aksakov's popularity reflected to a great extent the mood and the expectations of a large section of the Russian public. It is not an easy task to analyze in detail the reasons for the display of national grief which accompanied Aksakov to his grave, yet it is possible to say that he was remembered, most of all, for his role in Balkan affairs. He stood out as the symbol of pan-Slavism and as the catalyst of the nationalist and pro-Slav fervor that swept Russia in the 1870's and 1880's and gave her a glimpse of radiant glory. He had been the right man for this role. As Vengerov reminisced:

[44] "K biografii I. S. Aksakova," *Istoricheski vestnik* (1886), no. 9, pp. 569–575. The quotation is from pp. 571–572.
[45] S. Vengerov, *Kritiko-biograficheski slovar russkikh pisatelei i uchenykh* (St. Petersburg, 1889), I, 319.

Aksakov had all the ability of a good orator: a powerful voice, the physique of a legendary hero [*bogatyr*], majestic gestures, and a remarkable mastery of the art of declamation inherited from his father. Thus, it is not difficult to understand the reason why he always made an overpowering impression on his listeners . . . It is said about Victor Hugo that he was not a person but an institution in France. The same can be said with even a greater right about Aksakov in the period of the pro-Slavic exaltation. The voice of Aksakov acquired all of a sudden such an influence that each word of his was interpreted as a political event. After each of his speeches, telegrams were sent to all parts of the world and the western press tried to guess [from Aksakov's speeches] the next step in Russia's foreign policy . . . The fiery speeches and addresses delivered by Ivan Aksakov were among the decisive causes of the war. No one among those who lived through these years of pro-Slav excitement and who, consequently, knew through personal experience, would question the importance of the far-ranging impact of Aksakov's heated appeals and the influence they had on the minds and hearts of all.[46]

In another place, Vengerov testified that Aksakov was "a man of enormous journalistic talent; the unusual beauty and force of his speech made him truly a prophet of Slavophilism about whom one can say without any rhetorical exaggeration that he knew how to enflame with his words the hearts of men." [47]

For many people Aksakov was a link with the past. On learning about his death, Pobedonostsev hastened to write to the tsar: "It is a loss beyond repair. We have few men who are so honest and pure and who love Russia and all that is Russian as Aksakov did. He took with him to the grave a body of traditions that were bequeathed to us by previous generations." Alexander answered in the same vein: "It is indeed in many respects an irreparable loss. He was a truly Russian man with a pure soul and, although he was a maniac on certain questions, he knew how to defend always and under any circumstances the interests of Russia." [48] From these testimonies it becomes obvious that Aksakov was appreciated as a champion and apostle of nationalism. If this was his real meaning

[46] *Ibid.*, pp. 335–336.
[47] *Ibid.*, p. 320.
[48] C. Pobiedonostsev, *Mémoires politiques, correspondance officielle* . . . (Paris, 1927), p. 358.

for the society of his time, then the nature of his nationalism must be thoroughly investigated.

Vladimir Solovev has given us an excellent criticism of Slavophile nationalism. He points out that the Slavophiles and their followers confused the notions narodnost and nationalism. Solovev explains:

> We distinguish narodnost from nationalism according to results. The fruits of English narodnost are Shakespeare and Byron, Berkeley and Newton, whereas the fruits of English nationalism are a worldwide plundering, the exploits of Warren Hastings and Lord Seymours, in other words—destruction and murder. The fruits of the great German narodnost are Lessing and Goethe, Kant and Schelling, whereas the fruit of German nationalism is the forceful Germanization of their neighbors from the times of the Teutonic knights to our own days.[49]

In other words, for Solovev narodnost represented the spiritual qualities of a people, and nationalism a concept with which to justify violence and aggression.

These points are extremely important because, had the Slavophiles, who posed as champions of narodnost, agreed entirely with Solovev's definition, Slavophilism would have been a contemplative and fatalistic doctrine. Indeed, the Slavophiles might have remarked philosophically that some nations were capable of producing a great culture and great men while other nations were not, because they did not have in them the divine spark of narodnost or because their time had not come yet. But the Slavophiles were neither contemplative nor fatalistic in outlook. They claimed that Russia, if led in the right direction, would create and develop a colossal culture, thus contributing to the enrichment of world civilization. In order to support their ideas, they had to define and, at the same time, convince themselves and others of the superiority of the Russian narodnost. Conversely, to speak of one's own superiority meant to demonstrate that the creative capacities of other nations were either exhausted or nonexistent. Thus, the Slavophiles spoke of the "decaying West" and of "historical" and "unhistorical" peoples. In brief, they devised a proto-racist philosophy in which the world was

[49] V. Solovev, *Sobranie Sochineni,* 2 ed., V, 12–13.

divided into peoples who were instrumental in shaping the destiny of the world and into other peoples who were clay waiting to be molded in the image of their superior neighbors.

The Slavophiles firmly believed that the most outstanding feature of the Russian narodnost was that Russia had preserved the purity of the Apostolic Church and that Russia was appointed by Providence to restore Christianity in the world in its Orthodox form. This was the basis for the messianism of the Slavophiles. Speaking on this subject P. N. Miliukov has remarked:

There was an inner contradiction at the base of the old Slavophilism. The idea of nationality precluded the natural development of the messianic idea and the messianic idea hindered the flowering of the idea of nationality. They [the old Slavophiles] valued the religious essence of the Russian narodnost, yet, at the same time, they valued only the popular form of the religious essence of this narodnost.

After pointing out that Slavophilism could not but split as a result of this inner contradiction, Miliukov continues:

In theory, this development led Russian nationalism to the metaphysical conception of a "universal historical type" and led Russian messianism to a chimeric universal theocracy. In practice, however, our nationalists finished by defending systematically reaction and obscurantism; our messianists saved themselves from following in their footsteps by adapting their world views, for better or for worse, to the theory of progress.[50]

This statement contains some truth and yet it seems that such a cleavage was not unavoidable, as Miliukov claims. Indeed, it is possible to imagine the Slavophile doctrine as being "Russian in form but messianic in content." But the disintegration of Slavophilism did, in fact, occur, roughly as Miliukov has stated, and it is important here to evaluate the transition of Ivan Aksakov from a liberal to a reactionary position on many questions.

Aksakov was conscious of the changes that were occurring in the Slavophile camp, and he accepted the idea of a reinterpretation of Slavophilism. In his biography of Tiutchev, Aksakov wrote:

[50] P. N. Miliukov, "Razlozhenie slavianofilstva," in *Voprosy filosofii i psikhologii*, year IV, Book 3 [18] (Moscow, 1893), pp. 92–93.

The very name "Slavophilism" may be abandoned and forgotten, and it is possible that the spiritual bonds that connect the first Slavophiles to the modern ones will be lost sight of. Many things that are happening under the influence of Slavophile ideas but which take place at a certain given time and under certain historical conditions will even seem to deviate from the purity and the orthodoxy of certain Slavophile ideals. There is no doubt also that some of the extreme fascinations which were, so to speak, organically connected with the personal character of the first preachers [of Slavophilism] or which were the outcome of a passionate struggle have now been superseded. Certain formulas which were too rigidly constructed and in which the Slavophiles projected the historical materialization of their favorite ideas and hopes have proved, or will prove to be, incorrect. It is possible, however, that history may perhaps arrive at the same principles, but by completely different and unfathomable ways and in an altogether different form.[51]

This tolerant appraisal of the evolution of Slavophilism clashes somewhat with the sectarian and bigoted tone of many of his articles. In order to understand this last point, it is necessary to investigate the nature of his attitude toward Slavophilism in general.

Ivan Aksakov was an idealist, but his idealism was not born out of optimism and hope. On the contrary—and this fact is crucial for understanding this tormented man—his idealism was the product not exactly of despair (although elements of despair were often present in his mind) but at least of a profound feeling of impotence. Although a practising Orthodox, his faith was not strong enough to ameliorate his inner turmoil. He found a partial solution to his problem by accepting the idealism of the Slavophile teaching. But although Aksakov liked to repeat again and again that life was impossible without idealization, he continued to waver and doubt. In his own words, describing Tiutchev's state of mind, one hears the echo of the letters that Aksakov wrote from Kaluga or Iaroslavl:

A thinking mind, undeviatingly realizing the limitations of the human brain in which the consciousness and the feeling of these limitations were insufficiently matched by the life-giving principle of faith—a faith accepted by the mind, recognized by the heart but which did not

---

[51] I. S. Aksakov, *Biografiia F. I. Tiutcheva* (Moscow, 1886), p. 62. This work was written in 1874 but published later.

possess him entirely, which did not direct his will, and which did not sanctify his life and which therefore was incapable of introducing into it [the life] either harmony or unity. In this duality, in this contradiction lay the tragic meaning of his existence.[52]

In Chapter II earlier we suggested that Aksakov's conversion to Slavophilism was the result, to a certain extent, of the emotional qualms that assailed him at the death of his father and his brother. Slavophilism had acquired two functions for Ivan Aksakov: it was a way of expiating his feelings of guilt toward the departed and it provided him with the discipline he needed to maintain his inner balance. These reasons were not altogether "healthy," and hence were bound to produce a sense of frustration. As soon as he embraced Slavophilism, Aksakov stopped writing poetry and shortly after this he began to persecute the Jews. His anti-Semitism might simply have coincided with his conversion, but it is also possible that the Jews were a most convenient scapegoat with which Aksakov could displace his repressed dislike of Slavophilism. In fact, he was the most anti-Semitic of all the Slavophiles. It is also true that anti-Semitism could not be a real issue until the Jews and the Gentiles could directly compete with each other in every field of human endeavor. This possibility was introduced by the reforms and the democratization of Russian and European societies in the second half of the nineteenth century. Moreover, Aksakov may have felt that the Jews were bad because they had succeeded in developing qualities which the Slavophiles felt the Russians had failed to acquire. Slavophilism was based on a belief in the particular virtues of the Slavic race; yet what race was more attached to the cultivation of its particular virtues than the Jewish race? The Slavophiles viewed the Russians as a chosen people with a mission to fulfil in the world—the Jews also believed that they were a chosen people and had a long tradition of messianic prophecies. For the Jews religion was the essence of their nationality—for the Slavophiles, the words Orthodox and Russian were interchangeable. The Slavophiles dreamed of a peasant commune based on Orthodox principles, but the Jews already had communities ruled by their religious lead-

[52] *Ibid.*, pp. 47–48.

ers. Finally, the Slavophiles preached Slavic solidarity at a time when Jewish solidarity was proverbial in Russia.

From this brief comparison one can see that the Jewish way of life had a great deal in common with the Slavophiles' vision of the future Russian society. There is, however, not enough room for two in any fantasy, and this is why, perhaps, Slavophilism was potentially anti-Semitic. Besides, the similarity between the basic strivings of Slavophilism and Judaism were conducive to antagonism and hatred.[53]

Vladimir Solovev has described how the Slavophiles constructed their ideology by means of concepts that did not belong to the heritage of the Slavic peoples but rather to the hated West. The Slavophiles were against the omnipotence of the government, which was a feature of western liberalism just as were their repeated demands for freedom of speech and enterprise. In short, the Slavophiles can be viewed as crypto-westernizers and this contradiction made their ideology very brittle and difficult to use. Indeed, they were forced to exaggerate their originality by praising Russian autocracy in the name of "true democracy" and by claiming barbarous Muscovy as a proof of the democratic nature of the Russian people. This awkwardness in their ideology was due to a great extent to their nationalism which was also imported just as was their taste for antiquity, a western romantic trait. In other words, the Slavophiles wanted to remold Russia, past and present, according to western patterns, whether liberal or romantic. It follows that their dislike of the West was only natural. The Slavophiles wanted to be original (*samobytnye*) and yet they could not wean themselves away from the West; conversely, they were doomed to be unoriginal as long as western patterns existed.

The letters that Ivan Aksakov wrote in the forties and the fifties testify to a certain extent to his awareness of the basic contradiction in Slavophile ideas. He sensed that Slavophilism stood on two

---

[53] This possibility was suggested by N. Berdyaev in his pamphlet *Khristianstvo i antisemitizm: religioznaia sudba evreistva* (Paris: Izd. Religiozno-filosofskoi akademii, n. d.), translated as *Christianity and Anti-Semitism* (New York, 1954). Berdyaev said: "The Russian people, because of its polarized nature and its messianic consciousness, shows certain similarities to the Jewish" (p. 5).

pillars—liberalism and conservatism. To discard one of these pillars —either conservatism or liberalism—meant the collapse of the originality that the Slavophiles valued so much. Yet, to keep both of them meant great intellectual confusion for the disciples of Slavophilism and great frustration for the teachers. In order to become a popular movement, Slavophilism would have had to be simplified.

At this point it is necessary to make once more a connection between this feature of Slavophilism and Aksakov's state of mind. The frustration which Aksakov experienced was a result of his inability either to withdraw from Slavophilism or to admit that the human mind is often an incompetent tool for solving all the problems with which it is faced. Aksakov's frustration unassuaged by Christianity was bound to result in destructiveness. He popularized Slavophilism by simplifying it to the point of making it a brutal appeal to hatred. In his articles for almost twenty years he taught his readers to hate, in the name of Slavophile purity, the Poles, the Jews, the Catholics, the Austrians and the Hungarians, the liberals and the conservatives, the government and those who were against it, as well as many others. In this respect, Aksakov adumbrated the ideologies of the twentieth century which demanded holocaust in the name of some unattainable purity of race or of polity.

Slavophilism as a current of Russian thought, by its very nature, could either lend itself to a mystical interpretation or could be viewed as a sanction for hatred and aggression. In fact, however, the exultant appeal to hate was often justified by the belief that hatred was demanded by the religious and mystical principles preached by Slavophilism. Such an attitude was found in the writings of Ivan Aksakov and, to some extent, in those of Dostoevski, Leontev and others.[54] P. N. Miliukov thus was right when he described very pragmatically the polarization that occurred during the "disintegration" of Slavophilism, but he was wrong to put Ivan Aksakov among the orthodox Slavophiles; besides, he did not show to what extent Slavophilism had a different psychological function for each of its exponents or followers.

In the case of Ivan Aksakov one is tempted to conclude that this

[54] On the other hand Vladimir Solovev refused this solution and had to break, therefore, with this kind of Slavophilism.

temperamental, idealistic, and unhappy Slavophile belonged to that extreme category of people who strive to purify and reshape the world according to the image which their often diseased minds have elaborated. Such a man, for instance, was Robespierre. The cruel irony is that these would-be benefactors or saviors of society are usually destroyers of life because their ideals demand bloody sacrifices. Aksakov, of course, never reached this extreme; nonetheless, he had all the features of the inquisitor. In the name of Slavophilism and for the sake of the salvation of the Slavs, in particular of the Russians, he taught men to hate. Still he did not go all the way along this path, for his teachings were always blunted somewhat by remnants of Christian ethics. When Christianity would no longer be adequate to control the morality of the peoples, the world would then, as the German pessimist E. Hartmann prophesied a century ago, "betray Christ and go and hang itself like Judas . . ."

Bibliography
Index

Bibliography

THE WRITINGS OF IVAN S. AKSAKOV

Collected Works

Sochineniia (Works) 7 vols., Moscow, 1886—1887.

Vol. I: *Slavianski vopros, 1860–1886* (The Slavic Question, 1860–1886).

Vol. II: *Slavianofilstvo i zapadnichestvo, 1860–1886* (Slavophilism and Westernism, 1860–1886).

Vol. III: *Polski vopros i zapadno-russkoe delo; Evreiski vopros, 1860–1886* (The Polish Question and the West-Russian Cause; The Jewish Question, 1860–1886).

Vol. IV: *Obshchestvennye voprosy—po tserkovnym delam, svoboda slova, sudebnyi vopros, obshchestvennoe vospitanie, 1860–1886* (Social Questions—Church Affairs, Freedom of Speech, Legal Question, Social Education, 1860–1886).

Vol. V: *Gosudarstvennyi i zemski vopros—Stati o nekotorykh istoricheskikh sobytiiakh, 1860–1886* (The State and Zemstvo Question—Articles on Certain Historical Events, 1860–1886).

Vol. VI: *Pribaltiiski vopros (The Baltic Question)*. This volume contains many articles on the conditions in Russia (*O vnutrennikh delakh Rossii*, pp. 171–542) as well as the introduction to his work on the Ukrainian fairs.

Vol. VII: *Obshcheevropeiskaia politika, 1860–1886.* (General European Politics, 1860–1886). This volume contains in addition many articles and speeches written or pronounced on various occasions.

Note: It appears that there exists another edition of the *Sochineniia* published in St. Petersburg in the early 1890's. See the bibliography at the end of M. Petrovich's book: *The Emergence of Russian Pan-Slavism*, New York, 1956.

Ivan Sergeevich Aksakov v ego pismakh (Ivan Sergeevich Aksakov in

His Letters), Moscow-St. Petersburg, 1888–1892, 4 vols. Most of this correspondence covers the period 1844–1856; in vol. IV, however, are most of his letters from the early 1860's. At the end of each of the first three volumes, there is an appendix with Aksakov's poetical works, distributed chronologically.

Books and Articles

Moskovski sbornik, vol. I: *Sochineniia K. S. Aksakova, I. S. Aksakova* . . . Moscow, 1852.

Izsledovanie o torgovle na ukrainskikh iarmarkakh (Izdano na izhde-venie sanktpeterburgskago kupechestva). St. Petersburg, 1858.

"Das Volksleben und die Messen in der Ukraine, Ein Bild aus der Gegen-wart," in Bodenstedt, F. M., ed., *Russische Fragmente,* Leipzig, 1862, I, 161–259.

"Uber die Arbeiterassociationen im Governement Jaroslaw (Schreiben an den Herausgeber der *'Russischen Unterhaltungen'* " in Boden-stedt, F. M., ed., *Russische Fragmente,* Leipzig, 1862, II, 305–316.

"Kratkaia zapiska o strannikakh ili begunakh," *Russki Arkhiv,* 1886, no. 3. Also in *Sochineniia,* VII, 834–848.

"Pismo k izdateliu Russkago Arkhiva po povodu stati E. Mamonova: 'Slavianofily,' " *Russki Arkhiv,* 1873, no. 2. Also in *Sochineniia,* VII, 766–784.

Prisutstvennyi den ugolovnoi palaty. Sudebnyia stseny iz zapisok chinov-nika ochevidtsa. Leipsig: E. L. Kasprowicz, 1874, 119 pp.

"Epizod iz istorii slavianofilstva," *Russkaia starina* 14:367–379 (1875). The story of the ill-fated *Moskovski sbornik.*

Condensed speech of Mr. Ivan Aksakoff, October 1876 (London, n.d.) 12 pp.

"Fedor Vasilevich Chizhov (Iz rechi I. S. Aksakova, proiznesennoi 18 dekabria 1877 g.)," *Russki Arkhiv,* 1878, no. 1, pp. 129–137. Also in *Sochineniia,* VII, 800–813.

"Rech pri otkrytii v Moskve pamiatnika Pushkinu," *Russki Arkhiv,* 1880, no. 2. Also in *Sochineniia,* VII, 813–834.

Biografiia Fedora Ivanovicha Tiutcheva, Moscow, 1886. A very sensitive understanding of Aksakov's father-in-law, perhaps the greatest poet Russia ever had.

Sbornik stikhotvoreni, Moscow, 1886.

"K biografii I. S. Aksakova," *Istoricheski vestnik,* 1886, no. 9, pp. 569–575. This item contains a letter that Aksakov wrote in 1883 to some students and in which he explained the difference that existed between Populism and Slavophilism.

"Ivan Sergeevich Aksakov—Neizdannyia ego stikhotvorennia." Soobshchil baron F. A. Biuler. *Russkaia starina* 52:639–652 (1886).

"Iz perepiski I. S. Aksakova s N. M. Pavlovym o drevnei Russkoi istorii," *Russki Arkhiv*, 1887, no. 8, pp. 469–494. Aksakov's views on certain problems of ancient Russian history.

Barsukov, N., *Zhizn i trudy M. P. Pogodina*, St. Petersburg, 1888–1910, 22 vols. This monumental work contains a wealth of primary sources on Ivan Aksakov.

Koliupanov, N., *Biografiia A. I. Kosheleva*, Moscow, 1889–1892, 2 vols. The second volume contains several letters written by Aksakov in the early 1850's.

"K voprosy o slavianskom edinenii (Pismo I. S. Aksakova o propagande pravoslaviia v Chekhi)," *Istoricheski vestnik*, September 1891, pp. 775–777. Written in July 1870. Shows the role of Ivan Aksakov in helping to build an Orthodox church in Prague.

"I. S. Aksakows Briefe an A. I. Herzen (1857–1861)" in *Konstantin Kawelins und Iwan Turgenjews Sozial-politischer Briefwechsel mit Alexander Iw. Herzen. Mit Beilagen und Erläuterungen herausgegeben von Prof. Michail Dragomanow*, Stuttgart, 1894.

"Ob istoricheskikh bumagakh ostavshikhsia posle A. N. Popova—Iz pisma I. S. Aksakova k K. P. Pobedonostsevu," *Russki Arkhiv*, 1894, no. 1, pp. 103–104.

"Pisma Aksakovykh k Turgenevu," *Russkoe Obozrenie*, 1894, Aug., Sept., Oct., Nov., and Dec. issues.

"Perepiska Aksakovykh s N. S. Sokhanskoi (Kokhanovskoi)" *Russkoe Obozrenie*, February 1897, pp. 569–616. These letters contain in particular Aksakov's opinions on Belinski (pp. 591–592), Nicholas I (p. 594) and Pushkin (p. 589).

Trubetskaia, O., *Materialy dlia biografii kn. V. A. Cherkasskago*, 2 vols., Moscow 1901. Vol. I contains 14 letters of I. Aksakov written in 1852–1859. Vol. II contains 1 letter of I. Aksakov written in 1861.

"Pismo I. S. Aksakova v Orlovskuiu derevniu," *Russki Arkhiv*, 1901, no. 6, pp. 297–299. This letter contains some candid views of Aksakov on the emancipation of the serfs.

Biograficheski ocherk poeta s prilozheniem ego stikhotvoreni, Moscow, 1902.

"Rech," *Russki Vestnik,* 1902, no. 8, pp. 477–488. A reprint of Aksakov's speech on the Congress of Berlin, in July, 1878.

"Perepiska P. D. Golokhvastova s I. S. Aksakovym o Zemskom sobore," *Russki Arkhiv,* 1913, I, 93–111 and 181–204. Extremely important for understanding the role that Aksakov played in the attempt to convince the tsar to grant a zemski sobor to Russia.

de Vollan, G. A., "Poezdka v Bosniu i Gertsegovinu v 1878 g.," *Golos Minuvshego,* 1914, no. 9, pp. 110–131. This item contains two letters of Ivan Aksakov to the author who was entrusted to deliver supplies to the insurgents of Bosnia and Herzegovina. In the second letter Aksakov shows how little faith he had in the Serbs and how much hope he staked on the Bulgarians.

Bukhgeim, L. (ed.), *Pisma I. S. Aksakova, N. P. Barsukova etc. k bibliografu S. I. Ponomarevu,* Moscow, 1915. This book contains just one letter of Aksakov in which the latter exposes his purpose in publishing *Rus.*

"Pisma I. S. Aksakova k N. A. Elaginu," *Russki Arkhiv,* 1915, no. 1, pp. 5–13.

"Pismo k grafine A. D. Bludovoi," *Russki Arkhiv,* 1915, no. 6, pp. 130–132. A letter written in 1860, in which Aksakov relates his trip through the Habsburg Empire.

"Pisma I. S. Aksakova k N. A. Chaevu—Iz arkhiva N. A. Chaeva," *Russki Arkhiv,* 1915, no. 9, pp. 63–64.

"Iz perepiski A. F. Gilferdinga s I. S. Aksakovym," *Golos Minuvshego,* 1916, no. 2, pp. 201–208.

"Melochi proshlogo: Nakaz redaktora-slavianofila (Ot I. S. Aksakova pri sdache N. A. Popovu redaktsii upravleniia *Moskvy* na letnie mesiatsy 1868)," *Golos Minuvshego,* 1916, no. 11, pp. 205–206.

"Perepiska dvukh slavianofilov (I. Aksakov i V. Lamanski)," *Russkaia Mysl,* September 1916, pp. 1–32; December 1916, pp. 85–114; February 1917, pp. 82–89.

Pobedonostsev, K. P., *K. P. Pobedonostsev i ego korrespondenty,* Moscow-Petrograd, 1923. This *recueil* contains a couple of letters written by I. Aksakov to Pobedonostsev.

S. O. Iakobson: "Pisma Iv. Aksakova k Putsykovichu," *Na chuzhoi storone* (Berlin and Prague), 1924, no. 5, pp. 129–157. Written from Varvarino—his place of exile—after his speech against the Congress of Berlin, in 1878.

"Moskovski adres Aleksandru II v 1870 g. (Iz perepiski K. P. Pobedonostseva s I. S. Aksakovym)," *Krasnyi Arkhiv* 6:144–154 (1928). This contains a letter written by Aksakov in protest against the reprimand that the Moscow city-duma received for lauding the tsar for his unilateral breach of the Treaty of Paris in 1870. The address to the tsar was written by Ivan Aksakov himself.

"Pismo I. S. Aksakova k A. F. Gilferdingu" in "F. I. Tiutchev i problemy vneshnei politiki tsarskoi Rossii," *Literaturnoe nasledstvo*, 1935, no. 19–21, pp. 177–256.

"Perepiska I. S. Aksakova s kn. V. A. Cherkasskim (1875–1878)," in *Slavianski sbornik—Slavianski vopros i russkoe obshchestvo v 1867–1878 godakh*, N. M. Druzhinin ed., Moscow, 1948, pp. 132–188. Very important correspondence between two men who did a great deal for the liberation of the Slavs.

Stikhotvoreniia i poemy (Leningrad, 1960).

OTHER SOURCES AND SECONDARY WORKS

"I. S. Aksakov i kritiki slavianofilov," *Russkaia beseda*, St. Petersburg, 1896, no. 4, pp. 21–44.

Aksakov, Vera S., *Dnevnik Very Sergeevny Aksakovoi*, St. Petersburg, 1913. The diary of Ivan Aksakov's sister during the years of the Crimean War. Very important for judging the relation of Ivan to his family in these years.

Anonymous, "Iz obshchestvennoi khroniki—I. S. Aksakov," *Vestnik Evropy*, 1886, no. 3, pp. 430–444. See also Arseniev K. K. *Za chetvert veka*.

Antonovich, M. A., *Izbrannye stati*, Leningrad, 1938. See the article "Suemudrie Dnia" on pp. 398–430, which offers a very harsh criticism of the Slavophiles in general and of Ivan Aksakov in particular.

Arseniev, K., "Doreformennaia Rossiia v perepiske I. S. Aksakova," *Vestnik Evropy*, 1888, no. 12, pp. 744–780. A review of the first 2 vols. of Aksakov's letters. Also included in Arseniev's *Kriticheskie etiudy*, vol. II.

———*Za chetvert veka (1871–94)*, Petrograd, 1915. Contains the necrology of Ivan Aksakov published anonymously in *Vestnik Evropy*, 1886, no. 3, pp. 430–444. A very good criticism of the activities of Ivan Aksakov.

———*Kriticheskie etiudy*, 2 vols., St. Petersburg, 1888, II.

Balaklyev, I., "Pamiati I. S. Aksakova," *Russkaia beseda*, St. Petersburg, 1896, no. 2, pp. 76–106.

Belinski, V. A., *Provintsial publitsist-mechtatel—Po povodu sobraniia pisem Aksakova*, St. Petersburg, 1894.

Belozerskaia, N. A., "N. I. Kostomarov v 1857–1875 gg"—Vospominaniia N. A. Belozerskoi," *Russkaia starina* 47:609–636 (1886).

Bernstein, H., *The Truth about the "Protocols of Zion,"* New York, 1935.

Bobchev, N., "Slavianofilskoto dvizhenie v Russiia i novobulgarskoto obrzovanie," *Proslava na osvoboditelnata voina 1877–1878 g.*, Sofia, 1929.

Bodenstedt, F., "Poet i professor Fridrikh Bodenshtedt—Otcherk ego biografii." *Russkaia starina* 55:571–591 (September 1887). This contains Bodenstedt's memoirs about Ivan Aksakov's visit to Germany in 1860. Very valuable for this study.

Bogucharski, V., *Aktivnoe narodnichestvo 70-kh godov*, Moscow, 1912.

Borozdin, A. K., "I. S. Aksakov v Iaroslavle (Otryvok iz vospominani)" *Istoricheski vestnik*, 1886, no. 3, pp. 622–633. Superficial but, nonetheless, valuable.

Brodski, L., *Rannie slavianofily*, Moscow, 1910.

Cherniaev, M. G. and P. A. Kulakovski. "Pisma M. G. Cherniaeva i P. A. Kulakovskago k I. S. Aksakovu o Serbii v 1880–1882 g.," *Golos Minuvshego*, 1915, no. 9, pp. 232–249.

Chicherin, B. N., *Moskva 40-kh godov—Vospominaniia*, Moscow, 1929. Indispensable for this work.

——— *Zemstvo i Moskovskaia Duma—Vospominanie*, Moscow, 1934.

Chmielewski, Edward, *Tribune of the Slavophiles: Konstantin Aksakov*, Gainesville: University of Florida Press, 1962.

Christoff, Peter K., *An Introduction to Nineteenth-Century Russian Slavophilism; A Study in Ideas*, vol. I: *A. S. Khomiakov*, Gravenhage: Mouton, 1961.

Danilevski, N. Ia., *Rossiia i Evropa*, St. Petersburg, 1888.

Derzhavin, N. S., *Istoriia Bolgarii*, 4 vols., Moscow-Leningrad, 1945–1948, IV (M., L., 1948).

Dimitrov, Mikhail, "K voprosu ob ideologii Liubena Karavelova," *Uchenye zapiski instituta slavianovedennia*, XVI, 1958, pp. 78–108. This article mentions the early influence that Aksakov had on the political views of Karavelov.

Dmitriev, S., "Arkhiv redaktsii 'Selskogo blagoustroistva' (1858–1859)" in *Zapiski otdela rukopisei vsesoiuznoi biblioteki im. V. I. Lenina. Vypusk 10—Krestianskaia reforma 1861*, Moscow, 1941, pp. 33–43. On the economic views of the Slavophiles on the eve of the emanci-

pation. The *Selskoe blagoustroistvo* was a short-lived journal to which contributed most of the Slavophiles including Ivan Aksakov.
───── "Slavianofily i slavianofilstvo" (Iz istorii russkoi obshch. mysli sered. XIX veka), *Istorik-marksist*, Moscow, 1941, Book I (89).
───── "Zapadniki i slavianofily," *Molodoi bolshevik*, 1941, no. 11.
Dmitriev-Mamonov, E., "Slavianofily–Istoriko–kriticheski ocherk," *Russki Arkhiv*, 1873, col. 2488–2508. Written by a man who deplored the degeneration of Slavophilism after the death of Khomiakov. Aksakov took offence and answered him. See "Pismo k izdateliu Russkogo Arkhiva po povodu stati E. Mamonova 'Slavianofily.'" In the same volume of *Russki Arkhiv* or in Ivan Aksakov, *Sochineniia*, VII, 766–784.
───── "Nauka i predanie—Pismo k N," *Otechestvennye zapiski*, 1875, no. 8, pp. 245–265.
Dostoevski, F. M., *Pisma*, 4 vols., Moscow, 1928–1959. 1928, vol. I—1832–1867; 1930, vol. II—1867–1871; 1934, vol. III—1871–1877; 1959, vol. IV—1878–1881. The four volumes contain a great amount of letters from Dostoevski to Ivan Aksakov.
Dubnow, S. M., *History of the Jews in Russia and Poland*, 3 vols., Philadelphia, 1918. This is the standard and very excellent work on Russian Jewry.
───── *Evrei v Rossii i Zapadnoi Evrope v epokhu antisemitskoi reaktsii*, Petrograd, 1923.
───── "Furor judophobicus v poslednie gody tsarstvovania Aleksandra III," *Evreiskaia Starina*, Petrograd, 1918, X, 27–59.
Dubnow, S. M. and Krasnyi-Admoni, *Materialy dlia istorii antievreiskikh pogromov v Rossii*, 2 vols., Petrograd–Moscow, 1919–1923. Volume 2 is important for the study of the pogroms in the years 1881–1882.
Dunin, A. A., "I. S. Aksakov v Iaroslavle," *Russkaia Mysl*, Moscow, 1915, no. 8, pp. 107–131. This article contains the letters written by Sergei Aksakov to his son Ivan in Iaroslavl as well as a few letters of Aksakov's mother.
Durylin, S., "Gogol i Aksakovy," *Zvenia*, vols. 3–4, 1934, pp. 325–364.
Elk, J., *Die Judischen Kolonien in Ruszland, Studie und Beiträg zur Geschichte der Juden in Ruszland*, Frankfurt, 1886.
Evgenev, V., "Tsenzurnaia praktika v gody Krymskoi voiny," *Golos Minuvshego*, 1917, no. 11–12.
Fischel, A., *Der Panslawismus bis zum Weltkrieg* (Berlin, 1919).
Friedlaender, I., *The Jews of Russia and Poland*, N. Y., 1915.

Garmiza, V. V., *Podgotovka zemskoi reformy 1864 goda*, Moscow, 1957, 263 pp. An excellent little book. The author took great pains in showing the various currents of opinion existing in the early 1860's in Russia.

———"Zemskaia reforma i zemstvo v istoricheskoi literature," *Istoriia SSSR*, 1960, no. 5, pp. 82–107. A very fine article on the subject of zemstvo.

Georgievski, A. I., *Ivan Sergeevich Aksakov i sovremennaia deistvitelnost*, Kazan, 1915, 47 pp.

———"Moskovski Slavianski blagotvoritelnyi komitet i ego sudba," *Zapiski istoriko-filologicheskogo fakulteta*, Vladivostok, vol. I, sect. I, 1919.

Gilferding, A. F., "Iz perepiski A. F. Gilferdinga s I. S. Aksakovym," *Golos Minuvshego*, 1916, no. 2, pp. 200–214. Gilferding (Hilferding) was a prominent Slavicist. He helped to spread pan-Slavic ideas by acquainting the Russian public with the Slavic peoples.

Giliarov-Platonov, N. P., "Pisma N. P. Giliarova-Platonova k kniaziu Sh." *Russki Arkhiv*, 1889, Oct., pp. 267–269.

Golitsyn, V., "Moskva v semidesiatykh godakh," *Golos Minuvshego*, 1919, no. 5–12, pp. 111–162. This article mentions the political activity of Ivan Aksakov during the 1870's.

Goncharov, I. A., "I. A. Goncharov, kak chlen soveta glavnago upravleniia po delam pechati," *Golos Minuvshego*, 1916, no. 11, pp. 117–156; no. 12, pp. 140–179. Goncharov was very ill-disposed to Aksakov and his *Den*. As a censor Goncharov tried to have the *Den* banned.

Granjard, Henri, *Ivan Tourgenev et les courants politiques et sociaux de son temps*, Institut d'études Slaves de l'Université de Paris, 1954.

Gratieux, A. A., *Khomiakov et le Mouvement Slavophile*, Vol. I: *Les hommes;* Vol. II: *Les doctrines*, Paris, 1939. One of the finest books on Slavophilism.

Greenberg, Louis, *The Jews in Russia*, New Haven: Yale University Press, 1944. This work contains an extensive bibliography on the Russian Jewry in the nineteenth century. It is particularly good for the reign of Alexander II.

Golovshchikov, K. D., *Deiateli Iaroslavskogo kraia*, Izd. Iarosl. uchen. arkhiv, komis. Vyp. 1–2. Iaroslavl, 1898–1899.

Haxtshausen, Baron von, *Studien über die inneren Zustände, das Volksleben und insbesondere die ländlichen Einrichtungen Russlands*, 3 vols., 1843–1852. Haxtshausen became acquainted with the Slavophiles in 1843 and fell under their influence. See "Pisma Iu. F. Samarina" in *Russki Arkhiv*, 1880, no. 2, pp. 241–332, in particular p. 311. His work was published simultaneously in French.

Iakobson, S. O., "Pisma Iv. Aksakova k Putsykovichu," *Na chuzhoi storone*, Berlin–Prague, 1924, vol. 5, pp. 129–158.

Iazykov, D., "Literaturnaia deiatelnost I. S. Aksakova," *Istoricheski vestnik*, 1886, no. 4, pp. 134–139. A succinct but good résumé of Aksakov's literary activities with the dates of his publications.

Jelavich, C., *Tsarist Russia and Balkan Nationalism—Russian Influence in the Internal Affairs of Bulgaria and Serbia 1879–1886*, Berkeley, Calif., 1958.

Khomiakov, A. S., "Pisma k Aksakovu," *Russkii Arkhiv*, 1893, no. 3, pp. 197–208.

Khomutov, A., "Otryvok iz vospominani," *Istoricheski vestnik*, 1886, no. 7, pp. 47–56. A very touching recollection of Aksakov's stay in Iaroslavl.

Khristov, Kh., "Russkata obshchestvenost i blgarskato natsionalno-osovo-boditelno dvizhenie v navecherieto na russko-turskata voina ot 1877–1878," *Osvobozhdenieto na Blgariia ot tursko igo 1878–1958*, Sofia, 1958.

Kireev, A., *Slavianofilstvo i natsionalism*, St. Petersburg, 1890. In defense of the Slavophiles against the attacks of Vladimir Solovev.

——*Kratkoe izlozhenie slavianofilskago ucheniia*, St. Petersburg, 1896.

Kizevetter, A., "Chekhi v Moskve v 1867 g.," *Na chuzhoi storone*, 1925, no. 10, pp. 251–269.

——"Zapiski po istorii politicheskikh idei v Rossii, Slavianofilstvo i anarkhism," in *Travaux scientifiques de l'Université populaire russe de Prague*, vol. I, Prague, 1928.

Klevenski, M. M., "Gerstsen-izdatel i ego sotrudniki," *Literaturnoe nasledstvo*, vols. 41–42, 1941, pp. 572–620.

Knorring, N., *General Mikhail Dmitrievich Skobelev*, 2 vols., Paris, 1939–1940. The latest and most complete biography of the "white general."

Kochubinski, A. A., "Nashi dve politiki v slavianskom voprose," *Istoricheski vestnik*, 1881, June, pp. 201–232; July, pp. 455–486. A good survey of the Russo-Slav relations with a pan-Slavic slant.

Koliupanov, N., "Ocherk filosofskoi sistemy slavianofilov," *Russkoe obozrenie*, 1894, vol. 28, pp. 6–22, 489–504; vol. 29, pp. 85–104, 547–567; vol. 30, pp. 48–71. A very detailed study.

Kolosov, E., "M. A. Bakunin i N. K. Mikhailovski v narodnichestve,"

Golos minuvshego, 1913, no. 5, pp. 61–89. Discusses the similarity between the Populists and Ivan Aksakov.

——"P. L. Lavrov i N. K. Mikhailovski o balkanskikh sobytiakh 1875–1876 gg.," *Golos Minuvshego,* 1916, no. 5–6, pp. 301–339.

Kornilov, A., *Obshchestvennoe dvizhenie pri Aleksandre II,* Paris, 1905.

Koshelev, A. I. *Zapiski Aleksandra Ivanovicha Kosheleva (1812–1883),* Berlin, 1884.

——"Pisma A. I. Kosheleva k I. S. Aksakovu," *Sbornik "O minuv-shem,"* St. Petersburg, 1909, pp. 406–416.

——"Iz perepiski moskovskikh slavianofilov—A. I. Koshelev i I. S. Aksakov," *Golos Minuvshego,* 1918, no. 1–3, pp. 231–250 (for 1853); no. 7–9, pp. 163–181 (1854–1860).

——"Iz perepiski moskovskikh slavianofilov—A. I. Koshelev i I. S. Aksakov 1861–1878 gg." *Golos Minuvshego,* Moscow, 1922, no. 2, pp. 59–90.

Kozlovski, L. S., "Mechty o Tsargrade," *Golos Minuvshego,* 1915, no. 2 (I: Dostoevski i K. Leontev), pp. 88–116, 1915, no. 11 (II: Konstantin Leontev), pp. 44–74.

Kozmenko, I., "Russkoe obshchestvo i aprelskoe bolgarskoe vosstanie 1876 goda," *Voprosy istorii,* 1945, no. 5, pp. 95–108.

Kravtsov, N. I., "Russko-iugoslavskie literaturnye sviazi" in *Obshchest-venno-politicheskie i kulturnye sviazi narodov SSSR i Iugoslavii—Sbornik statei,* ANSSSR, Moscow 1957, pp. 200–289.

L., "I.S. Aksakov i Dzh. St. Mill," *Mysl,* 1881, no. 4, pp. 85–89.

Lebedev, M., *Vzaimnoe otnoshenie tserkvi i gosudarstva po vozzreniiu slavianofilov,* Kazan, 1907.

Léger, Louis, "Panslavisme," *La Grande Encyclopédie,* Paris, n. d., col. 954.

Malia, Martin, *Alexander Herzen, and the Birth of Russian Socialism 1812–1855,* Cambridge: Harvard University Press, 1961.

Melgunov, S. P., "Iz obshchestvennykh nastroeni 1863 goda," *Golos Minuvshego,* 1916, no. 3, pp. 232–242. On Aksakov, see pp. 236–241.

M-ev, "Zhosef de Mestr i ego politicheskaia doktrina," *Russki vestnik,* May 1889, pp. 220–238; June 1889, pp. 74–95. Mentions de Maistre's influence in Russia, in particular on Ivan Aksakov. Not very conclusive.

Miliukov, P., "Razlozhenie Slavianofilstva," *Voprosy filosofii i psikho-logii,* year IV, May 1893, pp. 46–96.

——*Iz istorii russkoi intelligentsii,* St. Petersburg, 1902. Contains a discussion of S. T. Aksakov and his family.

—— "Slavianofistvo," *Entsiklopedicheski slovar Brockhaus and Efron,* XXX, 307–314.

Miliutin, D. A., *Dnevnik D. A. Miliutina, 1873–1882,* 4 vols., Moscow, 1947–1950. Volumes II, III, and IV contain passages dealing with Ivan Aksakov.

Molchanov, A., "Vospominaniia ob I. S. Aksakove," *Istoricheski vestnik,* 1886, no. 8, pp. 365–379. Written by a friend of Ivan Aksakov, this article contains many valuable opinions of the Slavophile on the *Zemki sobor* and Skobelev.

Mordovtsev, D. L., "Razvitie slavianskoi idei v russkom obshchestve XVII–XIX vv." *Russkaia Starina,* 21:65–78 (1878).

—— "N. I. Kostomarov v posledniia desiat let ego zhizni 1875–1885," *Russkaia starina* 47:323–360 (1886).

Nevedenski, S., *Katkov i ego vremia,* St. Petersburg, 1888.

Nikitenko, A. V., *Zapiski i dnevnik,* 2 vols., St. Petersburg, 1904.

Nikitin, S. A., "Vozniknovenie Moskovskogo Slavianskogo Komiteta," *Voprosy istorii,* August 1947, pp. 50–65.

——"Slavianskie sezdy shestidesiatykh godov XIX veka," *Slavianski sbornik. Slavianski vopros i russkoe obshchestvo v 1867–1878 godakh,* N. M. Druzhinin, ed., Moscow, 1948, pp. 16–92.

—— "Iuzhnoslavianskie sviazi russkoi periodicheskoi pechati 60-kh godov XIX veka," *Uchenye Zapiski Instituta Slavianovedeniia,* Moscow, 1952, VI, 1952, vol. 6, pp. 89–122.

—— *Slavianskie komitety v Rossii,* Moscow, 1960, 361 pp. The latest and the most complete work on the Slavic committees between 1858 and 1876.

—— "Russkoe obshchestvo i natsionalno-osvoboditelnaia borba iuzhnykh slavian v 1875–1876 gg.," in *Obshchestvenno-politicheskie i kulturnye sviazi narodov SSSR i Iugoslavii—Sbornik statei,* ANSSSR, Moscow, 1957, pp. 3–77.

Nikolski, A., "Nekrolog," *Istoricheski vestnik,* 1886, no. 3, I–XX. A very good biographical sketch and a good account of the impression produced by Aksakov's death in Russia and abroad.

Nolde, B., *Iuri Samarin i ego vremia,* Paris, 1926.

"Panslavianskoe obshchestvo, osnovannoe Petrashevskim," *Istoricheski vestnik,* 1880, no. 11, pp. 633–637.

Petrovich, M., *The Emergence of Russian Panslavism, 1856–1870,* New York, 1956. A very fine work and an excellent background for this study. Includes a detailed biography.

———— "Russian Pan-Slavists and the Polish Uprising of 1863," *Harvard Slavic Studies,* I (1953), 219–247.

Pigarev, K., "F. I. Tiutchev i problemy vneshnei politiki tsarskoi Rossii," *Literaturnoe nasledstvo,* 1935, no. 19–21, pp. 117–218.

Plekhanov, G. V., "Zapadniki i slavianofily," in *Sochineniia,* XXIII, Moscow–Leningrad, 1926.

Pogodin, A., "Imperator Aleksandr II i ego vremia v otsenke serbskago obshchestvennago mnenia, shestidesiatye gody," *Zapiski russkogo nauchnago instituta v Belgrade* (Vypusk 13), Belgrade, 1936, pp. 1–38.

Ponomareva, O., *Pamiati I. S. Aksakova,* Moscow, 1886. A collection of necrologies gathered in one book.

Popova, A. A., "Russkaia pressa o bolgarskom osvoboditelnom dvizhenii v 1867–68 gg.," *Vestnik istorii mirovoi kultury,* September–October 1960, pp. 98–109.

Predtechenski, A., "Slavianofily," in *Ocherki istorii istoricheskoi nauki v SSSR,* 2 vols. published in 1955–1960, I, M. N. Tikhomirov et al., eds., pp. 325–331. On the historical views of the Slavophiles.

Pushkarevich, K. A., "Balkanskie slaviane i russkie 'osvoboditeli,' " *Trudy In-ta Slavianovedeniia ANSSSR,* II, Leningrad, 1934, pp. 189–229.

Pypin, A. N., *Panslavizm v proshlom i nastoiashchem,* St. Petersburg, 1913.

———— "Russkoe slavianovedenie v XIX–m stoletii," *Vestnik Evropy,* 1889, no. 7, pp. 238–274; 1889, no. 8, pp. 683–728; 1889, no. 9, pp. 257–305.

———— "Iz istorii panslavizma," *Vestnik Evropy,* May 1893, pp. 267–313.

———— "Davnost slavianskoi idei v russkom obshchestve," *Vestnik Evropy,* May 1878, pp. 283–316.

———— "Slavianski vopros po vzgliadam Iv. Aksakova," *Vestnik Evropy,* 1886, no. 8, pp. 763–807. A review of the first volume of Ivan Aksakov's collected works.

Riasanovsky, N. V., *Russia and the West in the Teaching of the Slavophiles,* Cambridge, Mass., 1952.

Riasanovsky, V., *Obzor russkoi kultury—Istoricheski ocherk,* New York, 1947–1948. The Slavophiles are discussed in Part II, issue I, pp. 310–322.

Rossolovski, V. S., "Ivan Sergeevich Aksakov v ego pismakh," *Istoricheski vestnik,* 1888, no. 11, pp. 448–464. A review of the first two volumes of Ivan Aksakov's letters. A good biographical sketch.

Rubinshtein, N., "Istoricheskaia teoriia slavianofilov i ee klassovye korni,"

Trudy In-ta Krasnoi Professury. Russkaia istoricheskaia literatura v klassovom osveshchenii. Sbornik statei, Moscow, 1927, I, 53–118.

———*Russkaia istoriografia,* Moscow, 1941.

Schenrok, V., "S. T. Aksakov i ego semia," *Zhurnal Ministerstva Narodnago Prosveshcheniia,* 1904, no. 10, pp. 355–418; no. 11, pp. 1–66; no. 12, pp. 229–290. Excellent, but goes only to 1860.

Schmurlo, E., "From Krizanic to the Slavophiles" in *The Slavonic Review* 6:321–335 (1927–1928).

Segel, B., *The Protocols of the Elders of Zion: The Greatest Lie in History,* New York, 1934.

Semevski, V. I., "Nikolai Ivanovich Kostomarov, 1817–1885," *Russkaia starina* 47:181–212 (1886).

Shpet, G., *Ocherk razvitiia russkoi filosofii,* Petrograd, 1922.

Siuzor, D. D., *Ko dniu LXXV iubileia imperatorskago uchilishcha pravovedeniia 1835–1910,* St. Petersburg, 1910.

Sladkevich, N., "K voprosu o polemike N. G. Chernyshevskogo so slavianofilskoi publitsistikoi," *Voprosy istorii,* 1948, no. 6, pp. 71–79.

Slavic Benevolent Committee, *Otchet o deiatelnosti slavianskago blagotvoritelnago Obshchestva v Moskve,* Moscow, 1876.

Smirnov, V., *Aksakovy, ikh zhizn i literaturnaia deiatelnost,* St. Petersburg, 1895. Hostile to the Aksakovs but interesting. Smirnov was one of the first to examine the class-nature of Slavophilism.

Smirnova, A. O., "Perepiska s Aksakovymi," *Russki Arkhiv,* 1895, no. 3, pp. 423–480; 1896, no. 1, pp. 142–160; 1905, no. 3, pp. 210–212.

Snytko, T. G., "Iz istorii narodnogo dvizheniia v Rossii v podderzhku borby iuzhnykh slavian za svoiu nezavisimost 1875–1876 gg.," in *Obshchestvenno-politicheskie i kulturnye sviazi narodov SSSR i Iugoslavii—Sbornik statei,* ANSSSR, Moscow, 1957.

Solovev, V., *Sobranie Sochineni,* V, St. Petersburg, 1901. The entire volume is dedicated to the disavowal of nationalism in Russia. It contains articles directed at Ivan Aksakov.

———"Iz vospominani—Aksakovy," in *Pisma Vladimira Sergeevicha Soloveva,* 3 vols., St. Petersburg, 1911, III, E. L. Radlov, ed.

[Spectator], "Rossiia i evropeiskie soiuzy," *Russkoe obozrenie,* October 1890, pp. 873–886. The author recollected his conversation with Ivan Aksakov and the views of the latter on the French revolution.

Steppun, F., "Nemetski romantism i russkoe slavianofilstvo," in *Russkaia mysl,* March 1910, pp. 65–91. Steppun's article provides the best discussion of the relation between the Slavophiles and the Western romanticists.

Strakhov, N., *Borba s Zapadom v nashei literature,* 2 ed., 2 vols., St. Petersburg, 1890.

Strukova, K. L., "K istorii russko-bolgarskikh otnosheni v 1876 gg.," *Slavianski arkhiv,* ANSSSR, Moscow, 1959, pp. 116–125. This article tries to prove that the Slavic Committee was more interested in Chernyaev's expedition than in a new Bulgarian revolt.

Struve, P., "Aksakovy i Aksakov," *Russkaia mysl,* Prague-Berlin, 1923, no. 6–8, pp. 340–358.

—— "Ivan Aksakov," *Slavonic Review* 2:514–518 (1924). Eulogy written on the one hundredth anniversary of Aksakov's birth.

Sukhomlinov, M. I., "I. S. Aksakov v sorokovykh godakh," *Istoricheski vestnik,* 1888, no. 2, pp. 324–348. Contains Aksakov's answers to the Third Department during his arrest in 1849.

Sukhotin, S. M., "Iz pamiatnykh tetradei S. M. Sukhotina," *Russki Arkhiv,* 1894, no. 2, pp. 225–266; no. 3, pp. 417–436; no. 4, pp. 599–610; no. 5, pp. 139–149. Diary of a Muscovite who participated in the political life of Moscow in the 1860's.

Sumner, B. H., *Russia and the Balkans, 1870–1880,* Oxford, 1937, pp. 56–80 on pan-Slavs.

Svatikov, S., *Obshchestvennoe dvizhenie v Rossii,* 2 vols., Rostov-on-the Don, 1905.

—— "Proekty narodnago predstavitelstva v Rossii v 1882 g.," *Golos Minuvshego,* 1913, no. 7, pp. 242–248.

Talin, V., "I. S. Aksakov, kak tserkovnyi publitsist," *Russkaia budushchnost,* Prilozhenie, St. Petersburg, 1916, no. 9, pp. 50–58.

Tatishchev, S. S., *Imperator Aleksandr II—Ego zhizn i tsarstvovanie,* 2 vols., St. Petersburg, 1903.

Timanskaia, L. Ia., "Gosudarstvennyi istoricheski arkhiv leningradskoi oblasti-Obzor dokumentalnykh materialov fonda S. Peterburgskago slavianskago blagotvoritelnago obshchestva (1868–1921)," *Slavianski sbornik,* 1947, pp. 359–365.

Timofeev, S., "Cherta iz zhizni I. S. Aksakova," *Istoricheski vestnik,* 1886, no. 3, pp. 640–643. A superficial eulogy written after Aksakov's death.

Tiutcheva, A. F., *Pri dvore dvukh imperatorov—Dnevnik 1855–1882,* Moscow, 1929. This volume, written by the daughter of F. I. Tiutchev and the wife of Ivan Aksakov, follows a volume published in 1928 under the same title. These two volumes contain the remnant of the copious diaries of A. F. Tiutcheva. The second volume is very important for this study.

Trubachev, S., "Aksakov, Ivan Sergeevich," *Russki bibliograficheski slovar,* St. Petersburg, 1896, I, 97–100.

Trubetskaia, O., *Materialy dlia biografii kn. V. A. Cherkasskago,* 2 vols., Moscow, 1901. This collection of documents contains letters of Ivan Aksakov to Prince Cherkasski.

Turgenev, I. S., "Iz perepiski I. S. Turgeneva s semeiu Aksakovykh," *Vestnik Evropy,* 1894, no. 1, pp. 329–344; no. 2, pp. 469–499. From this correspondence it appears that Turgenev was very friendly with Ivan Aksakov.

Ulanova, V. Ia., "Slavianofily i zapadniki o krepostnom prave," *Velikaia reforma,* 6 vols., Moscow, 1911, III, 175–193, A. K. Dzhivelegov, S. P. Melgunov and V. I. Picheta, eds.

Ustrialov, N., "Natsionalnaia problema u pervykh slavianofilov," *Russkaia mysl,* 1916, no. 11, pp. 1–22.

—— "Politicheskaia doktrina slavianofilstva (Ideia samoderzhaviia v slavianskoi postanovke), *Izvsetiia Iuridicheskago Fakulteta* (Harbin), Year I, 1925, pp. 47–74.

Valentin, Hugo, *Anti-Semitism,* New York, 1936.

Vengerov, S. A., *Kritiko-biograficheski slovar russkikh pisatelei i uchenykh,* St. Petersburg, 1889, vol. I. On Ivan Aksakov see pp. 318–344 and 905–916. This is the best biographical sketch available on Aksakov.

—— *Istochniki slovaria russkikh pisatelei,* St. Petersburg, 1900, I, 24–26. This work contains a good bibliography on Ivan Aksakov.

Veniukov, M. I., "Russkoe obshchestvo v tsarstvovanie Aleksandra II," *Na chuzhoi storone* (Paris), 1926, no. 1, pp. 81–100; no. 2, pp. 113–128; no. 3, pp. 197–208.

Vetrinskii, T. (Cheshikhin, V.), *V sorokovykh godakh—Istoriko-literaturnye ocherki i kharakteristiki,* Moscow, 1899. Contains an essay on Ivan Aksakov and A. V. Nikitenko as two representatives of the Russian intellectual class.

V-n, A., "Novye tomy sochineni I. S. Aksakova," *Vestnik Evropy,* 1887, Book I, pp. 413–430.

—— "Na kanune reform—I. S. Aksakov v ego pismakh," *Vestnik Evropy,* 1893, Book V, pp. 291–342. A review of vol. III of Aksakov's letters and an appraisal of their author. An intelligent essay.

Zaionchkovski, P. A., "Popytka sozyva zemskogo sobora i padenie ministerstva N. P. Ignateva," *Istoriia SSSR,* 1960, no. 5, pp. 126–139. A very important article for the last chapter of this work.

Index

Adam, Juliette, 160
Aksakov, Gregory, 15, 27, 117
Aksakov, Ivan: childhood, 15–17; education, 17–18, 20; work with Moscow Senate, 21–26; assignment to Astrakhan, 21–22; assignment to Kaluga, 22–26; work with Ministry of Interior, 26–33; assignment to Bessarabia, 26–27; arrest in St. Petersburg, 27–29; assignment to Iaroslavl, 29–33; editing *Moskovski sbornik*, 34–35; investigating Ukrainian Fairs, 36; first trip to Europe, 37; publication of *Parus*, 37–38; death of father, 38–39; second trip to Europe and "Address to the Serbs," 39; conversion to Slavophilism, 38–42; character described by friends and acquaintances, 40–42; publication of *Den*, 43–45, 73; marriage, 73–74; publication of *Moskva* and *Moskvich*, 74–75, 133, 144; forced retirement from journalism, 75; publication of *Rus*, 141, 144–146, 160; death, 152, 162–163

thoughts and views: anti-Semitism, *see* Jews; aristocracy, 49–50; autocracy, 60–62, 67–69; Baltic Germans, 73, 75, 109–110; Catholicism, 90, 92–94, 99, 126–127, 131; Crimean War, 36–37; democracy, 59–60; education, 56–57, 146–151; England, 58; Finland, 111–112; gentry, 46, 48–55, 66–69, 70–71; Jews and Judaism, 27, 94, 95–110, 167–168; legal reforms, 70–73; marriage, 25, 27; *obshchestvo*, 55–63, 87; peasant commune, 62, 69; Polish question, 75, 76–95, 96–97, 129–130; Populism, 161–162; Protestantism, 94n; revolutions of 1848–49, 25–26, 30; Russian imperialism, 114–115, 151; serfdom and abolition of serfdom, 27, 36, 44–45, 51; Slavophilism, 1–3, 13–

14, 28–29, 125, 161–162, 165, 168–169; Slavs, 92–93, 117–118, 121, 123–124, 125, 126–129, 131–132, 133–134, 137–138, 142–143; state, 58–59; Ukrainians, 27, 112–114
Aksakov, Konstantin, 1, 6, 15–17, 19, 21, 24, 25, 29, 31–33, 34, 35, 38–40, 43, 55n, 61n, 84, 119, 122, 151, 152
Aksakov, Michael, 20
Aksakov, Sergei, 15, 17, 18, 22, 24, 25, 38–40
Aksakova, Olga, 16
Aksakova, Vera, 15n, 39
Alexander I, 6, 79
Alexander II, 1, 76, 77, 102, 130, 138, 144, 152, 153, 156, 158
Alexander III, 1, 132, 136, 153, 157, 158, 162, 163
Alexander of Bulgaria, *see* Battenberg
Alvensleben, C., Count, 78, 130
Axelrod, P., 97n

Bakunin, M., 84
Battenberg, Alexander von, 61, 142
Beguny, see Runners
Belinski, V., 19, 23, 24
Berdyaev, N., 4, 161
Bezobrazov, P., 46–47
Bludov, Count Dmitri, 43, 89
Bludova, Countess Antonina, 43, 73, 94n
Bogucharski, V., 161
Brafman, J., 103, 104

Catherine the Great, 6, 31, 50, 51
Charter of Nobility, 6, 46, 50; *see also* Gentry
Cherkasski, Princess E., 124, 134
Cherkasski, Prince V. A., 119
Cherniaev, General M., 128, 135, 136, 137
Chicherin, B., 11, 29, 40, 41, 53, 67, 74, 154

HARVARD HISTORICAL MONOGRAPHS

43. Ottoman Imperialism and German Protestantism, 1521–1555. By Stephen A. Fischer-Galati. 1959.
44. Foch versus Clemenceau: France and German Dismemberment, 1918–1919. By Jere Clemens King. 1960.
45. Steelworkers in America: The Nonunion Era. By David Brody. 1960.
46. Carroll Wright and Labor Reform: The Origin of Labor Statistics. By James Leiby. 1960.
47. Chōshū in the Meiji Restoration. By Albert M. Craig. 1961.
48. John Fiske: The Evolution of a Popularizer. By Milton Berman. 1961.
49. John Jewel and the Problem of Doctrinal Authority. By W. M. Southgate. 1962.
50. Germany and the Diplomacy of the Financial Crisis, 1931. By Edward W. Bennett. 1962.
51. Public Opinion, Propaganda, and Politics in Eighteenth-Century England: A Study of the Jew Bill of 1753. By Thomas W. Perry. 1962.
52. Soldier and Civilian in the Later Roman Empire. By Ramsay MacMullen. 1963.
53. Copyhold, Equity, and the Common Law. By Charles Montgomery Gray. 1963.
54. The Association: British Extraparliamentary Political Association, 1769–1793. By Eugene Charlton Black. 1963.
55. Tocqueville and England. By Seymour Drescher. 1964.
56. Germany and the Emigration, 1816–1885. By Mack Walker. 1964.
57. Ivan Aksakov (1823–1886): A Study in Russian Thought and Politics. By Stephen Lukashevich. 1965.

* *Out of Print*